The ManDak League

The ManDak League

Haven for Former Negro League Ballplayers, 1950–1957

BARRY SWANTON

McFarland & Company, Inc., Publishers
Jefferson, North Carolina, and London

LIBRARY OF CONGRESS CATALOGUING-IN-PUBLICATION DATA

Swanton, Barry
 The ManDak league : haven for former Negro league ballplayers, 1950–1957 / Barry Swanton
     p.   cm.
 Includes bibliographical references and index.

 ISBN-13: 978-0-7864-2510-5
 (softcover : 50# alkaline paper) ∞

 1. Manitoba-Dakota Baseball League — History.
 2. Semi-professional baseball — History. 3. African American baseball players — History.   I. Title.
 GV875.M36S93   2006
 796.357'64097127 — dc22   2006006095

British Library cataloguing data are available

©2006 Barry Swanton. All rights reserved

No part of this book may be reproduced or transmitted in any form or by any means, electronic or mechanical, including photocopying or recording, or by any information storage and retrieval system, without permission in writing from the publisher.

On the cover: Two unidentified Brandon Greys enjoy some warmup hijinks *(courtesy of Lillian Lowe)*

Manufactured in the United States of America

McFarland & Company, Inc., Publishers
  Box 611, Jefferson, North Carolina 28640
  www.mcfarlandpub.com

For my Dad, Cecil Swanton, who took me to the ManDak League games when I was a youngster

Contents

Introduction	1
I. History of the League	5
1. The 1950 Season	5
2. The 1951 Season	22
3. The 1952 Season	29
4. The 1953 Season	35
5. The 1954 Season	42
6. The 1955 Season	49
7. The 1956 Season	54
8. The 1957 Season	59
9. The End of the ManDak League	63
II. Player Profiles	65
Appendix I. 1950 Minot Mallards Team Rules	182
Appendix II. Batting and Pitching Records	183
Appendix III. Rosters	204
Bibliography	211
Index	213

Introduction

Before 1950, many small towns in Manitoba would hire two or three Negro League baseball players for their town teams. This was done to give their teams a competitive edge in league and tournament play. The towns had no trouble attracting players who were glad to get away from the prejudice in the United States. Ron Teasley, for one, stated that in Canada the players were judged by their baseball ability, not by their color.

Before 1950, teams in the Manitoba Senior Baseball League (over 21 years of age) were allowed to sign up to three "import players." These players would come from the Negro Leagues, and most teams exceeded the three-player unwritten import rule. It appeared that teams who could afford to pay import players could have as many as they wished.

Jackie Robinson, who was playing in the Negro Leagues, signed with the Brooklyn Dodgers in 1945 and entered organized baseball in 1946. This started the demise of the Negro Leagues. With the steady decline in attendance, the leagues would cease operation. The talented young Negro players would go into organized baseball and the older players would journey north to Manitoba and North Dakota to continue their careers in the newly formed ManDak League. In 1950, the league consisted of the Winnipeg Buffaloes, the Winnipeg Elmwood Giants, the Carman Cardinals, the Brandon Greys and (in North Dakota) the Minot Mallards. Along with the Negro League players, the ManDak League attracted a number of ex–major leaguers, minor league stars and some of the best Manitoba-, North Dakota- and Minnesota-born players. After the birth of the ManDak League, the Manitoba Senior Baseball League continued to operate, and still operates today, in cities and towns in Manitoba.

The ManDak League operated from 1950 to 1957. At the end of the 1957 season, the league folded. All the teams were suffering financially in a sea of red ink. Many old fans were of the opinion that teams such as Williston and Bismarck, North Dakota, with their oil money, had exceeded the salary cap, which caused the ManDak League to cease operation.

Over the eight years of operation, the ManDak League provided fans in Manitoba and North Dakota with quality baseball. Many historians write stories up to the end of the players' careers in the Negro Leagues, not knowing that they continued playing in the ManDak League. This book takes baseball fans to the end of many Negro League players' careers. The league is truly one of baseball's best kept secrets. Not many leagues had three players who eventually would be selected to the baseball Hall of Fame in Cooperstown, New York—but the ManDak League had Willie Wells, Leon Day, and Ray Dandridge. You could count Satchel Paige as a fourth, as he pitched very briefly for Minot in 1950. In 2005, the Manitoba Baseball Hall of Fame will honor the players who played in the ManDak League with a special presentation.

I was 12 years old when the ManDak League started in 1950. My dad was a big baseball fan and took me to many games at Osborne Stadium in Winnipeg. He would buy me a scorecard and I would keep score in my own way. The next day I would cut out the game report from the newspaper, place it in the scorecard and throw it into a box. Many years later, I found the box that, fortunately, my mother hadn't thrown away.

On some nights my friends and I would jump on the streetcar and head downtown to watch a game at Osborne Stadium. After the game, we would hang around waiting for the players to come out so we could get their autographs. The ex–Negro League players would always talk to us and sign autographs eagerly, and not rush away to get back to their hotels or rooming houses. They always made time for us, and to this day, I remember that well.

Years later, when I found the box of programs, I realized how many great players were in the ManDak League. Because the league was in North Dakota and Manitoba, Canada, it is forgotten by many baseball historians. James Riley, the well-known Negro League historian, mentioned to me that we have to make sure these old players get their place in baseball history. That is why I have written this book.

My favorite ManDak players were Hall of Famer Leon Day and Minot's star hurler, Sugar Cain. I also liked Mickey Rocco, who was a marvelous fielder. My favorite Manitoba player was Ian Lowe of the Brandon Greys, a good hitter and fielder. To me, as a 12-year-old, the ManDak players *were* the major leaguers.

Here are the players I would pick as my ManDak League All Stars:

Catcher—Joe Massaro (Minot Mallards, Williston Oilers) was a durable player who could hit. He averaged .305 over his five seasons in the league.

First Base—Lyman Bostock (Winnipeg Buffaloes, Carman Cardinals) had a .312 batting average over his four seasons in the league and was also a good defensive player.

An unidentified Carman Cardinals player shows the local Little Leaguers some batting tips (courtesy of Dufferin Historical Museum of Carman, Manitoba).

Second Base — John Kennedy (Winnipeg Buffaloes, Minot Mallards) had a .289 average over his three seasons and played well defensively.

Shortstop — Zoonie McLean (Minot Mallards) averaged .322 over his eight years in the league. Won the batting championship in 1952.

Third base — Ray Dandridge (Bismarck Barons) played only one season, but what a season it was. He batted .360 and played well in the field.

Outfield — Butch Davis (Winnipeg Buffaloes, Minot Mallards) was a batting champion twice and runner-up once.

Outfield — Roy Weatherly (Williston Oilers, Bismarck Barons) was batting champion in 1954 and 1955. In his four seasons he hit 46 home runs and drove in 167 runs.

Outfield — Cowan Hyde (Elmwood Giants, Brandon Greys) averaged .303 for his four seasons in the league.

Utility — Leon Day (Winnipeg Buffaloes, Brandon Greys) was at the top of his game on the mound, infield or outfield.

Pitcher — Sugar Cain (Minot) won 62 games and lost 31 in his Man-Dak career. He led the league in strikeouts and ERA a number of times.

Pitcher — Gentry Jessup (Carman Cardinals) was a workhorse for the Cardinals. He won 27 games in his three seasons in the ManDak League.

Pitcher — Hal Price (Winnipeg Giants) won only 25 games, as in 1952 the Giants' team was not that strong. Price led them with a 10–5 record and led the league in strikeouts with 130.

I. History of the League

1
The 1950 Season

In 1950, baseball was in what has been called its Golden Era (1946–1951). There were 59 leagues in over 400 cities. The Brooklyn Dodgers had 24 teams in their minor league system. Fans flocked to the ballparks and baseball interest was at an all-time high.

Before 1950, the top baseball league in Manitoba was the Manitoba Senior League (players 21 years old or older). In 1948 the senior league comprised the Brandon Greys, Winnipeg Reos, Elmwood Giants, and ANAF Vets. The Carman Cardinals joined the league in 1949 to make it a five-team circuit. The Minot team, the Merchants, played in North Dakota.

At a meeting on December 10, 1949, in Brandon, Manitoba, a semi-professional baseball league was formed. Five teams accepted offers to join the new league: the Minot Mallards of North Dakota, the Brandon Greys, the Carman Cardinals, the Winnipeg Elmwood Giants, and the Winnipegers, all from Manitoba. At the next meeting, the Winnipegers became the Winnipeg Buffaloes. A constitution was discussed, as was umpiring and the length of the schedule. The league was to be called the International League. The executives realized there already was a league with that name in organized ball, and placed the naming of the league on the agenda for the January 15, 1950, meeting in Winnipeg, at the then-posh Royal Alexandra Hotel.

At the January 15th meeting, it was agreed that the league would be known as the Manitoba-Dakota Baseball League, and would be referred to as the ManDak League. With a few changes, the constitution of the Southern Manitoba Baseball League was adopted. The teams would play a 48-game schedule. Four of the five teams would make the playoffs. The first-place team would play the fourth, and the second and third place teams would meet, with the winners playing for the championship. There would be no limit on the number of imports. The league would have a 16-man player limit and a salary cap of $8500 a month.

Player salaries would range from $300 to a high of $1000 a month. It was rumored that Carman's Gentry Jessup was paid $1000 a month in 1950. In 1953 ex–major leaguer Mickey Rocco also was making $1000 a month.

Minot released him when he wouldn't take a pay cut. He later joined the Winnipeg Royals.

ManDak paid higher salaries than other leagues. That was the reason it attracted so many good players, both from the Negro Leagues and from organized baseball. Ron Teasley recalled that when he was at a Negro League reunion in Louisiana with Andy Porter, Pee Wee Jenkins, and Frank Evans, they all agreed that they were paid more money in Canada than anywhere else. Besides playing their regular schedule, the teams played several exhibition games. Minot played teams from towns in North Dakota, Minnesota, and Saskatchewan. The Buffaloes and Greys also played teams in Saskatchewan. That first season, the two teams played an exhibition game in the resort area of Clear Lake, Manitoba. Traveling teams like the Brooklyn Cuban Giants, Memphis Red Sox, House of David, Harlem Globetrotters, Minneapolis Clowns, Omaha Rockets, and New Orleans Creoles played against ManDak League teams. The Creoles' drawing card that season was second baseman Toni Stone, the first woman to play professionally. When these barnstorming teams played in Winnipeg, it was a good money maker for all teams.

The teams also played in tournaments in both the United States and Western Canada. Tournament play was very popular, as it generated more revenue for the teams and players. Prize money varied, with the average tournament money being $1500 to $3000. At times these tournaments were held in conjunction with a town's country fair and also would feature rodeo events, fireworks and a barn dance. The tournaments always were well attended and a money maker for the local community.

The June 8, 1950, *Lacombe Globe* (Alberta) newspaper stated that the ladies of the town and district were planning to set up four eating areas on the baseball grounds. Here's a partial list of what was ordered for the hungry tournament fans: potatoes, 1500 lbs.; cold meats, 1100 lbs.; tomatoes, 300 lbs.; and Parker House rolls, 6000. Indian Head, Saskatchewan, hosted a big tournament every baseball season. One would have a hard time finding Indian Head, as it is just a small dot on the map. At one such tournament they attracted a record 16,000 fans for a two-day tournament. They had 209 local people working at the event and whereas Indian Head was a small farming community, you can bet there wasn't much work done on the farm that weekend.

The Stadiums for the Initial Season

Municipal Stadium in Minot was the home park for the Mallards. Before the start of the first season, the city of Minot spent $60,000 in upgrades to the lighting system, grandstand roof, and billboards. The stadium had a fairly large seating area down both baselines. In 1951, the grandstand interior was painted a cream color and the scoreboard was painted black with white numbers, and on July 22, 1953, new and bigger lights were installed in the scoreboard.

Osborne Stadium in Winnipeg was the home for the Winnipeg Buffaloes and (Winnipeg) Elmwood Giants. It also was the home for the Winnipeg Blue Bombers football team. There was seating down both baselines and a large grandstand in center field. The right-field fence was the wall of the hockey arena. The stadium was flanked by Shea's brewery on one side and the Margaret Rose Tea Room on the other. Across the street were the Manitoba Parliament buildings. Osborne had the largest seating capacity in the league. In 1951, the city added 50 more lights.

Carman Stadium also underwent upgrading. Local business people from Carman and the surrounding area put up the money for new bleachers, and a new lighting system was installed. The lights cost $22,000 and were reported to be the best in Western Canada.

The Brandon Stadium had seats down the first- and third-base lines. The dugouts were real dugouts. Players went down four steps in the ground to the bench, and the tall ones had to duck for fear of hitting their heads.

None of the grandstands in these ballparks were very high, and a lot of foul balls would fly over into the surrounding grounds and parking lots. There were always a lot of young kids hanging around outside the stadiums hoping to get a baseball. In an effort to get some of these balls back, the teams offered to let the kids into the game free if they returned the balls. This paid off most of the time, although on many occasions, the lure of having a baseball was too great. The kids would hide the ball and get it after the game. In their yearly souvenir book, the Carman executive stated the balls were costing them $36 a dozen, and that they usually used 10 balls a game and were hoping that the balls would be returned.

The Personnel

Officials

James "Jimmy" Dunn was elected league president for the first season. His work in baseball and hockey had been of a very high order. At the time, he was the vice president of the Canadian Amateur Hockey Association. With his leadership, Manitoba and North Dakota were destined to have the best baseball in their history.

Stanley Zedd was the owner of the Winnipeg Buffaloes. He owned the

Margaret Rose Tea Room, which was a nice restaurant at that time. Besides the restaurant, he also ran floating card games. Every so often the Winnipeg police would raid one of his gambling sites, and he would pay a small fine and be back in business the next night. Stanley was a character right out of Damon Runyon. He sponsored a number of minor hockey and baseball teams in North Winnipeg. He was of stocky build, always dressed smartly and carried a trademark cigar in his mouth at all times.

Alex Turk was the owner of the Elmwood Giants. Turk was a local businessman who owned a coal company, was a real estate broker, and was also a wrestling promoter. He was a local politician and sat as a city councilor.

Curly Haas owned the Giants and Royals in 1952 and 1953. He had a long love affair with local Winnipeg baseball.

The first president of the Minot Mallards was Roy Reimer. Minot, Brandon and Carman were run by local baseball officials. As the years passed, no teams were owned by a single individual, such as Zedd, Turk and Haas. Over the remaining years, the various teams would be headed by sports-minded businessman in their areas.

Players

In that first season, the league teams were stocked with many stars from the Negro Leagues, ex–major leaguers, minor league veterans, college players, and some local players. Many of these players had been restricted by baseball's reserve clause and were looking for another chance. With the Negro Leagues in decline, many of their stars came north to continue their careers. Jackie Robinson had broken the color barrier, but many of these players were just too old for the majors. It is believed that Abe Saperstein, of basketball's Harlem Globetrotters fame, helped Alex Turk with stocking the Giants team. Saperstein, who at times owned teams in the Negro Leagues, knew many of the baseball players. Turk had Winnipeger Curly Haas as his manager. A story circulated that Zedd knew Chicago racketeer Mickey Cohen, that Cohen had introduced Zedd to Willie Wells, and so the Buffaloes were formed. This was probably not true, as Wells had played the 1949 season for the Elmwood Giants in the Manitoba Senior League. It is believed that Turk introduced Zedd to Wells and that Wells became the Buffaloes' playing manager. Percy Fenwick was hired as business manager, and local player Ian Lowe as playing manager of the Brandon Greys. Red House took over the reins of the Carman Cardinals. Ex–major leaguer Lefty Lefebvre was the manager of the Minot Mallards. The Winnipeg Buffaloes were all ex–Negro League players, such as Butch Davis, Spoon Carter, Leon Day, Lyman Bostock Sr., Frazier Robin-

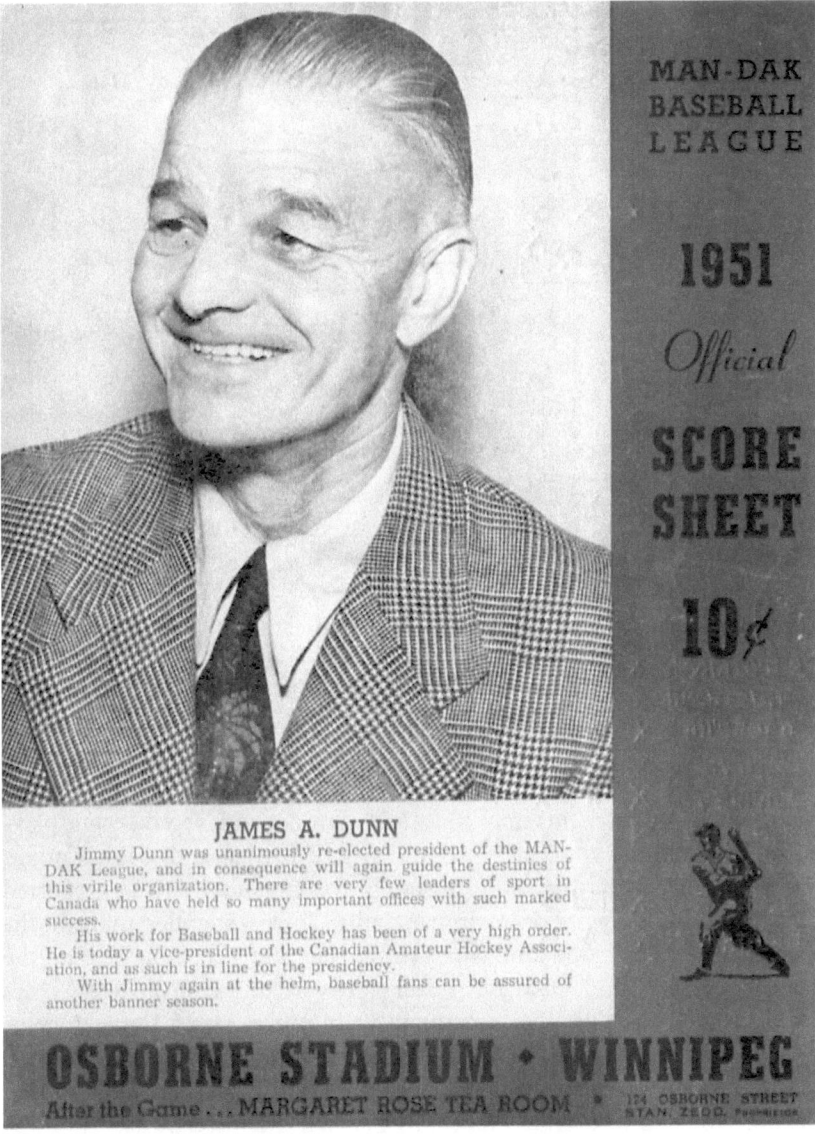

ManDak League official 1951 scorecard, featuring league president Jimmy Dunn.

son, and John Britton. They also had young players such as John Kennedy and Joe Taylor, who eventually would make it to the major leagues. The Giants had a great young center fielder named Solly Drake. Three years later, he would be playing center field for the Chicago Cubs. They also had veteran Negro League star Cowan Hyde. The bulk of the team appeared to be fringe Negro League players or players of advanced age. Brandon had

Ron Teasley's 1950 contract.

a Cuban flavor with Rafe Cabrera, Manuel Godinez, Pedro Naranjo and Armando Vasquez. Local standouts Ian Lowe and Gerry MacKay complemented a strong lineup. Carman had stars such as Lillard Cobb, Gentry Jessup, and Ron Teasley. Local boy Almer McKerlie was a team leader and a very good catcher. Minot had a mix of minor and Negro League players such as Zoonie McLean, Ted Strong, Jack Bruton and Willie Cathey. Ex–National Leaguer Joe Mack (Boston Braves) was signed. It was reported that Syd Pollack, owner of the Indianapolis Clowns, supplied many of the players for the Brandon and Minot teams that first year. Ron Teasley, the Carman player, said that "Black Jack" Stewart, the Detroit Red Wings hockey player, put the Carman executive in touch with a Detroit agent. He recommended several players from the Detroit area to Carman.

In the initial season, players stayed at the local hotels and the YMCA or were billeted in private homes. In Carman, Manitoba, the Whiteside family put up several Cardinal players, and lasting friendships were formed. Lyman Bostock, Al Spearman, and Chick Longest stayed at the Whiteside home when they were playing in Carman. Mrs. Whiteside cooked their meals and washed their clothes and provided a family atmosphere for the players, all for $50 a month. Lyman Bostock told me the Whiteside family took good care of them. Mrs. Whiteside would always send fresh pies with the players when they went on the bus for a road game.

Over the eight years that the league operated, the teams would continue to have a mix of ex–major leaguers, minor league stars and local players. It was not uncommon in those years for a player to have a 10-year minor league career. Many of the players in the league fit into that category.

Managers

Most of the teams hired playing managers. With a salary cap, this gave more money to the players. In 1950, Stanley Zedd, the owner of the Buffaloes, hired the legendary Willie Wells to manage the Winnipeg Buffaloes. He led them to the first league championship and managed them again in 1951. When the Buffaloes ceased operation, Wells moved on to manage the Brandon Greys from 1952 to 1953. After the 1953 season Wells returned for one season to the Negro League.

Ian Lowe, a local player, managed Brandon in 1950 and 1951. After the 1951 season he retired from the league and continued to manage local teams in the Brandon area. He managed the Kenton Midgets (16 years old) team to the Manitoba Provincial championship in 1955. Ex–major leaguer Dee Moore managed the Greys in 1954 and 1957.

Curly Haas managed the Elmwood Giants in their inaugural season. Haas had some help from Cy Snead. Haas had been involved in the Winnipeg baseball scene for many years. In 1951, Wes Barrow lasted 14 games, then Ted "Double Duty" Radcliffe took over as the Giants manager. In 1952, the team became the Winnipeg Giants and Bill Peterson was the new manager. He had previously managed the Moultrie Athletics in the Georgia-Florida League. Two weeks into June, Peterson was replaced and Radcliffe was back at the helm. Radcliffe lasted until July 14, when he was replaced by Jesse Douglas. In 1953 the Winnipeg Giants again had a name change and became the Winnipeg Royals. Ken Myers started the season as manager. Myers had managed Las Vegas in the Sunset League in 1948, 1949 and 1950. In 1949 he led Las Vegas to a first-place finish and was the league's All-Star manager in 1948. Myers lasted three weeks and was replaced by ex–major leaguer Dee Moore, who became the playing manager. Moore had managed the Ogden Reds of the Pioneer League in 1952.

Red House started the 1950 season as Carman manager and was replaced on June 8th by Ed Novak. Negro League great Chet Brewer managed the Cardinals in 1953. Before the 1953 season he had been manager of the Porterville Comets in the Southwest International League. Jack Schaefer was the Cardinals' playing manager in 1952. Ed Albosta managed the Cardinals in 1954. He had managed Minot to the league championship in 1953.

Ex–major leaguer Lefty Lefebvre managed the Minot Mallards in their first season. Otto Huber took over in 1951. Huber had managed the Mt. Vernon Braves in the Illinois State League in 1947. Midway through the 1951 season he threatened to quit if the Mallards didn't give him more money. The Mallards refused his request, so he quit and Zoonie McLean and Wally Jako co-managed for the remainder of the season. McLean took over the managerial duties in 1954 and 1955. Bernard Busse had to take over the reins of the Mallards midway through the 1955 season when McLean had to return to his high-school coaching job. Under McLean and Busse, the Mallards were just as good as ever, and won the championship again.

Minot hired Joe Lutz to manage Minot in 1956, but Lutz became ill. He was replaced by pitcher Joe Piercey, who was replaced midway through that season by second baseman Hal Daugherty. McLean managed the Mallards again in the 1957 season.

Ron Bowen guided the Dickinson Packers in their first season. Bill "Red" Rose managed the Packers in the 1956 season. Ex major leaguer Al Cihocki managed Bismarck in 1955 and 1956 and Bill Hockenbury managed the Barons in their last season. Lloyd Gearhart was playing manager in 1954, the first season that Williston Oilers were in the league. Roy Weatherly started the 1955 season as the Oilers' manager, then gave way to ex–major leaguer Bobby Hogue (Boston Braves). Dee Moore was playing manager in 1956, and led the Oilers to their only league and playoff championship. Preston Elkins then took over as playing manager for the Oilers in 1957.

Umpires

The ManDak League used many a local umpire. The league also hired umpires from the North Western Minnesota–Wisconsin Umpires Association. One of the good Canadian umpires was Jack "No No" Carrigan. He was described as quiet and stern, but with a great sense of humor, and was a fan favorite. He got his start as an umpire in Halifax, Nova Scotia, while in the Navy during World War II. He became Umpire-in-Chief of the Winnipeg Senior league in 1947 and was a respected umpire that first ManDak season. He was selected to the Manitoba Baseball Hall of Fame in 1999.

Another well-known umpire was Ed Claussen, who over the years umpired many games in the three American cities. He was from the Minot area. He was a standout baseball and basketball player in his early years and had pitched for the Minot Merchants before becoming an umpire.

Ab Richardson umpired many home games in Brandon. Before becoming an umpire he had been a good pitcher for the McConnell, Bradwardine and Hartney, Manitoba, baseball teams. He was the provincial and national Umpire-in-Chief and was selected to the Manitoba Baseball Hall of Fame in 1997. A 1957 article in the *Minot Daily News* stated that Brandon always had a ready pool of umpires. This would be a testament to Ab Richardson.

In 1950, Mark Van Buren was brought in from the United States to umpire games in Brandon. Before becoming an umpire he had played for the Memphis Red Sox in the Negro Leagues.

After a career-ending car accident, Steve Molinari became the only former ManDak player to umpire in the league. He went on to umpire in three U.S.A. American Legion National Championships.

Late in the 1957 season, Darcy MacKay, brother of the Greys' Gerry MacKay, would umpire in Brandon. Winnipeger Windy Lyndon also umpired in the league and was well known as a hockey referee. Newspaper reports indicated there was the odd rhubarb, but in general the quality of umpiring in the league was good.

The First Season

In 1950, the Red River overflowed and flooded much of Manitoba and North Dakota. The league openers were to be played May 20, 1950, but these games were canceled due to flooding. Minot was to play Brandon and Elmwood was to take on Carman. When the flooding was under control, the four league teams decided to play an All-Star game to raise money for the flood victims. The teams were named after the two local Winnipeg newspapers the *Winnipeg Free Press* and the *Winnipeg Tribune*. The Tribune won 8–4. Lillard Cobb was the winning pitcher and the loser was Bob Cunningham. Cliff Kempf, Rafe Cabrera and Sonny Andrews each belted a home run and Ron Teasley had two doubles. This worthy effort raised $2,643 for the flood victims. This was a substantial sum considering that tickets were in the .50 to $1.00 range. Yankee great Joe DiMaggio donated a signed baseball at the request of Winnipeg sports editor Maurice Smith. The *Free Press* indicated that DiMaggio said he was happy to help out such a worthy cause. The baseball was raffled off, and the raffle raised $266.25. The tickets were sold at 25 cents each.

The players in the All Star game were:

Free Press—Cliff Kempf, Minot (C); Jack Warwick, Elmwood (1B); Rafe Cabrera, Brandon (2B); John Britton, Buffaloes (3B); Sonny Andrews, Carman (SS); Gerry MacKay, Brandon, Minot (LF); Ed Leier, Elmwood (CF); Sam Hill, Buffaloes (RF); Taylor Smith, Buffaloes (P); Bob Cunningham, Elmwood (P); Frank Watkins, Brandon (P); Cy Snead, Elmwood (UT); Lyman Bostock, Buffaloes (UT); Willie Wells (Mgr.).

Tribune, Percy Howard, Buffaloes (C); Armando Vasquez, Brandon (1B); John Cowan, Elmwood (2B); Ian Lowe, Brandon (3B); Joe Wiley, Elmwood (SS); Solly Drake, Elmwood (LF); Ev Faunce, Minot (CF); Chuck Wilson (RF); Steve Wylie (P); Paul Jones, Elmwood (P); Lillard Cobb (P); Ron Teasley (UT); Almer McKerlie (C); Curly Haas (Mgr.).

The final score for the All-Star game was Tribune 8, Free Press 4.

The 1950 season had a 48-game schedule. Elmwood and the Buffaloes both played at Osborne Stadium, which was managed by Johnny Peterson. With two teams, there would be a game almost every night, but no games on Sunday, as the Manitoba teams didn't want to get on the bad side of the local churches. To increase fan interest, the Minot Mallards hired the legendary Satchel Paige to pitch three innings in their first three games. He didn't disappoint the fans, pitching nine scoreless innings, giving up three hits, and striking out 13. In an article in the August 2, 1997, *Minot Daily News*, Minot player Norm Felde said Satchel was going to start the game and didn't warm up beforehand. "He was standing beside me during the national anthem and I asked him why he hadn't warmed up. Satchel turned to me and said, 'I've been warmed up since 1936.'" During that season, the Louisiana Travellers, Harlem Globetrotters, Kansas City Monarchs, and Brooklyn Cuban Giants played exhibition games with the league teams.

Season Highlights

The initial season had several highlights. Ian Lowe sparked Brandon to an opening-day 12–1 victory over visiting Minot on May 24. Lowe hit a triple and a single. The game was played before 3,000 fans. That same day, Elmwood defeated Carman on a double by Willie Wells Jr. He was on loan from the Buffaloes. Taylor Smith was the winning pitcher. He was also on loan from the Buffaloes as some of the Giants players had yet to arrive in Winnipeg. Dan Webster took the loss for Carman. June 17 saw the Giants defeat Carman 9–5. Bob Cunningham was the winning pitcher and Roy McWorter took the loss. The game featured some outstanding defensive play. Solly Drake made an outstanding leaping catch, robbing Ron Teasley of at least a sure double in right center field. On June 20th, the Buffaloes' Taylor Smith and Brandon's Manuel Godinez engaged in a pitching duel. Both pitchers gave up four hits as the Buffaloes eked out a 1–0 victory. That same day, John Wingo pitched Carman to a 7–5 victory over Elmwood. It was his first start of the season. Carman was led at the plate by catcher Almer McKerlie, Lillard Cobb and Jack Schaefer. On June 24, the touring Harlem Globetrotters beat Brandon in an exhibition game, 10–4, in Brandon. The Trotters were led by Parnell Woods with four hits and Zell Miles

1—The 1950 Season

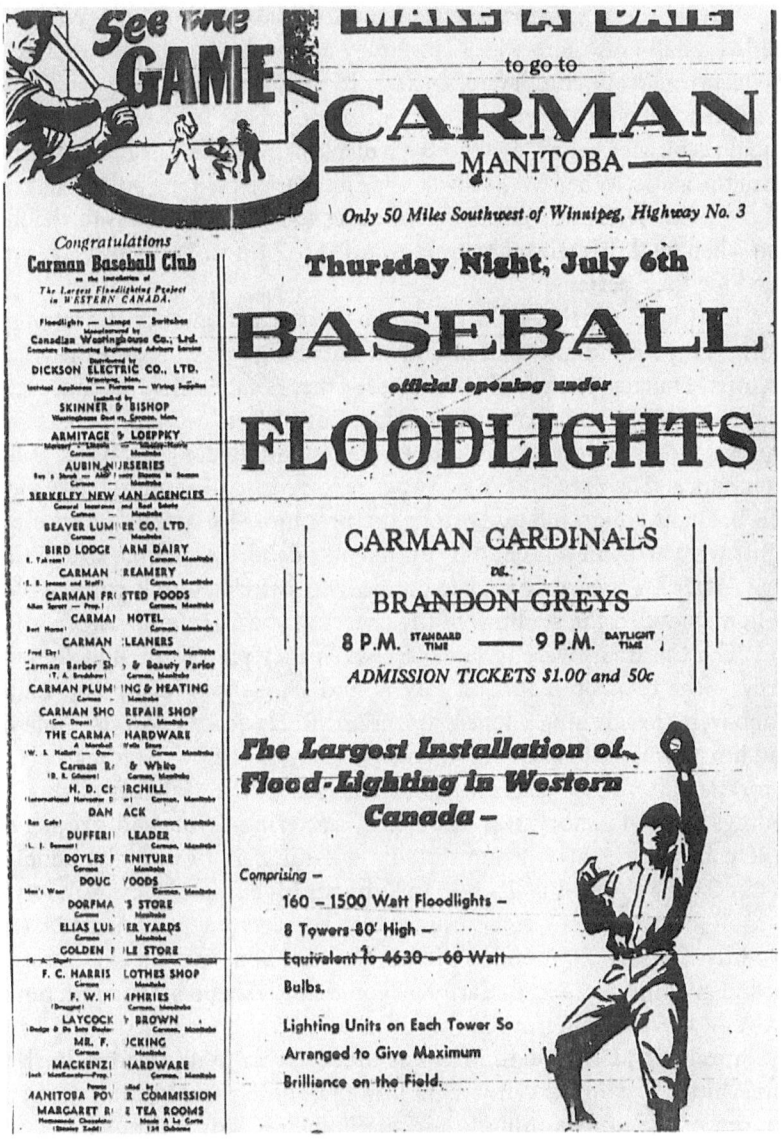

Carman Cardinals program from July 6, 1950, advertising the unveiling of the Cardinals' new lighting system.

with three hits. Hawaiian lefty Chris Mancao got the win for the Trotters. Baseball comedian Ed Hermman kept the crowd entertained with his comedic stunts.

In a July game between the Minot Mallards and Winnipeg Buffaloes, Minot was awarded a 9–0 forfeited game. The game was tied 5–5 after nine innings when the incident happened. Shortstop Willie Wells had fielded a ball and there was a close play at first base, which didn't go in Wells' favor. Wells complained bitterly to the base ump, to no avail. Then the Minot player attempted to steal second base and was ruled safe. Buffaloes pitcher Leon Day voiced his displeasure at the call and was tossed from the game. When Wells saw his ace pitcher ejected, he pulled his team off the field. Wells was given five minutes to return his team to the field and when he didn't, the game was awarded to Minot. Wells and Day were fined for their actions.

On July 6, the new lighting system was turned on at the Carman ball park. Many local dignitaries attended, including the Manitoba provincial premier, Douglas Campbell. There were other notables in attendance from provincial and municipal governments. Both Winnipeg newspapers were represented. Well-known Winnipeg sports announcer Jack Wells was in attendance. The *Free Press* newspaper reported that Premier D.L. Campbell brought congratulations from the province. He stated that the new lights were an achievement of great magnitude for a town the size of Carman. After his speech he clicked on the light switch. At that point, a blaze of lights flooded the stadium to the cheers of the Carman fans.

The Cardinals were in last place when they played the Buffaloes and Greys—the two top teams on July 17 and 18. Gentry Jessup and Lillard Cobb were the winning pitchers for the Cardinals. Jessup beat the Buffaloes and Jim Newberry 3–2. Cobb shut out the Greys 8–0 as the Cardinals played errorless ball. July 18 also saw Bob Danielson of the Mallards pitch all 14 innings in a 3–1 victory over the Giants, scattering 10 hits and striking out 14. On July 20, Gentry Jessup tossed a one-hitter in beating the Buffaloes 3–1 in Carman. The Buffaloes' John Kennedy hit a single in the fifth inning to spoil the no-hitter. Catcher Almer McKerlie led the Carman attack with two hits. On July 25, Brandon pitcher Dirk Gibbons made a wild throw to second base in a 4–3 loss to Carman. Gord Elliot's single in the ninth inning drove in the winning run. On July 27 Frank Watkins pitched a one-hitter for Brandon and lost 1–0 to Minot as the Mallards' Willie Cathey hurled a three-hitter to gain the victory. On July 28 Brandon scored two runs in the bottom of the ninth inning to nip the Buffaloes 5–4. Pedro Naranjo was the winning pitcher and Taylor Smith took the loss. Gerry MacKay, Armando Vasquez and Skeeter Watkins all had two hits.

Brandon beat the Buffaloes 2–1 on August 3 in Brandon. Although Brandon won the game, Buffaloes manager Willie Wells disputed the winning home run hit by Rafe Cabrera. Wells said the home run ball had gone under the right field fence instead of clearing the stands. Wells complained to umpire Mark Van Buren with no success, and the game was played under protest. An executive meeting was held the next day and Van Buren's decision was upheld. On August 4, Pedro Naranjo of the Greys hurled 12 shutout innings in a 1–0 victory over Carman's Lillard Cobb. Brandon scored the winning run in the 13th inning on a wild pitch by Cobb. Armando Vasquez and Skeeter Watkins each had two hits for the Greys. On the same day, Taylor Smith carried a no-hitter into the eighth inning as the Buffaloes beat Elmwood 6–2. Smith got the first two batters out in the eighth, then gave up three hits. He finished up with a four-hitter with seven strikeouts and two walks. The Buffaloes took advantage of seven Elmwood errors. Hot-hitting Butch Davis paced the winners with three hits.

On August 9, Manager Ian Lowe of Brandon drove in five runs in a 12–3 victory over the Buffaloes. On August 10, Brandon beat the Elmwood Giants 16–3, in a fight-filled game. The fights resulted from alleged "bean balls." In the first incident, Giants pitcher Ray Finch hit Brandon's Rafe Cabrera. The next batter, Ramon Rodriguez had to back off the plate on an inside pitch. He charged the mound with his bat in hand and attempted to get at Finch. Order was restored, and to everyone's surprise there were no ejections, although the league did suspend the players involved. On August 11, Ian Lowe singled in the 12th inning to give Brandon its tenth straight victory. Art Hunt entered the game in the eighth inning and retired 13 straight batters for the win. On August 13, there was a 17-strikeout performance by the Buffaloes' Taylor Smith against the Carman Cardinals. The final score was 9–1. The game was part of an afternoon and evening doubleheader. In the second game, the Buffaloes beat Carman 5–4. Jim Newberry got the win and Carman's ace, Gentry Jessup, took the loss. The Winnipeg fans showed their disapproval with Newberry when he threw a wild pitch that allowed the tying run. When he got the ball back he chucked it into right field. In the afternoon game, Buffaloes manager Willie Wells had four hits in five at-bats, then went 1 for 3 in the nightcap. Ron Teasley led Carman with a double and three singles in the afternoon-game and followed that with two singles in the evening game.

On August 14, Leon Day tossed a three-hit 9–0 shutout over the Minot Mallards. He faced 30 batters, fanned 11, and walked one. He also drove in three runs with a bases-clearing double. Carman beat Brandon 4–3 on August 16 behind the pitching of Lillard Cobb. Dirk Gibbons took the loss for Brandon. It was Brandon's first loss since July 27. Gord Elliot knocked in two runs to pace the Cardinals. Gentry Jessup pitched a two-hitter for Carman on August 17 in a 12–1 victory over Elmwood. On August 23, Brandon snuffed out a ninth-inning Carman rally with a triple play to gain a 7–5 victory. Ian Lowe at third base scooped up the hard-hit ball and rifled it to second baseman Murray Watkins, who threw the ball to first baseman Armando Vasquez, who threw home to catch Bob Johnson trying to score from third base. Dirk Gibbons was the winner and Joe Adams took the loss. Carman shaded Elmwood 12–11 on August 24 to clinch a playoff spot. Each team used three pitchers. John Wingo picked up the victory and Paul Jones took the loss. Ron Teasley, Solly Drake and Cowan Hyde all hit home runs.

Tournament Play

Tournament play was popular in 1950. On June 14, the Winnipeg Buffaloes took first prize in the $1,400 Brandon Invitational Tournament. Taylor Smith was the winning pitcher in the final game beating host Brandon 8–1. Wilfredo Gonzales and Pedro Naranjo, both Cubans, pitched for Brandon. Gonzales took the loss. Butch Davis and Lyman Bostock led the Buffaloes in the hitting department. The Regina Caps and Muskogee Cardinals were the other teams in the tournament.

On June 29, the Brandon Greys won top prize in the $2,000 Moosomin, Saskatchewan, tournament before 4,500 fans. Frank Watkins won the final game, beating Carman's John Wingo. Skeeter Watkins and Ian Lowe were the hitting stars for the Greys. The Brooklyn Cuban Giants and Elmwood Giants were the other teams in that tournament. On July 1, Brandon hosted the Dominion Day Tournament. The touring Harlem Globetrotters beat Brandon 3–2 in the final. First prize was $500. Jimmy Williams gave up three hits to win for the Globetrotters. On July 3, Brandon beat the Louisiana Travelers 5–4 in the Minot, North Dakota, tournament. The Regina Caps played in that tournament. The July 4 Holiday Tournament saw newcomer Art Hunt, formerly with the Brooklyn Cuban Giants, pitch Brandon to a 6–5 victory over Minot. Rafe Cabrera led Brandon with three hits and Ted Strong homered for Minot. Brandon won the Virden, Manitoba, tournament on July 5, defeating the Minot Mallards 13–7. Tom Johnson was the winning pitcher in the final game. The Regina Caps finished third, beating the touring Muskogee Cardinals 9–0. That victory gave Brandon three tournament wins in a busy week of baseball. On August 7, the Buffaloes took home first prize money in the $1500 Portage La Prairie tournament. Buffaloes manager Willie Wells went the distance on the mound, scattering 11 hits for the win. Brandon won the pennant that first season, with a seven-game lead over the Buffaloes.

The final standings for 1950:

	W	L	GBL
Brandon Greys	32	16	
Winnipeg Buffaloes	25	23	7
Minot Mallards	24	24	8
Carman Cardinals	21	27	11
Elmwood Giants	18	30	14

The Buffaloes' Butch Davis won the batting title with a .456 average. He had led the league from start to finish. He also led the league with 78 hits and tied with Brandon's Ian Lowe for the most RBI with 39. Gentry Jessup led the pitchers with 10 wins and Brandon's Art Hunt had a perfect 9–0 record.

Playoffs

The first round of the playoffs was a best-of-five series that started on August 29. The Winnipeg Buffaloes played the Minot Mallards in the first round. In game one, Minot's best hurler, Willie Cathey, held the Buffaloes in check until the ninth inning, when Lyman Bostock hit a two-run single that gave the Buffaloes a hard-fought 3–2 victory. Bostock hit the ball hard at shortstop Zoonie McLean. It took a high bounce and went over McLean's outstretched arm. The Minot infield had been pinched in. Leon Day was the winning pitcher, with a five-hitter. He struck out eight and walked four. Cathey gave up nine hits, striking out three and walking none. McLean was spectacular at short for the Mallards. He handled 14 chances and turned 13 of them into outs. Davis and Bostock each had two hits for the Buffaloes. In Game 2, in Minot, the Buffaloes came from behind to take a 6–5 victory. Butch Davis tripled in Sam Hill with the winning run. Jim Newberry was the winner with two innings of fine relief. In Game 3, the Buffaloes crushed the Mallards 13–4 to advance to the league final. Jim Newberry went the distance for the win and Cathey took the loss. Joe Taylor knocked in four runs, including a home run, and Bostock and Frazier Robinson also homered.

Carman pushed league-leading Brandon to five games before Brandon beat them, three games to two. In the first game, Gentry Jessup hurled a two-hitter and lost 2–1 to the Greys. In that game, the Cardinals made five errors and ruined a good pitching job by Jessup. Jessup fanned 11 and walked six. Art Hunt was the winner with a three-hitter. Carman bounced back in Game 2 as Lillard Cobb beat Frank Watkins 6–3. Dirk Gibbons came on for Watkins in the seventh inning and finished the game. Brandon made five errors, which didn't help their cause. Cobb helped himself when he belted a two-run home run. Sonny Andrews and Ron Teasley each had three hits for the Cardinals. Brandon took Game 3 as 18-year-old Pedro Naranjo beat Carman 8–2 before 3,500 Brandon fans. John Wingo took the loss for Carman. Brandon manager Ian Lowe led the Greys with three hits. The Cardinals again tied the series with a 4–3 Game 4 win before 3,000 happy Carman fans. This game featured an argument between the umpire, the managers, and the players. In the fifth inning, Carman's Ron Teasley hit a ball which appeared to clear the right field fence. A dispute arose as to whether the ball had bounced over the fence and should have been ruled a ground-rule double, or was a home run. When things settled down, Teasley was awarded a home run. The Cardinals made five errors in the game, but Brandon couldn't take advantage of it. Ron Teasley had a double and two singles for Carman. Gentry Jessup bested Manuel Godinez in the pitching department. This forced a fifth and final game. Brandon won the series as their ace, Art Hunt, blanked the Cardinals 7–0. Lillard Cobb took the loss. Cobb was supposed to leave the day before to start his new job in Detroit. The win was Hunt's eleventh straight and was played before a record crowd of 5000 in Brandon.

The best-of-seven final featured the Brandon Greys and Winnipeg Buffaloes. This series got under way on September 6. The opening game produced a 13-inning 9–7 Buffaloes victory. There were 26 hits, 15 errors, and three ejections. Frazier Robinson and Lyman Bostock were the big hitters for the Buffaloes. Jim Newberry got the win in relief and Dirk Gibbons took the loss also in relief. Game 2 saw the Buffaloes nip the Greys 7–6 in a come-from-behind victory. Joe Taylor drove in Leon Day with the winning run. Jim Newberry was again the winner in relief and Art Hunt took the loss in relief. An 8–2 victory in Game 3 left the Buffaloes one win away from the championship. Day and Bostock led the Buffaloes' hitting in this game as each drove in two runs. Jim Newberry again was the winning pitcher. Newberry came into the game in the sixth inning for Andy Porter. With two on and one out, Brandon's Charley Peete got on base when second baseman John Kennedy made an error to load the bases. Newberry then struck out Gerry MacKay and Dirk Gibbons to end the threat. Andy Porter got the win. Newberry was becoming the series star, having won in relief in the first two games and saved the third. A 7–3 Brandon victory kept their fragile playoff hopes alive in Game 4. Dirk Gibbons gave up two hits in four innings of relief for the win. Ian Lowe had two hits for Brandon.

The fifth and final game saw one of the best pitching duels fans could wish to see. Not many baseball historians know about this game. Both pitchers, Leon Day of the Buffaloes and Manuel Godinez of the Greys, hurled all 17 innings in a 1–0 Buffaloes win. Day gave up six hits, had eight strikeouts, and walked only six. Godinez gave up nine hits, had three strikeouts, and gave up no walks in his 17 innings of work. Buffaloes manager Willie Wells wasn't around to see the final result, as he was tossed from the game in the 10th inning. The argument developed when Brandon had runners on first and second base. Chuck Wilson hit an infield roller to second baseman John Kennedy. Kennedy attempted a double play, but the umpire ruled the runner safe. The umpire said that Kennedy had stepped over the bag and his throw was not in time to catch the speedy

Wilson at first. Wells was out of the dugout in a flash and the argument was on. Umpire Mark Van Buren gave Wells two minutes to leave the field, and when he didn't, he was tossed from the game. That left the bases loaded with two out. Brandon was going to try a squeeze play. Buffaloes catcher Frazier Robinson stole the sign and called for a pitchout, and they caught Godinez at home trying to score from third. In the 17th inning, Buffaloes slugger Butch Davis smashed a single and went to second when right fielder Charlie Peete let the ball get away from him. Lyman Bostock laid down a perfect sacrifice bunt to move Davis to third. Day then grounded out, and that brought Joe Taylor to the plate. Taylor singled, driving in Davis with the only run of the game. Day shut the door in the bottom of the 17th and the Buffaloes became the first ManDak League champions. Following the game, the Buffaloes held a victory party at one of the fancy eating establishments in Brandon.

At season's end the *Winnipeg Tribune* announced its ManDak League All-Star team:

Catcher	Ramon Rodriguez	Brandon
First Base	Lyman Bostock	Winnipeg
Second Base	John Kennedy	Winnipeg
Third Base	Ian Lowe	Brandon
Shortstop	Rafe Cabrera	Brandon
Left Field	Butch Davis	Winnipeg
Center Field	Solly Drake	Elmwood
Right Field	Jack Schaefer	Carman
Utility	Leon Day	Winnipeg
Pitchers	Dirk Gibbons	Brandon
	Art Hunt	Brandon
	Taylor Smith	Winnipeg
	Gentry Jessup	Carman
Manager	Lefty Lefebvre	Minot

With the season over, the American and Cuban players returned south to their homes. Some went on to play winter ball in Mexico and South America. The Carman Cardinals had a going-away chicken supper at the Carman Memorial Hall. C.N. Bedford, the club president, thanked the players for getting the team into the playoffs. He complimented them on their fine sportsmanship, both on the diamond and in the community. The following day, before leaving, Gentry Jessup, Joe Adams, and Bob Johnson visited the school grounds in Carman to say goodbye to their young fans and signed many autographs.

2
The 1951 Season

Jimmy Dunn was reelected league president. Optimism in the league ran high. The league increased the number of games to 64. Owner Stanley Zedd was optimistic that the Buffaloes could repeat their success. He thought the Buffaloes were as good as any team in Canada, and that included the Triple A teams in Toronto and Montreal. The Buffaloes signed Pee Wee Butts to play shortstop. Many considered him the greatest shortstop in the Negro Leagues. Charlie White, a young third baseman, also was signed. He had been a .300 hitter the year before with the Chicago Colored Giants, and eventually played parts of two seasons with the Milwaukee Braves. Giants owner Alex Turk thought his team would be on top when the season ended. The Giants still had Negro League star Cowan Hyde, and added Ducky Davenport and Jesse Douglas. Ted "Double Duty" Radcliffe joined the Giants shortly into the season. Carman, Brandon and Minot all thought their clubs had improved and would be challenging for the championship. It looked like a banner season ahead. Minot was expecting good things for its ball club. Hard-hitting Othello Renfroe was signed and midway through the season Minot acquired young Canadian Gerry MacKay. He had played the previous season with the Brandon Greys. The pitching staff appeared strong with the return of Willie Cathey. Hal Schacker, who had had a brief appearance with the Boston Braves, and Sugar Cain were signed. Jonas Gaines was added to an already strong pitching staff which was expected to carry Minot to the championship. Brandon still had its Cuban contingent, with Pedro Naranjo, Rafe Cabrera, and Manuel Godinez, and slugging first baseman Alonzo Perry. The team still featured local player Ian Lowe. Lowe was considered a standout. Before coming to the ManDak League, he had played several years in organized ball. Carman's pitching staff was headed by former Negro League stars Gentry Jessup, Al Spearman, and Gene Smith. Herb Souell and Sonny Andrews led the hitting attack. Local player Almer McKerlie returned as catcher. Besides being good defensively, he had a strong arm. Midway through the season he broke his toe when hit by a pitch, and was finished for that year.

The 1950 Carman Cardinals (Dufferin Historical Society).

The season opener attracted over 6,028 fans at Osborne Stadium, in a game between the Buffaloes and Brandon. Newcomer Charlie White and Joe Taylor each had three hits and Taylor Smith, with the help of Jim Newberry, pitched the Buffaloes to an 11–4 victory.

Season Highlights

The Winnipeg Buffaloes played their home opener against Brandon on May 19 before 6,000 happy fans. Centerfielder Leon Day had three hits and three RBI. Charlie White and Joe Taylor each hit three-run home runs. On May 26th, Day got tossed from the game in the fourth inning of a Buffaloes 9–6 win over Brandon. Jim Newberry came on in relief and pitched no-hit ball the rest of the way. Alonzo Perry made his Brandon debut on May 29 and hit a home run, double, and a single, and had two walks in an 8–6 win over Elmwood. Perry continued his hot hitting on May 30 with four hits, including a home run and three RBI. In that game, Minot playing manager Otto Huber was ejected for arguing ground rules. Huber was allowed to stay in the game when he explained to the umpire that he had no one to take his place on the bench, and apologized to the umpire.

Jim Newberry pitched a six-hitter on June 1 beating Brandon 3–0. Lefty McKinnis took the loss. The night was very cold and the game was over in 1 hour 37 minutes. Leon Day and Alonzo Perry each had a triple and single for their respective teams. On June 10, Perry hit a tremendous home run over the center-field wall. It was the first time a ball had been hit over the wall since 1933. In Perry's next game, he had four hits. He played 14 more games for Brandon and was hitting at a .397 clip, with five home runs and 19 RBI, when he jumped the team for the Dominican League and a reported salary of $1,500. On June 11, Double Duty Radcliffe struck out eight and walked only three in going the distance in a 13–4 win over Minot. He also helped himself at the plate with two doubles and a single. On June 14, Brandon was awarded a 9–0 forfeit decision. Brandon had the bases loaded when Pepper Bassett swung at a ball that was ruled "catcher's interference." Minot's manager, Otto Huber, thought the ball had been tipped foul. After an umpire meeting, the decision remained the same, and Minot packed up their equipment and left the field. Two days later, Huber was fined $100 and suspended for two games. The ManDak executive ruled that any manager in the future who would pull his team off the field would be suspended for the season and the club fined $1,000. At the same meeting, in an unrelated incident, Giants manager Double Duty Radcliffe was fined $25 for abusive language and disregard for an umpire in another June 14 game. On June 23, there was a report in the Winnipeg paper that some ManDak clubs were complaining about umpire Mark Van Buren. The complaint stated that Van Buren had helped stock the Brandon Greys club with players. Van Buren had been a player in the Negro Leagues before coming to Manitoba to umpire. The allegations were not proven and no action was taken. On June 27, Leon Day pitched shutout ball and stroked a three-run homer in a 7–0 victory over Minot.

On July 1, outfielder Connie Juelke and catcher Chuck Wiles left the Mallards overnight without telling anyone. At the time, Juelke was batting .280 and playing well. Wiles was not a great loss, as he was batting only .202 at the time. Cleveland Indians scout Stan Lucas came to Winnipeg on July 3 to scout the ManDak League talent and specifically to look at Buffaloes third baseman Charlie White. On July 4, the *Free Press* reported that 8 ManDak League players had been charged with disorderly conduct from an early-morning altercation, and all appeared in City of Winnipeg Police Court. The players involved were Lou Louden and Paul Jefferson of the Elmwood Giants and Jim Newberry, Leon Day, Taylor Smith, Frazier Robinson, Al Wilmore, and Pee Wee Butts of the Winnipeg Buffaloes. Each player was fined $50. At a league hearing that followed, the players were fined an additional $50 and the league stated that any similar actions would result in permanent suspensions. In early July, the Toronto Maple Leafs of the International League were looking for some player help and sent scout Bill Welsh to Winnipeg to look at the Buffaloes. It was reported that he was there to scout the Buffaloes' hot-hitting Butch Davis and shortstop Pee Wee Butts. The scout was very impressed and contacted Rip Collins, Toronto head scout. Collins came to Winnipeg and within days he headed back to Toronto with Charlie White. The Maple Leafs were the Triple-A farm team for the St. Louis Browns. The Buffaloes then made a deal with Browns owner Bill Veeck for the rights to Leon Day, John Kennedy, Jim Newberry, and Butch Davis. They were regarded as the best and youngest of the Buffaloes players. On July 10th the *Free Press* reported that at a Buffaloes practice, Leon Day was being called "Bonus Baby" for his impending signing with the St. Louis Browns. Willie Wells was quoted as saying that Davis received $1,000 and Day $800 to sign. Day headed to Toronto and Davis to Albany. Their departure ruined the Buffaloes' chance of repeating as champions. Owner Stanley Zedd became disillusioned with the loss of those players, and that led to his folding the Buffaloes at season's end. During the season, the Elmwood Giants sold Jesse Douglas to the Chicago White Sox, who assigned him to Colorado Springs in the Class A Western League. On July 5, Brandon pulled off a triple play in a 7–2 victory over Minot. Skeeter Watkins started the triple killing. With two men on the bases, Zoonie McLean hit what appeared to be a single, but Watkins made a spectacular catch and threw to second to catch Harvey Beaster off base. Willie Cathey was tagged out coming late to second base. On July 15, Minot manager Otto Huber resigned in a financial dispute with management, and McLean took over the club. On July 19, Carman's Gentry Jessup blanked Minot 1–0 in Carman. He struck out six and issued no walks. Walt Thomas doubled in the winning run. On July 20, Willie Wells pinch-hit in the ninth inning and hit a home run to give the Buffaloes a 4–3 win over Brandon.

Johnny Jones the famous baseball clown, put on his show of laugh-provoking stunts on August 4 in Winnipeg at a game between the Royals and Mallards. Armando Suarez fired a three-hit, 1–0 victory on August 10 in an exhibition game against the California Mohawks. The winning run scored on an error by future Boston Red Sox infielder Pumpsie Green. Al Spearman pitched a one-hitter on August 12 against Minot in a 2–1 win. On August 16 the Buffaloes' O.B. Robison beat Minot 2–1 on a one-hitter.

Tournament Play

Tournament play again proved to be popular and profitable. On July 2, the Buffaloes won the $1,500 Brandon Holiday Tournament, defeating the Elmwood Giants 3–2. Willie Wells doubled and Lyman Bostock hit a hard drive that brought in the winning run. Leon Day was the winning pitcher and Ray Finch took the loss. On July 6, Moosomin, Saskatchewan, hosted its $2,200 tournament. The Brandon Greys beat the Indian Head Rockets 13–9 and the Estevan Maple Leafs 12–5 to take the first prize money. Clarence King and Pepper Bassett hit home runs for the Greys. Pedro Naranjo and Armando Suarez were the winning pitchers. On July 12, the Elmwood Giants' Ray Finch beat Brandon 1–0 on a one-hitter in the Brandon Invitational Tournament. Pedro Naranjo had a two-hitter in a losing cause. The Carman Cardinals scored six runs in the ninth inning to beat the Estevan Maple Leafs 13–9 to win the Virden, Manitoba, tournament and first prize money. Fred Brenzell was the winning pitcher. Brandon and Yorkton, Saskatchewan, participated in the tournament. Estevan, Saskatchewan, held a $1,200 tournament on July 25. Estevan beat Minot 6–3, before 7,000 cheering fans. The final standings for 1951 were:

	W	L	GBL
Brandon Greys	37	26	
Winnipeg Buffaloes	34	29	3
Minot Mallards	32	32	5½
Carman Cardinals	34	34	7½
Elmwood Giants	26	38	11½

Even though the Buffaloes' Butch Davis went into organized ball, he still had enough at-bats to win his second batting championship. Davis batted .406 and led the league in RBI with 53. Gread McKinnis of Brandon led the league with 11 wins. Bob Harvey of Elmwood led the league with nine home runs. At season's end there was talk of Minot ceasing operation, as the club had a $13,000 debt. With the season over, Minot held a fan appreciation exhibition game which reduced the debt by $5,000 and was looking to get 100 stockholders to donate $100 each towards the next season's operation.

Playoffs

The 1951 playoffs were a best-of-seven series. The Buffaloes faced the Mallards and Carman played Brandon in the semi-finals. Those were the same matchups as in the previous year. Elmwood was out of the playoffs for the second straight year. Both of these series would go the full seven games. The Buffaloes also got lucky, as Minot's top pitcher, Sugar Cain, left after the third game to pitch in the Dominican Republic. Newspaper reports indicated that Cain was being paid $1,500 a month. O.B. Robison pitched a three hit 11–0 opening-game Buffaloes victory. Zell Miles drove in three runs for the Buffaloes. The Mallards made eight errors. Games two and three were part of a doubleheader in Minot. The Buffaloes won the opener 7–5 and Minot took the nightcap 9–8. In game one, Al Wilmore was the winning pitcher and John Kennedy had three hits for the Buffaloes.

Willie Wells, Pee Wee Butts, and Frazier Robinson had two hits each. In game three, Sugar Cain made his final appearance on the mound before leaving for the Dominican Republic. He wasn't very effective, but his five hits in five at-bats helped his own cause in a 9–8 victory. Minot tied the series in game four as Willie Cathey pitched them to a 6–4 victory and O.B. Robison took the loss. Wally Jako hit a three-run homer and Zoonie McLean had three hits for the Mallards. Minot took a three games to two lead, as Frank Watkins, a Canadian, beat the Buffaloes 6–2. Watkins was a late-season replacement. Another Canadian, Gerry MacKay, hit a three-run homer that drove in the winning runs for Minot. Willie Wells took the loss in a rare pitching performance. Needing a victory in game six to win the series, the Mallards lost to the Buffaloes 10–6. Pee Wee Jenkins was the winner and Willie Cathey, working on two days rest, was the losing pitcher. The Buffaloes won game seven 5–2 and advanced to the finals. Winner Al Wilmore was sharp in relief of O.B. Robison. Othello Strong had three hits and drove in three runs to lead the Buffaloes in the hitting department. The Buffaloes, despite the loss of Day, Davis, and White, still had enough talent to beat the Mallards.

The Brandon-Carman series would prove most interesting. Gentry Jessup's pitching and Gene Smith's hitting led Carman to a 2–1 victory in game one. Jessup gave up four hits and fanned 11. Pedro Naranjo gave up six hits in the loss. Carman jumped into a two-game lead with a 4–1 win in game two. Al Jacowski pitched the complete game victory and Gread McKinnis took the loss. Carman shut out Brandon 6–0 in game three, putting them one game from the league finals. Willie Hutchinson pitched shutout ball and Herb Souell, Joe Wiley, and Bob Johnson had two hits each for the Cardinals. Armando Suarez took the loss. With their backs to the wall, Brandon eked out a 2–1, ten-inning victory. Pedro Naranjo bested Gentry Jessup in the pitching department. Ramon Rodriguez singled in Pepper Bassett with the winning run. In game five, Brandon pounded out 14 hits and beat Carman 10–3 before 4,000 fans. Gread McKinnis was the winning pitcher and Gene Smith took the loss. Manager Ian Lowe had four hits for the Greys. This forced a sixth game. In game six, Lowe drove in Rafe Cabrera with the winning run in Brandon's 3–2 victory. Armando Suarez was the winning pitcher. This forced a seventh and final game. In game seven, 18-year old Amancio Ferro allowed only four hits and fanned seven in a 1–0 Brandon victory. Ed Finney, in his first game back from a broken leg, drove in the only run in the seventh inning. Willie Hutchinson pitched well in defeat, giving up only four hits. This capped a great Brandon comeback after the Greys had lost the first three games. They went on to meet the Buffaloes in the final series.

Brandon demolished the Buffaloes in four straight games. In the first

I. History of the League

game, Brandon edged the Buffaloes 3–1. Brandon's two 18-year old Cuban lefties, Pedro Naranjo and Armando Suarez, pitched the Greys to victory. Pee Wee Jenkins took the loss. Game two was a wild affair that Brandon won 17–8. Gread McKinnis was the winner in relief. Ian Lowe and Skeeter Watkins each had three hits and Clarence King drove in four runs. Lyman Bostock stroked three hits for the Buffaloes. Lowe drove in three runs with a double and a single to pace Brandon to a 5–4 game three win. Amancio Ferro was the winning pitcher. During the season he had failed to win a game. Leon Day took the loss. Day had just returned from the Toronto Maple Leafs of the International League. Brandon won game four 5–3 to sweep the Buffaloes. Armando Suarez was the winning pitcher and O.B. Robison took the loss. Joe Mitchell and Skeeter Watkins led the Greys with home runs. Frazier Robinson hit a round-tripper for the Buffaloes. This was Brandon's first and only league championship.

3
The 1952 Season

Before the start of the season the Buffaloes ceased operation. This left the Giants as the only Winnipeg team. Elmwood had finished last in the two previous ManDak seasons. The Elmwood Giants changed their name to the Winnipeg Giants. Minot was assured of operating when they got 100 investors at $100 each, which cleared up their debt from the previous season. The league voted to make all teams eligible for the playoffs. Minot's Roy Reimer became the league President and Coleman Traub took over as president of the Mallards in Minot. On May 23, Carman held an auction to raise money for the team. They auctioned off items such as trucks, tractors and refrigerators.

The Giants improved themselves. They had such stalwarts as Ray Finch, Cowan Hyde, Lester Lockett, Lou Louden and Othello Strong. Lyman Bostock joined Sam Hill, Herb Souell, Gentry Jessup, Harry Rhodes, and Almer McKerlie in Carman. Carman finished five games behind Minot at season's end. Brandon finished in last place with their Cuban players. Willie Wells was signed to manage the Greys and Pee Wee Butts and Frazier Robinson joined Wells in Brandon for the 1952 season. Minot finished in first place with mostly new players. Holdovers Sugar Cain and Jonas "Lefty" Gaines headed a strong pitching staff. Quincy Barbee, a 13-year Negro League veteran, was at first base. Zoonie McLean returned at short. He was regarded by many as the premier shortstop in the league. Newcomers added were catcher Joe Massaro, former Buffaloes player John Kennedy, outfielders Don Corcoran, and Yogi Giammarco, a 7-year minor league veteran.

The final standings for 1952 were:

	W	L	GBL
Minot Mallards	32	22	
Carman Cardinals	27	25	5
Winnipeg Giants	25	29	7
Brandon Greys	24	30	8

The Minot Mallards' hitting and home run power led them to their first of four straight championships. The Mallards led the league in all hitting departments. Zoonie McLean won the batting championship with a .369 average. The home run leader was Yogi Giammarco, with 11, and the RBI leader was Joe Massaro, with 55. The Winnipeg Giants' Hal Price led the pitchers with 10 wins and 130 strikeouts.

SEASON HIGHLIGHTS

One highlight of the 1952 season was the league's decision to play four league tournaments, one in each of the four member cities. On May 24, Gentry Jessup shut out the Winnipeg Giants 4–0 in the season opener in Carman. Both teams lined up on the basepaths and were introduced. Along with the game, a 125-piece band, gathered from Carman and five surrounding towns, performed before the start of the games. A majorette corps also performed and the concession stands did a booming business. The game was attended by 3,500 in a town of 1,500 people.

Another highlight came early in the season, when Sugar Cain beat Brandon 10–0 on a 3-hit, 15-strikeout performance. The season also featured a pitching duel between the Mallards' Jonas Gaines and the Giants' Hal Price. The game went 13 innings and ended in a 1–1 tie, called because of the curfew. Both pitchers went the distance.

In July, the Chicago American Giants and the Memphis Red Sox played three league games at Osborne Stadium in Winnipeg. With the Negro Leagues in decline, they had attendance problems in their home parks, so they took their show on the road. On July 4th, with Minot in first place, catcher Joe Massaro and hard-hitting outfielder Yogi Giammarco were offered more money and bonuses to return to their former Richmond team, but fortunately for the Mallards, they stayed in Minot. That month, Connie Juelke of Minot hit three home runs in a doubleheader against Carman. In another July game, Brandon's José Colas made 10 putouts in center field in a loss to Minot. Many of them were of the spectacular variety. Elmwood Giants General manager Curly Haas fired Double Duty Radcliffe and replaced him with Jesse Douglas on July 14. Haas thought that Radcliffe wasn't getting the most out of some of the veteran players. On July 18, Minot's Quincy Barbee hit five singles in an 11–2 victory over the Indian Head Rockets. On July 25, Carman's Willie Hutchinson fanned 11 in a 4–2 win over Minot. In that game, Minot's Yogi Giammarco hit his 16th home run, a 420-foot blast which, to that date, was a league home run record. On August 14, Brandon beat Minot 12–11 in 12 innings to keep their mathematical chance to finish in first place alive. Sam Williams was the winner and Willy Greene took the loss. Luther Clifford and Armando Vasquez led Brandon at the plate with four hits each. Minot's Don Cor-

Man-Dak Baseball League

Opening Game

OSBORNE STADIUM
SATURDAY, MAY 24th, 1952

CARMAN CARDINALS	WINNIPEG GIANTS
A McCURLIE c	2—LOU LOUDIN c
L BOSTOCK 1b	15—MEL GELLEGES c
P CARLISLE .... ss	4—JESSE DOUGLAS 2b
RIDDLEY 2b	6—JERRY POWELL .... ss
C LONGEST .... of	5—NICK CORNULLI 3b
S ANDREWS .... of	7—CLIFF GONZALES .... of
SAM HILL .... of	8—AL TEHRO .... of
H RHODES .... of	9—BOB HARVEY .... of
RICHARDSON .... p	10—ELL ENDRESS 1b
G JESSUP .... p	11—DON LOWEEN .... of
W HUTCHISON .... p	15—BILL COX .... p
E. BOUCHET 1b	17—HAL PRICE .... p
SHAFFER .... mgr.	16—KAVIN KING .... p
BRENDELL	BILL PETERSEN, p. & mgr
	ARN. FERNANDEZ

NEXT GAME—
Winnipeg Giants vs. Minot Mallards
WEDNESDAY, MAY 28th

The Winnipeg Giants' Opening Day program, 1952.

coran hit two home runs and drove in six runs on August 15 against the Winnipeg Giants.

TOURNAMENT PLAY

In the first tournament of the year in Brandon, Bob Landers pitched a no-hitter for the Mallards over the Cardinals. After a few more starts he was released. Minot beat Elmwood Giants in the final of its tournament 10–4. Warren Martin picked up the win and Walt McCoy took the loss. Quincy Barbee had a home run, triple, and two singles and Wally Jako hit two doubles and two singles for the Mallards. On July 8 and 9, the Mallards won the $2,000 first prize in the Foam Lake, Saskatchewan, tournament. Sugar Cain was the pitching star as Minot beat the Brandon Greys 15–3 in the final. It was reported that 7,000 fans attended the tournament. In August, Winnipeg hosted a $3,000 tournament. Brandon beat Carman 2–1 in the final game before 4,000 fans. Armando Vasquez was the star at the plate for Brandon. In the ninth inning he singled, then stole second and third base, and came home when catcher Leonard Pigg threw wildly when he tried to catch Vasquez stealing third. Pee Wee Jenkins was the winner and Jerry Cobb, a minor league pitcher from Roblin, Manitoba, got the loss.

During the season, ManDak teams played several exhibition games. The Indian Head Rockets entertained ManDak teams at home and on the road, and a number of barnstorming teams played in ManDak League parks. As the ManDak schedule was increased, tournament play was not as popular, and the teams played more exhibition games to gain more revenue.

Playoffs

In the semifinals, Minot swept Brandon in four straight. Sugar Cain fired a six-hitter for Minot to win the first game 7–2. Pee Wee Jenkins took the loss. Yogi Giammarco blasted a 420-foot, two-run home run for the Mallards. The game featured some great fielding plays by Joe Massaro, John Kennedy, Duke Bowman, and Zoonie McLean. In game two the Mallards came from behind for an 8–5 victory. Jonas Gaines picked up the win and Mario Amero took the loss. Catcher Joe Massaro had two hits and drove in two runs for Minot. A triple play highlighted game three as the Mallards crushed Brandon 9–3. Warren Martin, with relief help from Ed Albosta, picked up the win and Barney Brown took the loss. John Kelly won game four 5–4, on a misplayed fly ball by T.W. Richardson, normally a pitcher, was pressed into service in left field. Mario Amero took the loss. Zoonie McLean and Quincy Barbee were the big hitters for the Mallards and Joe Mitchell hit a grand slam for the Greys. With that win the Mallards advanced to the finals against Carman.

In the Carman-Winnipeg series, game one ended in a 7–7 tie and the game was called because of a local curfew. Carman beat Winnipeg in game two behind the pitching of Andy Porter. Chick Longest led Carman at the

3—The 1952 Season

Two unidentified Brandon Greys enjoy some warmup hijinks (courtesy of Lillian Lowe).

plate with three singles and a double. Winnipeg made six errors in game three on the way to an 8–6 loss. Murray Richardson gave up only seven hits for the Carman victory. Al Spearman took the loss. Lyman Bostock led Carman at the plate with two hits. In this series, Winnipeg general manager Curly Haas wanted to switch a game to the last remaining open date at Osborne Stadium in Winnipeg for a larger attendance instead of playing in Carman. Carman refused, and Haas threatened to pull his team from the playoffs, but then backed down. Carman won two more games and advanced to the finals.

In the first game of the final series, Sugar Cain pitched a three-hit, 1–0 shutout victory over Gentry Jessup. John Kennedy hit a sacrifice fly to bring in Don Corcoran with the only run. John Kelly fired a six-hitter in a 5–2, game two win and Murray Richardson took the loss. Zoonie McLean tripled in John Kennedy with the winning run and Duke Bowman hit an inside-the-park home run for the Mallards. Carman came back in game 3 to nip the Mallards 9–8 in 13 innings. Willie Hutchinson pitched all 13 innings for the win and Ed Albosta took the loss. The Cardinals scored the winning run in the 12th inning on a wild pitch, a passed ball and an error for the victory. Sonny Andrews had four hits for Carman and Zoonie

McLean, Quincy Barbee, and Yogi Giammarco all homered for the Mallards. In game four, Jonas Gaines pitched a strong game in a 4–3 Minot win and Andy Porter took the loss. Ed Bowman singled in the winning run and Yogi Giammarco stroked a home run for Minot. In game five the Mallards scored 8 first-inning runs to crush Carman 10–4 and win their first championship. Sugar Cain scattered eight hits for the win and Gentry Jessup took the loss. Quincy Barbee had four hits for Minot.

4
The 1953 Season

Roy Reimer was again the league president and the Winnipeg Giants became the Winnipeg Royals. They signed ex-major leaguer Mickey Rocco to play first base after his release from the Mallards. Pete Hughes, Bob Strader, and Chuck Gowett were signed from the Sunset League. All had been selected to the league's All-Star team the previous year. All were recruited by new Giants manager Ken Myers. Mickey Rocco had played four seasons for the Cleveland Indians and had averaged .250 in the major leagues and Pete Hughes had had a long and illustrious minor league career. He had been an all-star in many leagues and at many classifications. At one time he held the minor league record for the most walks during the season. He led the ManDak League that season with 13 home runs and a new league record of 66 RBIs. The Royals also added Dirk Gibbons and Bill Washburn to lead their pitching staff. The Royals still finished 7½ games out of first place. Carman added Jim Newberry to their pitching staff. Other newcomers were Lester Lockett, Joe Atkins, Benny Lott, and Bob Turner. They finished third, 6½ games out. Willie Wells managed the Brandon team again in 1953, his last season in baseball in Canada. New players were Cowan Hyde, John Washington, Tom Parker, Wilmer Fields, and Howard Easterling. Fields and Easterling played briefly for the Greys that season. Fields joined Brandon on July 24 and in his first game, belted a grand-slam homer and single to drive in six runs in a 13–5 Brandon victory. He continued his hot hitting for three more weeks, then up and left for more money. Howard Easterling was at an advanced age and had reached the end of his playing days. The 1953 Minot team had a number of new players at various positions. Shortstop Zoonie McLean, third baseman Duke Bowman, Othello Renfroe, who could play any position, and catcher Joe Massaro remained from the previous year. Sugar Cain (12–5) and ex-major leaguer Ed Albosta (8–2) were still the pitching stars. New players included first baseman Dean Scarborough, and outfielders Chuck Carroll and Connie Juelke. All the teams had many roster changes that year. Scarborough won the batting championship with a .356 average.

That year the ManDak league established an interlocking schedule with the Western Canada semi-pro league. That league had four Saskatchewan teams from Moose Jaw, Regina, North Battleford, and Saskatoon. Teams from each league played a home and home series. This was done with the possibility of both leagues joining into one strong league. Games were to count in the standings. The interlocking games were unique in that if the first game of the series was not played for some reason, the second game would count as two games in the standings. The ManDak League dominated the interlocking games by winning 28 of the 32 played. In an interlocking game in Saskatchewan between North Battleford and Brandon, Roy Dean of North Battleford punched the umpire. He had been called out on strikes and then threw the umpire to the ground and punched him several times. His actions resulted in a suspension.

Royals owner Curly Haas, in a June 5 *Free Press* interview, complained about the high cost of running a ManDak League team. There was talk that Winnipeg would vacate the ManDak League and join the Northern League for the 1954 season. The *Free Press* reported that the Brandon Greys already were $10,000 in the red. A month later it was reported that the Greys were $15,000 in the red. At the same time, there was a rumor that Ken Myers, who had started the season as the Royals manager, already was working on lining up a club in Brandon for the 1954 season. This didn't happen, as he had no official connection to the Brandon team, and in an odd twist, former Royals owner Curly Haas became the general manager for Brandon in 1954.

In an interview with the Mallards' Ed Albosta, he said that midway through the season, the Minot executive fired him. Zoonie McLean called a team meeting and the players voted to keep Albosta as manager. The executive relented and retained him as manager, and the Mallards went on to win the championship.

Jim Adelson was the voice of the Minot Mallards at radio station KCJB in Minot, starting in 1952. In a recent interview he told me an interesting and funny story that he originally told in his book, *Two Rolls ... No Coffee*. In 1963, the station manager decided it was too expensive to send Adelson on the road with the team and that Adelson would have to use his imagination to announce the games. He did just that and did it well.

Adelson got the local telephone companies to install phones in all the league teams' press boxes. He had someone in each city phone his station and describe pitch by pitch what was happening in the game. Adelson said he had an assistant sitting beside him taking the calls and relaying the information to him with a kind of shorthand that they had set up between them. Adelson would then go to work and describe the game as if he was there.

Adelson said the station had a disc jockey with a great sense of humor who would be running up and down the station halls yelling, "Programs Here" or "Get your Peanuts and Popcorn Here." Adelson said he was always a bit worried the disc jockey would get carried away and go too far.

Shortly into a game in Winnipeg, the phone lines went dead and the station was trying frantically to reconnect. Adelson didn't panic. He decided to make up a fight between the Mallards' mild-mannered third baseman, Duke Bowman, and the Winnipeg pitcher, and as time went by he had both benches involved. After about 15 minutes, the phone line was restored, Adelson reported that the altercation was over, and continued broadcasting the game.

When the Mallards returned to Minot the next day, Bowman was sitting in a favorite bar where the players hung out. A fan came in and commented to Bowman that he sure looked good considering the fight he was involved in. Bowman asked, "What fight?" When the fan explained about what he heard on the radio the previous day, Bowman then realized what Adelson had done.

Adelson said that things would be different with today's technology. There are probably still fans around today that think Adelson was at the ball park broadcasting the games. Adelson was that good.

SEASON HIGHLIGHTS

During the season, Minot's Duke Bowman had a 20-game hitting streak and teammate Dean Scarborough had an 18-game hitting streak Barney Brown fired a one-hitter for Brandon on May 21 in a 3–1 victory over Minot. On May 23, Chuck Carroll hit a single in the bottom of the 10th to score Minot's only run in a 1–0 victory over Winnipeg. Sugar Cain pitched a one-hitter for the win. Up to May 25, Minot's playing manager, Ed Albosta, pitching in relief, stretched his shutout string to $15\frac{2}{3}$ innings.

In an exhibition game on June 11, Indian Head, Saskatchewan, beat Carman 6–1. The losing pitcher was Negro League great Chet Brewer, who was making one of his rare pitching starts. Benny Lott's hitting led Carman to a 9–5 victory over the Regina Caps on June 12 in interleague play. Lott had a triple, two singles and two walks. Lyman Bostock chipped in with three hits and Walt McCoy went the distance on the mound. Chuck Wilson knocked in six runs and hit for the cycle as Brandon beat the Winnipeg Royals 13–3 on June 17. Minot scored an unearned run in the third inning for a 1–0 victory over Saskatoon in an interlocking game on June 24. Sugar Cain allowed five hits and struck out eight for the win. The victory was Cain's eighth shutout of his career with Minot.

On July 1, Connie Juelke blasted three home runs in a 9–2 Minot victory over Carman. On July 6, Brandon beat Saskatoon in an interlocking game 8–4. Detroit Red Wings hockey star Gordie Howe was on orders from Detroit not to play, but was at first base for Saskatoon. He hit a double in three plate appearances. On July 7, Brandon traveled to Indian Head for an exhibition game against the Rockets. Brandon won 10–9. Jim Banks had two home runs for the Greys. Willie Wells went six innings on the mound, and Gread McKinnes picked up the win in relief. On July 10 Minot's Sugar Cain was at it again, as he pitched a two-hitter in a 7–0 interlocking game against North Battleford. Joe Massaro and Zoonie McLean had three hits each for Minot. Wilmer Fields impressed his Brandon teammates on July 24. He drove in six runs with a grand slam home run and a single as Brandon wiped Winnipeg 13–5.

Minot's Neal Lettau pitched a one-hitter on August 1 in a 10–0 victory over Winnipeg. Baseball's old-timer, Barney Brown, beat Minot on August 5 for the fifth time that season, 5–3. In that game, Wilmer Fields led Brandon with two doubles. Sugar Cain pitched all 11 innings on August 10 as Minot beat Carman 5–4. It was Cain's tenth win of the season. On August 16, Carman beat Brandon 6–5. Wilmer Fields hit two home runs in a losing effort for Brandon.

At season's end Minot had to win its last six games to end up in a tie with Brandon. The league decided to have a best-of-three series to determine the league champion. The series opened in Brandon, and Neil Lettau fired a three-hitter to beat the Greys 8–2. Back home, Connie Juelke belted a three-run homer to power the Mallards to a 9–4 victory and move them into the first round of the playoffs. A tie for third place forced a one-game playoff between Carman and Winnipeg. Carman bested Winnipeg 3–2 behind the pitching of Jim Newberry and Joe Atkins' two-run homer to claim third place. The standings reflect the extra games played due to the teams being tied. The final standings for 1953 were:

	W	L	GBL
Minot Mallards	45	31	
Brandon Greys	43	33	2
Carman Cardinals	38	37	6½
Winnipeg Royals	37	38	7½

Minot's Dean Scarborough won the batting championship with a .356 average. Sugar Cain had the most pitching wins with 10. Ed Albosta had an 8–2 record and topped the league with an .800 winning percentage. Pete Hughes of the Winnipeg Royals led the league with 13 home runs and 66 RBI.

Playoffs

In the first round, the Minot Mallards met the last-place Winnipeg Royals, and second-place Brandon Greys met the Carman Cardinals in the other series. Sugar Cain fanned 11 Royals and Chuck Carroll and Duke Bowman cracked two-run home runs as the Mallards crushed Brandon 11–1. Dirk Gibbons was the losing pitcher. Fielding errors by Winnipeg led to a 12–3 Minot win in game two. Larry Dempsey got the win and Fred Parker took the loss. Winnipeg, with Bill Washburn and Neal Lettau pitching, won the next two games 10–6 and 5–4 to even the series. In game five, Larry Dempsey hurled a seven-hitter in a 6–1 Minot victory. Dirk Gibbons took the loss for Winnipeg. Joe Massaro had three singles for the Mallards and Lou Louden and Bill Cleveland each had two hits for the Royals. In game six, Sugar Cain struck out 10 in an extra-inning 6–5 Minot victory. Dirk Gibbons took the loss. Duke Bowman led the Mallards with a triple and three doubles. Pete Hughes hit a home run, two doubles and a single to lead the Winnipeg attack. Connie Juelke's sacrifice fly brought home the winning run in the eleventh inning.

In game one, Brandon whipped Carman 11–3. Big Bob Griffith was the winning pitcher and Felix Pine took the loss. Cowan Hyde, Jesse Douglas, and Joe Mitchell all had three hits for the Greys. In game two, Pee Wee Jenkins hurled Brandon to a 4–2 victory. Orlando Andux hit a 2 run home run for the Greys. Willie Hutchinson took the loss. Brandon beat Carman 12–5 in game three. Barney Brown went the distance for the win and Walt McCoy took the loss. Joe Mitchell had a three-run home run and Curly Williams a two-run homer for Brandon. With Brandon up three games to none, Carman whipped Brandon 13–4. Willie Hutchinson was the winner and Tom Parker took the loss. Chick Longest hit a two-run home run for Carman. In game five, Brandon advanced to the league final with a 6–1 win. Gread McKinnis was the winning pitcher and Walt McCoy took the loss. John Washington drove in four runs with a double and two singles.

In the league finals, Brandon, led by Bob Griffith and Barney Brown, crushed Minot in the first two games 9–4 and 10–4, to jump into a two-game series lead. Chuck Wilson knocked in five runs in game one and Cowan Hyde had three hits in game two. Minot came from behind to win game three 9–8. Larry Dempsey got the win and in the ninth inning, Ed Bowman made a sensational catch on a line drive to second base by Clarence King to save the game. In the next game, Sugar Cain evened the series with a 6–4 victory. Pee Wee Jenkins took the loss. Othello Renfroe hit a two-run home run to lead Minot. Game five provided a controversial win for Minot. The teams were tied 3–3 and Brandon had the bases

National Motors Ltd.
WINNIPEG'S MERCURY, LINCOLN AND METEOR DEALER

and

National U-Drive Ltd.
RENT A CAR DRIV-UR-SELF

By the day · Week · Month

PHONE 72-2411   276 COLONY STREET

OSBORNE STADIUM

Official 1953

 **SCORECARD**

10c.   Home of The Winnipeg Royals   **10c.**

Osborne Stadium Outfield Distances

LEFT FIELD WALL	320 FEET
CENTRE FIELD	370 FEET
SCORE BOARD	320 FEET
RIGHT FIELD WALL	270 FEET

All distances taken at ground level

Winnipeg Royals scorecard, 1953.

loaded. Brandon hit into a game-ending double play. Brandon argued that the winning run had scored. The Brandon players attacked the umpire, which resulted in first baseman John Washington being charged with assault and suspended for the remainder of the series. The umpire ordered play to resume and Brandon refused to take the field. The umpire then declared the game forfeited to Minot 9–0. Brandon won game six 6–4 to force a winner-take-all final game. Led by playoff hero Larry Dempsey, the Mallards won the deciding game 7–2 and claimed the league championship. Barney Brown took the loss. During that series the Mallards set a single-game attendance record of 3,700 fans.

At season's end, and before the players returned to their homes, Lou Louden was voted the most popular player for the Winnipeg Royals. Third baseman Bob Rittenberg was the runnerup. Both were presented with gifts from Miss Canada, Kathy Archibald.

5
The 1954 Season

Roy Reimer was re-elected for his fourth term as ManDak president. As expected, Winnipeg ceased operation, leaving Brandon and Carman as the only two Manitoba teams. Both Brandon and Carman had attendance and financial problems that season. Carman's problems were due in part to the weather and the construction of a new highway that bypassed the town. Both teams switched a number of home games to Winnipeg. The Williston Oilers entered the league, replacing the Winnipeg Royals. They signed ex–major leaguers Roy Weatherly, Lloyd Gearhart, Joe Lutz, and Dewey Williams to lead their attack and Harry Taylor to pitch. Minor league star Ed Williams was signed midway through the season to bolster Williston's pitching staff. In August, Oiler catcher Dewey Williams, a former Chicago Cub, was stabbed and beaten in downtown Williston. Williams knew his attacker, but the reason behind the attack was never revealed. Williams recovered, and returned for the playoffs. Brandon signed ex-Giants skipper and Royals manager Curly Haas as its general manager. He signed ex–major leaguers Dee Moore and Hal Daugherty. Moore was playing manager. Minor league star Ron Bowen was signed near the end of the season. He had started the season in Williston and had wanted more money. The Oilers, not wishing to pay, released him. Future Hall of Famer Leon Day was also signed by the Greys for his last season in baseball. Dirk Gibbons came over from Winnipeg to be the ace of the Brandon staff. After the problems he had had the previous year in Minot, Ed Albosta joined Carman as playing manager. Sammy Drake, John Washington, and Benny Lott were Carman's big hitters. Walt McCoy won eight games that season for the Cardinals. Minot returned most of the previous year's lineup. Having a core of returning players every season always helped the Mallards. They were led on the mound by the steady pitching of Sugar Cain and hitting of Othello Renfroe and Duke Bowman. At the start of the season, Minot's Neal Lettau was suspended for a month. This was later canceled and replaced with a fine. This was because he had sent a letter to the Brandon team asking them to make him a contract offer after he had already signed with Minot.

Season Highlights

On May 31, Joe Massaro knocked in five runs with a home run and two singles as Minot crushed Carman 14–0. Winning pitcher Neal Lettau fired a three-hitter for the win. Joe Massaro was back at it again on June 14 when he belted two home runs in a 13–7 Minot win over Williston. On June 21, Lettau fashioned his second shutout of the season, beating Carman 11–0 with a five-hitter.

Yogi Giammarco hit a grand slam home run, a double, and two singles for six RBI on July 7 in Minot's 9–4 win over Carman. Sugar Cain blanked Brandon 10–0 on July 16, scattering nine hits and striking out 12. On July 17, Giammarco jumped Minot to play with the semi-pro Rochester, Minnesota, club. The Mallards considered taking legal action, as they had given Giammarco $150 advance earlier in the day. Warren Martin tossed a one-hitter on July 19 as Minot beat Carman 4–0. On July 20, Williston's Roy Weatherly had a big day at the plate, going 5 for 6, including a home run, against Brandon. The game was a real slugfest as Williston beat Brandon 15–12. Bill Washburn fired a one-hitter for Minot on July 27 in a 2–1 victory over Carman.

On August 6, Washburn pitched a six-hit, seven-strikeout, one-walk 1–0 victory over Williston. Pitcher Ed Williams of Williston was not too shabby either, giving up the one run on six hits, striking out five. On August 9, the league held its second All-Star game. Six players each were picked from Brandon, Carman, and Williston to play the league-leading Minot Mallards. It was the first league All-Star game since the flood relief game in 1950. Williston representatives were Buddy Afremow, shortstop; Roy Weatherly, right field; Lloyd Gearhart, first base; Harry Taylor, pitcher; Dick Schoonover, pitcher, and Dewey Williams, catcher. Brandon's six players were Hal Daugherty, first base; Don Stewart, second base; Lou Louden, catcher; Dee Moore, catcher/manager; Dan Ahtipis, pitcher, and Dirk Gibbons, pitcher. Carman sent Sam Drake, third base; Jesse Douglas, shortstop; Benny Lott, second base; Chick Longest, outfield; Ed Albosta, pitcher, and Walt McCoy, pitcher. Don Stewart was injured and was replaced by Frank Mascaro. The All-Stars smacked out 18 hits as they crushed the Mallards 18–4 before 2,638 Minot fans. The All Stars were led by the pitching of ex–major leaguer Harry Taylor and Dick Schoonover, both from Williston. Along with Brandon's Dirk Gibbons, they each pitched two scoreless innings. Schoonover was credited with the victory. Carman's Sammy Drake led the All-Stars with three hits and Brandon's Frank Mascaro hit a long three-run homer for the All Stars.

All Star Game Box Score:

All Stars	AB	R	H		Minot	AB	R	H
Drake 3B	6	3	3		Corcoran OF	4	1	2
Douglas 2B	6	2	3		McLean SS	5	1	2
Longest CF	6	2	2		Scarborough RF	3	1	1
Weatherly RF	4	1	1		Greene RF	2	0	1
[1]Daugherty 1B	3	1	1		Renfroe 1B	3	0	2
Mascaro LF	4	2	3		D. Bowman 3B	5	0	1
Williams C	2	0	0		Massaro C	4	0	0
[2]Louden C	3	0	1		Juelke LF	3	0	0
Afremow SS	5	1	2		E. Bowman 2B	4	0	1
Taylor P	2	0	1		Lettau P	1	0	0
Gibbons P	0	0	0		Geisler P	1	0	0
Schoonover P	1	1	0		[4]Parker P	1	0	0
[3]Moore	1	0	0		[5]W. Bowman	1	1	1
Ahtipis P	1	0	0		Totals	37	4	10
Miller P	0	0	0					
Totals	46	14	18					

1. *Grounded out for Gearhart in the 5th*
2. *Grounded out for Williams in the 5th*
3. *Grounded out for Schoonover in 7th*
4. *Popped out for Geisler in 6th*
5. *Doubled for Parker in 9th*

```
ALL STARS    421 003 040 — 14 18 2
MINOT        002 000 002 —  4 10 5
```

E— Douglas, Daugherty; Greene, Renfroe, Massaro, E. Bowman 2, RBI— Drake, Douglas 3, Longest 2, Weatherly.

Gearhart, Daugherty 2, Mascaro 3, Afremow; McLean, Scarborough, Renfroe 2; 2B— Douglas, McLean, W. Bowman.

3B -Scarborough; HR— Mascaro, Daugherty; SB— Drake 2, DP— Minot 1; WP— Geisler; PB— Williams; SF— Renfroe, Weatherly; Left— All Stars 7 Minot 10; SO— Taylor 2, Gibbons

Brandon's Ian Lowe at bat (courtesy of Lillian Lowe).

2, Ahtipis 2 Geisler. Pitching Record— Taylor 1 hit for 0 runs in 2, Gibbons 3 for 2 in 2, Schoonover 1 for 0 in 2, Ahtipis 2 for 0 in 2, Miller 3 for 2 in 1, Lettau 7 for 7 in 3. Geisler 4 for 3 in 3, Parker 7 for 4 in 3. W— Schoonover L— Leteau. Umpires— Carrigan, Mann, Richardson, T 2:18, A— 2638

Othello Renfroe of Minot extended his 21-game hitting streak on August 15 with a single. During the streak he had 37 hits in 80 at-bats for a .463 average. Oddly enough, he was tossed from that game for fighting with Brandon catcher Lou Louden. On August 18, Carman and Winnipeg were tied 7–7 after 10 innings and the game was called because of a local curfew. Winnipeg made six errors on August 21 as Carman edged Winnipeg 8–6. Murray Richardson was the winning pitcher. In a game in late August, pinch-hitter Willie Wells drove in the winning run in the 11th inning as Brandon beat Carman 9–8.

Williston's Roy Weatherly won the batting title with a .412 average. Teammate Lloyd Gearhart hit 17 home runs and Minot's Joe Massaro drove in 66 runs to lead the league. Minot's Neal Lettau recorded the most wins with 13. At season's end, Sugar Cain recorded 11 straight wins, led the league in strikeouts with 98, and had the best ERA at 1.87. Minot finished in first place and was the class of the field, 10 games ahead of Brandon. Minot finished in first place for the third straight season.

The final standings for 1954 were:

	W	L	GBL
Minot Mallards	49	21	
Brandon Greys	40	32	10
Williston Oilers	28	42	21
Carman Cardinals	24	46	25

PLAYOFFS

Carman had a long losing streak near the end of the regular season, but in the first round of the playoffs, the Cardinals gave Minot all they could handle. This was sweet revenge for manager Ed Albosta of Carman, considering the problems he had had in Minot the previous season. This series was highlighted by several ejections and the suspension of Cardinals manager Albosta. Warren Martin won the first game for the Mallards by a 7–5 score and the Cardinals came roaring back with a 12–5 victory in game two. Buddy Woods beat Sugar Cain. Benny Lott put on a fielding exhibition and belted a 380-foot home run for the Cardinals. Almer McKerlie and Chick Longest each had three hits for the Cardinals. Minot took game three 13–6. Minot's Duke Bowman knocked in seven runs in that game, a ManDak League playoff record. Carman squared the series with a 6–2 victory, led by the four-hit pitching of Bob Miller. Benny Lott had a home run, two triples and a single and Norm Robinson had three hits, including a home run, to lead the Cardinals' attack. In game five, Carman took the series lead with a 4–3 victory behind winning pitcher Walt McCoy. With their backs to the wall, the Mallards got their bats working and pounded out 15 hits in 12–8 game six victory. Sugar Cain went the distance for the Mallards. Carman used four pitchers, with Buddy Woods taking the loss. Great pitching by Sugar Cain in game seven put Minot into the final as he beat the Cardinals 11–3. Joe Massaro and Duke Bowman each hit a triple, double, and single. Cain helped his own cause with an inside-the-park home run.

In the other series, Brandon beat Williston in seven games. Just as this series was getting started Dan Ahtipis and Red Rose bolted the Greys for organized ball, leaving them shy of pitching strength. The league allowed them to add local player Morley McFarlane and Minot loaned them pitcher Fred Parker. Brandon won game one 5–3. Gerry MacKay had two hits and knocked in two runs for the Greys. Joe Lutz homered for the Oilers. Dirk Gibbons fanned seven and was the winning pitcher. Harry Taylor took the loss. Williston took game two, 9–6, to even the series. Dick Schoonover was the winning pitcher and Fred Parker took the loss. The Oilers went up two games to one as they pounded out 17 hits on their way to a 14–6 victory. Ronnie Martin and Lloyd Gearhart had three hits apiece for the Oilers and Roy Weatherly and Joe Lutz each hit a home run. Ed Williams fanned seven to record the Oiler victory and Rod MacKay took the loss for the Greys. The Greys came back in game four to win 10–7. Dirk Gibbons again bested Harry Taylor and Ron Bowen and Lou Louden each homered for the Greys. Louden had a big day, driving in five runs. Back in Brandon the teams split games five and six. Brandon won game five 5–1 as Rod MacKay threw a five-hitter for the victory and Dick Schoonover took the loss. Hal Daugherty knocked in the winning run for Brandon. In game six, the Oilers came back to beat the Greys 14–8. Ed Williams was the winner and Morley McFarlane took the loss. Lloyd Gearhart homered to the Oilers and Gerry MacKay and Don Stewart hit home runs for Brandon. In game seven, Dirk Gibbons gave up six hits in a 6–0 victory that propelled Brandon into the finals. Vic Michalec took the loss. Williston's Kent Geisler came into the game with two out in the third inning and pitched no-hit ball for the rest of the game. Gibbons and Don Stewart each had two RBI for the Greys.

In the finals, Minot beat Brandon in a hard-fought series. That season, the Minot paper dubbed the Mallards the "Come Back Kids." The teams split the first two games, played in Minot. Brandon won the first

5—The 1954 Season

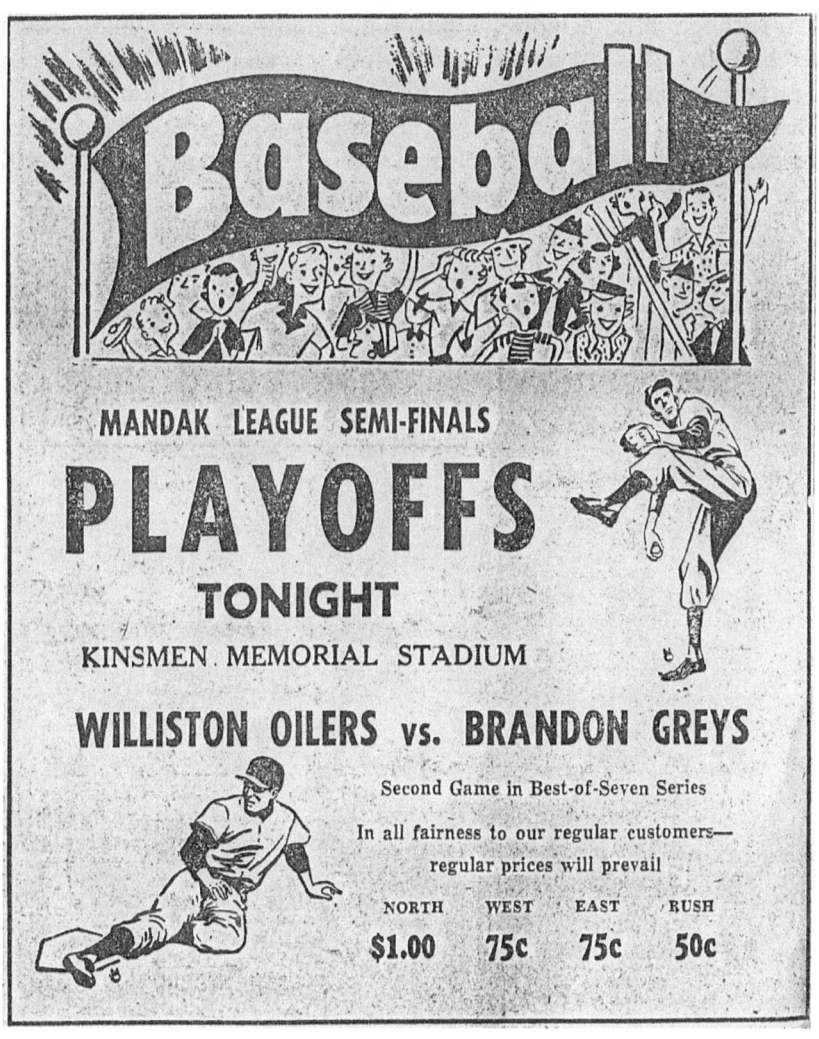

Playoff program, Williston vs. Brandon, 1954.

game 8–3 and the Mallards took game two 11–10. In that game, Brandon had a 10–4 lead when Minot scored five runs in the seventh and two in the eighth to cap a big comeback. The third game was highlighted by eight Brandon errors and a 7–2 loss to Minot. Brandon bounced back in game four with a 5–2 victory. In game five, Brandon was up 6–0 after two innings only to blow the lead and end up losing 9–8. Don Corcoran, with a homer, and Zoonie McLean, with a two-run single, were the hitting stars for Minot. In game six, saw Bill Washburn fashioned a six-hit, 9–0 shutout and Minot was crowned ManDak champs. Don Corcoran was the hitting star with four hits, including a home run. In this series the Mallards were led by Sugar Cain, Zoonie McLean, Don Corcoran, Duke Bowman, Dean Scarborough, and Joe Massaro. This was Minot's third straight league championship. At the 1997 Minot Mallards reunion, the 1954 team was regarded as the best and most talented team ever in Minot. This team held a special spot in the minds of many Minot fans.

6
The 1955 Season

Because of financial reasons, Brandon and Carman ceased operation in 1955. Many of the Carman townspeople who had bought shares in the ball club lost money. This left Minot and Williston and two new clubs—the Bismarck Barons and Dickinson Packers—in the league. The teams decided to keep the ManDak name and set an $8,000 a month salary cap.

Many of the Negro League players had played on the Manitoba teams. Most of these players were getting on in age and would retire before the 1955 season. The good young Negro players were now playing in organized baseball. The Negro Leagues would cease operation after the 1955 season. In 1955, they were considered to be "minor league" and only a few players came north to play. The ManDak League continued to attract ex–major leaguers and players who had excelled in the minor leagues. Many minor league players joined teams in the ManDak League for better pay and the opportunity to continue their careers. Minot still had most of the players returning from the previous championship season. The big addition to the Mallards was Butch Davis, the two-time batting champ of the ManDak League. Since leaving the ManDak League, he had played in Triple-A for the Toronto Maple Leafs and one season with Scranton in Double-A. He continued his hot hitting and finished the 1955 season as runnerup to Roy Weatherly for the batting championship. On April 22, Minot announced that their star pitcher, Sugar Cain, would be returning for his fourth season. Since joining, Minot Cain had started 63 games, including playoffs, and completed 56. The same day, Minot also announced it had signed ageless left-hander Barney Brown. Twenty-year-old pitcher Don Lee became a mainstay for the Williston Oilers. He would go on to a long major league career. Ex–major league pitcher Bobby Hogue (Boston Braves) was signed as playing manager. Minor leaguers Preston Elkins and Dolph Regelsky were added, and Roy Weatherly was still around to help in the hitting department. That season Williston set a single-game attendance record for its park of 2,689. Bismarck signed long time Negro League star Ray Dandridge. Also signed was Art "Superman" Pennington, who was considered to be one of the best long-ball hitters of the Negro Leagues in the late 1940's, and Preston Gomez (Washington Senators). To bolster their pitching staff, the Barons signed major league veteran Ken Heintzelman, minor league star Roger Higgins, and Detroit Tiger bonus baby Mike Lotz. The 1955 Barons were regarded as one of the strongest ever teams in the history of the ManDak League. Dickinson added minor league slugger Don Petschow and Don Lewandowski (St. Louis Cardinals) for its inaugural season. The *Minot News* reported that Dickinson might sign pitcher Dirk Gibbons if the club decided to hire colored players. By today's standards this would be considered racism. Dickinson remained all-white that season and not a word was said.

The Williston Oilers had been holding a fundraising drive during the season, and it was reported that they had raised $2,000. The Williston executives indicated that the results were a little disappointing. The executives then announced they would be holding a tag day on August 16 and tags would be sold door to door. The club set a goal of $8,000 to get the team out of the red at season's end.

Season Highlights

On June 2, Eldon Russell pitched four innings of shutout relief as Dickinson came from behind to nip Minot 9–7. Minot's Barney Brown had pitched six scoreless innings when the roof caved in. Manager Zoonie McLean belted three home runs and ended the game going 5-for-5 on June 20 in a 10–7 win over Williston. On June 28, Bismarck's Mike Lotz pitched a five-hit victory over Williston for his sixth straight win. Minot's Sugar Cain fanned 13 batters on June 30 in a 2–1 victory over Dickinson. Nine of the strikeouts were called strikes.

Minot beat Bismarck 6–3 on July 5 as Minot turned four double plays that snuffed out Bismarck rallies. That game saw Joe Montiero hit his fourth home run in four days to lead Minot, and Ray Dandridge had three hits for Bismarck. On July 10, Williston's Roy Weatherly hit his 17th and 18th home runs to break the old ManDak record of 16 held by Lloyd Gearhart. The mid–July stats showed Ray Dandridge leading the way with a .425 batting average. Bismarck's Jonas Gaines fired a one-hit, 2–0 shutout on July 17 in beating Bismarck. Minot catcher Joe Massaro was hit on the head July 19 while he was catching and missed some games. While he was on the mend, he stated that when he resumed playing, he would be wearing one of the new plastic safety helmets which just had been introduced. Dean Scarborough hit three doubles on July 21 in leading Minot to a 6–5 win over Dickinson. In the top of the 10th inning, Scarborough was tossed from the game due to a temper tantrum following an incident that had happened in the previous inning. Minot scored the winning run in the bottom of the 10th inning.

On August 1, Bismarck's Mike Lotz and Ken Heintzelman combined on a 1–0 shutout of Williston. That same day, catcher Joe Massaro and outfielder Joe Montiero informed the Minot executives they were leaving the club to join the Philadelphia Phillies organization. They were both promised an opportunity to play Triple-A ball. August 3 was "Roy Weatherly Night" and he and his wife were showered with gifts. His two hits helped Williston defeat Dickinson 7–6. August 4 was Canada night at the Minot ballpark, and all Canadians received free admission. On August 11, Minot's Don Corcoran hit a grand-slam home run in an 8–7 win over Dickinson. It was his second grand-slam home run of the season. Preston Elkins of Williston ran his record to 7–0 on August 14, with a five-hit, 5–0 win over Bismarck. On the last day of the regular season, Don Lee pitched a five-hitter for his fifth win as Williston beat Minot 6–2.

During the season the *Williston Herald* reported that five Williston players, Fran Healy, Bill Raehse, Carl Paylor, Pete Konyar, and Bill Sharp, all drank hot tea with honey before every game for energy. It was apparently an old trick of boxer Sugar Ray Robinson. There was no worry about steroids back then. The final standings for 1955 were:

	W	L	GBL
Bismarck Barons	47	31	
Williston Oilers	41	37	6
Minot Mallards	38	40	9
Dickinson Packers	30	48	17

Preston Elkins (Williston) led the league in pitching with a 7–0 won-lost record and Dickinson's Red Rose had the most wins with 10. Sugar Cain (Minot) had the most strikeouts with 91. Roy Weatherly won his second straight batting championship with a .371 average. He also had 21 home runs to lead the league. Bob Betz (Williston), Ron Bowen (Dickinson), and Bob Easterbrook (Bismarck) all tied for the RBI lead with 68.

Playoffs

In the playoffs, Williston played Minot and Bismarck met Dickinson in the first round. The ManDak executive ruled that Minot could pick up ex- Negro League players Mel Duncan, Willie Patterson, and Robby Cartledge. Minot also added hard-hitting minor league star Charlie Frey. This ruling was contrary to the league by-laws but the other league teams did not protest the decision. The first game of the Williston-Minot series featured a pitching duel between Preston Elkins and Sugar Cain. Cain gave up only five hits but Elkins was better, giving up only three hits in a 1–0 victory. Bob Betz hit a fourth inning home run, which was all the Oilers needed. The Oilers sparkled on the field with two double plays, and two runners were thrown out. The Mallards bounced back to take game two 12–6. The Mallards scored six runs in the ninth inning for the victory. Ted Edmunds was the winner, with relief help from Robbie Cartledge. Ed Williams took the loss. In game three, Dirk Gibbons gave up six hits on the way to a 7–2 victory. Don Lee took the loss for the Oilers. Zoonie McLean knocked in two runs for the Mallards. In game four, the Mallards beat the Oilers 6–5 and jumped to a three-to-one series lead. The Oilers stranded a lot of men on base. Ted Edmunds was the winner in relief and Dick Mulcahy starred in relief for Williston. He entered the game in the third inning and pitched one-hit ball the rest of the way. Bill Raeshe smacked two homers in a losing cause. The Oilers, facing elimination, won game five in a slugfest, 16–9. At one time they were down 9–2 and came roaring back with a 12-run seventh inning. Bobby Hogue was the winner in relief and Sugar Cain took the loss for the Mallards. In game six, Sugar Cain fanned seven and gave up seven hits in a 6–2 victory that put the Mallards into the league finals. Preston Elkins took the loss. Charley Frey led the Mallards with two hits including a triple. Dolph Regelsky had a home run in a losing cause for the Oilers.

The Dickinson-Bismarck series was a big upset, as the Packers knocked off the heavily favored Barons. In game one Fred Brenzell pitched a 5-hit 6–2 victory for the Packers. Roger Higgins took the loss. That game was Brenzel's only appearance, as he had to leave for a high school coaching job in Illinois. Dickinson again beat the Barons 4–3 in game two, handing the pennant winners a second straight loss. Red Rose was the winning pitcher, giving up six hits, and Ken Heintzelman took the loss. Ron Bowen and Dick Morgan belted homers for the Packers and Bill Hockenbury replied with one for the Barons. The clubs split games three and four, with the Packers taking a 3–1 lead behind the pitching of Dick Baxter. The score was 9–8. Ken Heintzelman again took the loss for the Barons. In game 4 the Barons, with their backs to the wall, bounced back behind the pitching of Roger Higgins. In game five, Bismarck blew out Dickinson 21–3. The Oilers scored 11 runs in the first inning and six in the second. The Barons pounded out 27 hits. Art Pennington had four hits, including two home runs. Ray Dandridge, Bob Easterbrook, and Pedro Gomez all homered for the Barons. Roger Higgins gave up six hits and was relieved by Ed Benecke. Benecke pitched three scoreless innings in relief. Jack Dean took the loss for the Packers. In game six, Dickinson scored two runs in the ninth inning to squeeze out a 3–2 victory and advance to the league final.

Don Orwiler was the winner and John Fitzgerald took the loss. Ev Johnson socked a homer for the Packers and Fred Vaughan hit a two-run shot for the Barons. Ray Tabacchi's single in the ninth drove in the go-ahead runs.

Dickinson met Minot in the final. In 13 meetings during the season, Dickinson had beaten Minot nine times. Minot's Dirk Gibbons struck out 11 to win the first game 3–1. Duke Bowman led the Mallards' hitting attack with three singles. In game two, the Mallards eked out a 4–3 win to go two games up. Newcomer Mel Duncan homered to give Minot the win. Tom Horton was the winner with relief help from Ted Edmunds. Don Orwiler went the distance for the Packers. George Wopnik hit a two-run homer for the Mallards. In game three, Sugar Cain smashed a two-run homer in the ninth to get Minot past the Packers 7–6. The Mallards completed the four-game sweep with an 11–6 victory and won their fourth straight championship. They were paced by home runs by Charley Frey, Willie Patterson, and Duke Bowman. During the regular season the Mallards couldn't catch Bismarck for the pennant, but once the playoffs started they got good pitching from Dirk Gibbons and Sugar Cain. They were led in the hitting department by Duke Bowman and late-season pickups Charlie Frey and Willie Patterson.

7
The 1956 Season

W.S. Davidson Jr. was the league president for the 1956 season. In 1955 and 1956 a sports writer for the *Fargo Forum* wrote a number of articles knocking the ManDak League and favoring the Northern League. Fargo had a team in the Class C Northern League at the time. In July 1956, Davidson wrote a two-column rebuttal to the sports columnist. He suggested that Fargo and Grand Forks join the ManDak League for the betterment of baseball in North Dakota. He acknowledged that in all probability it would be no contest in favor of the ManDak League team if a team from the Northern League were to meet them. Bismarck Barons pitching ace Roger Higgins stated that Bismarck had challenged Fargo to a game in which the winner would take all the gate receipts, but received no reply.

The 1956 season featured a renewal of the home-and-home series against teams in the Western Canada League. That league comprised teams in Edmonton, Lloydminster, Moose Jaw, Regina, North Battleford, and Saskatoon. The teams in the Western Canada League fared no better than when the two leagues had tried interlocking in 1953. The experienced ManDak teams steamrolled over the mainly college teams from Western Canada. The road trips were long and hard. The league also decided that the four league members would deposit $250 each, before the start of the season. At season's end the league champion would receive $500 and the playoff champion would receive $500.

The 1956 season again saw a number of new faces. Minot signed ex–major league pitchers Bill Oster (Philadelphia A's) and Mike Schultz (Cincinnati Reds) to help their pitching staff. On April 10th it was announced that Woody Johnson, a left-handed pitcher, had been signed as playing manager of the Minot club and that he had 12 years of organized baseball experience. He never did appear, and no reasons were given for his no-show. Williston added pitcher Al Lyons (Boston Braves) to an already strong pitching staff. Sam Hill returned from organized baseball to join the Bismarck Barons. Besides Hill, the Barons acquired two-time batting champ Roy Weatherly from Williston. With Hill, Weatherly, and Art Pennington, they led the league with a team batting average of .305.

Dickinson signed Gerald Fahr (Cleveland Indians), Rocky Krsnich (Chicago White Sox) and Garland Lawing (New York Giants) to bolster their team.

1956 was the year of the home run in the ManDak League. The teams hit 318 home runs. The sluggers were Al Leap (23), Sam Hill (20), Dolph Regelsky (19), Butch Lawing (19), Bill Hockenbury (18), and Bill Raeshe (17). Williston, Bismarck and Minot battled all season to finish in top spot. Williston edged Bismarck by two games.

Season Highlights

A highlight of the season was the strong relief pitching of Bismarck's Tony Garcia in a 6–5 victory over Williston. Down 5–1 in the second inning, Garcia entered the game and pitched $7\frac{2}{3}$ innings of no-hit ball. On May 30, Minot's Dirk Gibbons fired a 6-hit, 5–0 shutout against Bismarck.

Also on June 3, Dirk Gibbons pitched a 1-hitter in a 2–1 victory over Williston. On June 8, Sugar Cain pitched a shutout in a win over North Battleford in an interlocking game. Hal Daugherty hit an inside-the-park home run in a June 14th game. The ball bounced off the center field wall at the 460-foot mark. Preston Elkins pitched a one-hitter on June 15 as Williston crushed Dickinson 9–0. In an interlocking game on July 16 in Saskatoon, Saskatchewan, Williston's Ed Williams blanked Saskatoon 7–0 on five hits. Williams helped himself at the plate with three hits. Ex major leaguer Red Fahr beat the Regina Braves in Regina on June 25. Fahr had two men on and two outs and then struck out the opposing starter for the win in the bottom of the ninth inning. In July, Bismarck's ace, Roger Higgins, ran his record to 9–1 in beating the Regina Braves on five hits.

Fred Brenzel, in one of his last pitching assignments before leaving for his job, threw a one-hitter as Bismarck nipped Dickinson 3–2 on August 12. During the season Williston made a rare tournament appearance. The Oilers won the $1,300 Saskatoon Optimist Tournament. Preston Elkins was the winning pitcher in the final game before 7,000 fans.

The final standings for 1956 were:

	W	L	GBL
Williston Oilers	49	29	
Bismarck Barons	47	31	2
Minot Mallards	43	35	6
Dickinson Packers	30	46	18

Pitcher Preston Elkins (Williston), with 15 wins, led the league and also had the most strikeouts with 119. Sugar Cain (Minot) led the league in ERA with a 2.29 average, on the way to a 10–5 record. Roger Higgins had the best won-lost record at 12–1. Dolph Regelsky (Bismarck), won the batting championship with a .362 average. Art Pennington finished second with a .357 average. Al Leap (Bismarck) had 23 home runs and Sam Hill knocked in the most runs with 73.

Playoffs

Williston needed a strong pitching performance from Preston Elkins to clinch its first ManDak League pennant. In the first round of the playoffs, Williston again met Dickinson in the first playoff round. Dickinson again played tough and took Williston to seven games before bowing out. In game one Williston defeated Dickinson 12–5. Jack Sanoff was the winning pitcher and Jim Michalec took the loss. Ray Berns hit three homers and Bill Reashe went 3 for 5, including a home run, to pace the Oilers. Dickinson's Dan Chepkauskas had a bad day at the plate as he hit into three double plays. In game two, Dickinson tied the series with a 13–5 win. Gerald Fahr notched the victory and Al Lyons took the loss. First baseman Bill Jankowski paced the Packers with a homer and three singles and Butch Lawing had a home run. Third baseman Carl Paylor led the Oilers with a double and two singles. Preston Elkins pitched the Oilers to victory in game three by a 9–3 score. Walter Bryja took the loss for the Packers. Bill Raeshe went 3 for 5, including a home run, for the Oilers. The Packers evened the series again in game four with an 11–8 win. The game was a slugfest. Walter Bryja was the winning pitcher in relief of Jim Michalec. Jack Sanoff was the losing pitcher. Rocky Krsnich belted a three-run home run for the Packers and Dan Chepkauskas had three hits for the Packers. Gerald Fahr hurled the Packers to a close 5–4 victory in game five as Dickinson went up three games to two in the series. Jack Sanoff was the loser for the Oilers. All five Packer runs were scored by players who walked or reached base on an error. Bill Jankowski, Dan Chepkauskas, and Ev Johnson all had two hits for the Packers. With Williston facing elimination, the Oilers' Preston Elkins pitched them to a 4–0 shutout victory. Al Lyons, playing left field, had two hits and drove in two runs for the Oilers. The Oiler victory forced a seventh and deciding game. Lyons pitched Williston's second straight shutout with a 6–0 win. Preston Elkins, playing left field, was the hitting star with two Oiler hits, one a home run. For the Oilers, it was on to the league finals.

Minot beat Bismarck in six games in the other series. Minot beat the Barons in game one 9–8. Outfielder Ed Barr and first baseman Carl Bush

7—The 1956 Season

each homered for the Mallards. Dick Kelly was the winner and Dirk Gibbons did a great job in relief. Andy Anderson hit a grand slam in game two, but it wasn't enough to overcome an 8–7 Mallards loss. In game three, Ed Barr hit 2 more home runs, but Minot fell victims to an eight-run, eighth inning Baron explosion which beat the Mallards 13–10. Bill Oster fired a five-hitter on the way to a 7–2 game four win. He struck out ten. Harry Wise took the loss for the Barons. The next day Pete Taylor pitched them to a 3–2 win and a three games to two series lead. The Mallards were led at the plate by Andy Anderson's triple and home run and Duke Bowman's three hits. Roy Weatherly had four hits for Bismarck. The series moved to Bismarck for game six and the Barons had their backs to the wall. A win was not to be, as Minot's ace Sugar Cain fired a two-hitter and recorded twelve strikeouts in a 3–1 semi-final victory. Duke Bowman batted .650 in the series.

In the final, Williston ended Minot's streak of four league championships. Williston had timely hitting by Bill Raeshe, and Preston Elkins (15–4), Jack Sanoff (11–3), and Ed Williams (5–6. 3.37 ERA) were the pitching stars. Pete Taylor got Minot off to a good start in game one with a three-hit, 3–0 victory. Ed Williams took the loss for the Oilers. Hal Daugherty had a home run for the winners. In that game the Oilers made three errors, which didn't help them. Jack Sanoff got Williston back on track in game two with a 12–5 victory. He gave up six hits and helped his own cause with a home run. Sugar Cain took the loss for the Mallards. Jim Leavitt led the way for the Oilers with a grand-slam home run. In game three, Williston beat Minot 5–4 in twelve innings. Preston Elkins went the distance for the win and Dick Kelly took the loss. Bill Raeshe drove in the winning run in the twelfth inning with a single. Ex major leaguer Hal Daugherty left the Minot team after that game to return to his teacher/coaching job in Ohio. Bill Oster tied the series in game four as he fired a four-hitter on the way to a 3–1 Minot win. Oster struck out eight. Al Lyons took the loss for the Oilers. Zoonie Mclean and Dean Scarborough each had two hits. Ed Williams led the Oilers to a 7–3 win in game five. Ray Berns had two hits and knocked in three runs and Bill Raeshe hit a two-run homer that put the Oilers up three games to two. Pete Taylor took the loss for the Mallards. In game six the Mallards didn't have enough pitching and hitting to get them back into the series. Jack Sanoff pitched and batted the Oilers to their first championship. Sanoff fanned five and gave up eight hits on the way to a 7–3 victory. Dean Scarborough hit .409 in the finals for the Mallards. Manager Dee Moore was given a lot of credit for the Oiler championship. The Oilers never quit trying under his leadership and in every game a different Oiler would come to the front and carry the club. Sports writer Adrian Nelson of Williston wrote that he thought the Williston team was the best team in the league that season and possibly the best in the league's history. It would rank up there with the 1950 Winnipeg Buffaloes, the 1954 Minot Mallards, and the 1955 Bismarck Barons. The infield of Bill Raeshe (1B), Bill Sharp (2B), Dolph Regelsky (SS) and Carl Paylor (3B) was sound both in defense and offense. Regelsky hit 19 home runs and Raeshe hit 17 to power the Williston offense.

8
The 1957 Season

The 1957 season was the last for the ManDak League. The league president that season was Glenn Vantin, from Minot. The Dickinson Packers dropped out and the Brandon Greys returned to the league. Before the season started, the team executives lowered the salary cap from $8,500 to $6,000 and the rosters were cut from 16 to 14. The number of games was reduced from 78 to 72. They also agreed that only the top two teams in the league at the end of the schedule would play off for the $500 championship prize. The cut in salaries meant that not as many good pitchers would be hired. That had an effect on the high number of runs scored each game and the pitchers' high ERA.

Local player Gerry MacKay returned from organized baseball to play for Brandon, and Dee Moore was hired to manage the Greys. They picked up ex–major leaguer Al Lyons to anchor their pitching staff. He had pitched for the Yankees, Phillies and Braves. They also added the big bat of another ex–major leaguer, Butch Lawing, who had played for the Giants. Brandon used local players Don Hunter, Jim Slevin, Jerry Smith, and Mort Wright until July 10, when they were released. They had been recruited from the Brandon Cloverleafs until some of the regular players arrived. They then went back to the Manitoba Senior League. John André (Chicago Cubs) joined Minot along with Willard Brown (St. Louis Browns). Brown had been a long time Negro League star. He also was the first Negro player to hit a home run in the American league. They still had the core of their team with Zoonie McLean, Sugar Cain, and Dirk Gibbons. Williston signed catcher Joe Massaro who previously had starred in the league with Minot. Midway through the season, the Oilers signed Jerry Adair, who later had a major league career that lasted 13 years. The Oilers also signed minor league stars Steve Molinari and Pete Konyar and had high hopes that this would lead them to the championship. Bismarck had home run champ Al Leap back at shortstop to go along with many new faces. Eighty-four players played in the league in its last season.

In mid–June, three players from the Williston Oilers, returning from a game in Brandon, were injured when their vehicle went off the road and into a ditch. Star pitcher Jack Sanoff broke his neck, outfielder Steve Molinari received neck and hand injuries, and Pete Konyar had head injuries. Those injuries eventually ended their careers and had an effect on the Oilers' pennant hopes. Molinari and Konyar were leading hitters at the time of the injuries and Sanoff was rated as one of the league's best hurlers. Molinari gave this account of the accident. He said that after the accident, Sanoff walked to the highway and flagged down a passing vehicle, then collapsed from his broken neck. An ambulance arrived on the scene from Minot, but allegedly requested $15.00 before rendering assistance. By this time, Konyar was on his back on a stretcher, but he had the money. It was in his back pocket, and even with his head injuries, he was moved so they could get at the payment. Later that season Molinari returned to the league as an umpire.

All teams had attendance problems that season. Attendance averaged between 400 and 1,200 fans a game. The teams had many a promotional night in an effort to increase fan attendance. The clubs gave $100 merchandise awards and had "Ladies Day," when all ladies would get in free. Williston and Minot gave away a number of "good" used cars. Brandon had two raffles, one for a $5,000 house trailer and the other for a boat, motor, and trailer. During the season Brandon would celebrate its 75th Anniversary. Spectators at the game between Brandon and Williston dressed in clothes of the 1880s. It was reported that 800 fans attended the game.

Season Highlights

A 1957 season highlight was the Mallards' Sugar Cain getting knocked out of the box for the first time since 1955. In the first week of June, Molinari blasted two long home runs and drove in four runs as Williston defeated Brandon. On June 10, ex–major leaguer John Andre pitched a five hit, 10–0 shutout over Williston. In that game Gideon Jarvis, Minot's right fielder, hit two home runs and three doubles against Williston. Minot held "Ladies Night" on June 28 in an attempt to attract new fans. All ladies were offered free admittance. The game was attended by 1,955 fans of whom 1,033 were ladies.

Bismarck's Jack Bowes was a tough-luck hurler in July. He pitched 24 innings and gave up one earned run, and was charged with three losses. Sugar Cain pitched all 13 innings in a Minot 5–4 victory over Bismarck on July 29. Oiler catcher Joe Massaro ended an 18-game hitting streak in July. Also in July, Norm Johnson of Williston pitched a 4-hit, 2–0 shutout against Brandon. Because of the quality of pitchers, there were not as many well-pitched games as in previous seasons.

The finals standing for 1957 were:

	W	L	G
Bismarck Barons	38	33	
Minot Mallards	36	35	2
Williston Oilers	34	37	4
Brandon Greys	34	37	4

Bismarck's Len Van de Hey won the batting championship with a .404 average. Williston's Bill Raeshe set a league record for RBI with 88. Jack Bowes and Jim Ackers, both with Bismarck, had the most wins with 10. Brandon's Al Lyons led the league with a 3.08 ERA and teammate Bob Bennett had the most strikeouts with 98.

At season's end four games separated the first- and fourth-place teams. Due to the number of uneven games played, Minot ended up in second place. The league executive decided that the games would not be replayed when the outcome would not alter the final standings. Bismarck had finished in first place and only one game separated Minot, Brandon and Williston. Brandon and Williston had three games remaining and Minot had five. Minot was allowed to play two of its games and thus finished in second place and moved into the finals against the Barons. A protest and charges of "maneuvering" by the president were filed by Brandon and Williston. The league president stuck to his guns and ruled the protest invalid, and that Minot would meet Bismarck in the final.

Playoffs

In the first game of the playoffs, Bismarck opened with a 10–3 victory, behind the pitching of Jack Bowes. Bill Oster took the loss for the Mallards. Frank Neri and Gene Johnson hit two-run homers and Clyde McNeal stroked a solo shot to pace the Barons. Jesse Rogers led the Mallards with four hits. Minot nipped Bismarck 10–8 in game two. Jack Hale was the winner and Jim Ackers took the loss. Zoonie McLean had a home run and two other hits to pace the Mallards. Len Van De Hey and Bill Hockenbury each had three hits for the Barons. Game three featured a pitching duel between the Barons' Frank Schwartz and the Mallards' Dirk Gibbons. Gibbons threw a wild pitch in the ninth inning that allowed the winning run to score as the Barons came out on top 5–4. The victory gave Bismarck a one-game series lead. Batting champ Len Van De Hey led the way with a home run and double for the Barons.

Then Minot was hit with heavy rains. The league deemed the field unplayable and wanted to switch the remainder of the playoffs to Bismarck. Minot, not wishing to give up home-field advantage plus the gate receipts, refused to continue and forfeited the championship to Bismarck. As one Bismarck player stated, "That was the first time a championship series was decided in the board room."

At the completion of the season, Williston journeyed to Plentywood, Montana, to play an exhibition game against Notre Dame College from Saskatchewan. The game was played as a fundraiser for the Plentywood School. Minot's Zoonie McLean, who was the basketball coach at the school, played for the Oilers in that game. Hot dogs were sold and tickets to the game cost $1.00. That would be the last game a ManDak League team would play in.

With the season over, the *Williston Herald* picked its Mandak "Dream Team" for 1957. The selections were:

Manager — Zoonie McLean, smart, good handler of players, good hitter and fielder.
Pitchers — Al Lyons, Jim Ackers, Preston Elkins and Edmond Hahn.
Catcher — Joe Massaro, clutch hitter and handles pitchers well.
First Base — Bill Raeshe, ManDak League RBI champ with 88, top hitter and fielder.
Second Base — Clyde McNeal, good hitter, good fielder, Bill Sharp a close second.
Third Base — Ralph Wilcox, terrific glove man and good hitter
Shortstop — Al Leap, makes tough plays look easy. McLean and Jerry Adair close behind.
Left Field — Bob Rous, tough hitter, good arm.
Center field — Bill Lynn, ranges far to make catches, good competitor and hitter.
Right Field — Len Van De Hey, powerful hitter, good fielder. Has the edge on Willard Brown in the field but not as powerful.
Utility — Dennis Healy, plays the infield and outfield and is the top competitor in the league; fair hitter.

9
The End of the Mandak League

With attendance dwindling and operating costs rising, all teams were in trouble. The *Bismarck Tribune* on July 21, 1972, reported that in the year 1955, the Barons' expenses were over $54,000 and their goal was $25,000. Many Manitobans, to this day, believe that Williston and Bismarck exceeded the salary cap and that this eventually led to the league's demise.

The ManDak League was a glorious time for baseball in Manitoba and North Dakota. The quality of play was very high. To this day there's a lot of talk as to what classification the ManDak League would be. Many knowledgeable people believe the league was somewhere between Double A and Triple A. In 1957 ex–major leaguer Al Lyons was quoted in the *Williston Herald* as saying, "I could take a respective squad from the ManDak League into the Pacific Coast League and make a real race for the pennant." At the start of the 1950 season, Minot manager Lefty Lefebrve, who had pitched in the major leagues, was quoted as saying he thought the ManDak League was equal to Class B in organized ball. His view was that Brandon's Rafe Cabrera was the best all-around player and Gentry Jessup was the best pitcher. He hadn't seen the Buffaloes play yet. In 1951 Minot manager and former major leaguer Otto Huber was quoted in the Minot paper as saying he thought Zoonie McLean was a Class A shortstop and the Buffaloes' Al Wilmore was the best pitcher in the league. He thought the caliber of play was between Class A and Class B. In 1953, ex–major leaguer and manager of the Winnipeg Royals, Dee Moore, stated that the ManDak League was as good as the strongest Class B league in organized ball. In 1953, Maurice Smith, *Winnipeg Free Press* sports editor, questioned whether Winnipeg would be satisfied with Class C Northern League baseball after seeing the ManDak League. Winnipeg sports writer Ted Bowles echoed similar comments as Smith about Winnipeg going into the Northern League. It was his opinion that the ManDak League rated between Class A and Class B ball, and he wondered how Winnipeg fans would take to the lesser brand of ball. Winnipeg did join the Northern League in 1954.

In another article in the *Free Press*, Mickey Rocco, commenting on the league's pitching, said, "Some games are pitched like Class A ball and others are pitched like Triple-A." In an interview with Jim Adelson, sports announcer for Minot in the 1950's, he said that the ball was close to Triple-A. To this day, the argument continues as to what was the league's classification. It will never be decided and it doesn't matter that much, as the baseball was great. Fans got to see some of the big stars of the Negro Leagues and many talented ex–major and minor league stars. There are not too many leagues that can boast three Hall of Famers like Leon Day, Willie Wells and Ray Dandridge. There were four if you count Satchel Paige and his brief 1950 appearance with the Mallards. Day, Wells, and Dandridge were special players as were many who played in the league.

II. Player Profiles

Jim Ackers
Left Field

Akers played organized ball from 1950 to 1956 and played as high as Class B ball. His best season was 1952 in the Longhorn League, where he batted .331 with 20 home runs and 95 RBI. He joined the Bismarck Barons in 1957 and batted .304 with 9 home runs and 44 RBI.

Jerry Adair

Shortstop; Bats—Right; Throws—Right; Height—6'; Weight—175 lbs.; Born—December 17, 1936, Sand Springs Oklahoma; Died May 31, 1987, Tulsa Oklahoma

Adair was twenty years old when he was signed by the Williston Oilers midway through the 1957 season and batted .356 with no home runs and 8 RBI. He had been playing University baseball in Oklahoma and in the Basin League in South Dakota. In 1958, he led the Western Canada Baseball League in hitting with a .409 average and tied for the lead in home runs with 10. He received a $40,000 signing bonus from the Baltimore Orioles and played 11 games that season in the major leagues. In 1959 and 1960, he again played sparingly with the Orioles and in 1960 became a regular. In 1966, after 17 games, he was traded to the Chicago White Sox. In 1967, after 28 games, the White Sox traded him to the Boston Red Sox, and he played well for the Sox that season batting .291. Also that season he appeared in five World Series games for the Red Sox and batted .125. He played in 1968 for the Red Sox, batting .216 in 74 games. Before the 1969 season, he was a expansion draft choice of the new Kansas City Royals. In 1969 for Kansas City, he batted .250 and in 1970, after playing in seven games was batting .148 and then retired. His career major league batting average was .254. His best season was 1962 with the Orioles, when he batted .284. In 1964, Adair set the major league record for the fewest errors by a second baseman with five and had a .994 fielding average. That season he played 89 consecutive games without an error. After his retirement he coached for the Oakland A's and California Angels.

JOE "SMOKEY" ADAMS

Pitcher

Adams came from Toledo, Ohio, and had no Negro League experience when he joined the Carman Cardinals in 1950. He finished the season with a 2–4 record in his only season in the league.

BUDDY AFREMOW

Shortstop; Height — 5'10"; Weight —175 lbs.

In 1949 at Hopkinsville, he was selected to the All-Star team in the Class D Kitty League. He joined the Williston Oilers in 1954 and batted .188 with two home runs and 28 RBI. He joined the Dickinson Packers in 1955 and improved his hitting that season with a .264 average, one home run and 34 RBI. He was back with Dickinson in 1956 and batted .247 with two home runs and 21 RBI.

DAN AHTIPIS

Pitcher

The right-hander entered organized ball in 1949 in the Brooklyn Dodgers chain. He pitched three seasons for the Santa Barbara Dodgers in the California League. He joined the Brandon Greys in 1954 and had a 10–7 record. He played briefly in 1955 with Minot, when he developed a sore arm and asked for his release. His record at that time was 2–3 with a 4.98 ERA.

ED ALBOSTA

Pitcher; Bats— Right; Throws— Right; Height — 6'1"; Weight —175 lbs.; Born — October 27, 1918, Saginaw, Michigan; Died — December 7, 2003, Saginaw, Michigan

Albosta had the nickname of "Rube." In 1940, he was selected to the All-Star team with the Durham Bulls and led the league with a 1.73 ERA. In 1941 he was called up from Durham to the Brooklyn Dodgers at the end of the season. Durham was about to start their playoffs and had to play without Albosta. Albosta said he was surprised the Dodgers had brought him up as Durham was in the playoffs, not that he was complaining. He appeared in 2 games for the Dodgers and had a 0–2 record. With the Dodgers' season over, Albosta returned to Durham to collect the watch that was given to each of the Durham players. His wife said that years later he found the watch in a drawer and that it was showing signs of wear. Albosta then had the watch refurbished and gave it to one of his grandchildren. In an interview, he said even though he never won a game in the majors he was just happy to have made it. He said, "just think of how many players never get there." In 1942, he went to training camp with the Dodgers in Havana, Cuba, but was later sent down to the minor leagues. In 1946, he pitched in 17 games with the Pittsburgh Pirates and walked 43, struck out 24, and had a 6.15 ERA. He joined the Minot Mallards in 1952 when he was 34 years old. That season he had a 1–6 record. He was the Mallards' playing manager in 1953, led them to the league championship, and appeared in 18 games, mostly in relief. He posted an 8–2 record on the mound and did complete his only three starts. After a disagreement with the Minot executive, he signed on as playing manager with the Carman Cardinals in 1954. His record that season was 4–2. He pitched 71 innings for the Cardinals and walked 22 and struck out 30. That was his last season in baseball.

John Alexander
Pitcher

Alexander was a 20-year-old pitcher who came straight from the University of Michigan. He had been recommended to the University by a St. Louis Cardinals scout and received an athletic scholarship. He joined the Elmwood Giants shortly into the 1951 season and pitched briefly in recording a 0–1 record.

Ed Allen
Pitcher

Allen was a right-handed pitcher who attended the University of Southern California. He joined the Minot Mallards in 1952 and had a 3–1 record when he was released in mid–June. He also played in organized ball with Visalia in the California League.

Lou Almendariz
Shortstop

He was a player from Cuba who played briefly with Brandon in 1954 and was released. He played organized ball in 1956 with little success.

Mario Amero
Pitcher

He was a player from Cuba. He joined the Brandon Greys in 1953 and had a 2–6 record. He pitched in the Mexican League from 1955 to 1956; his best season was in 1956 with Mexicali where he was a 8–5, with a 4.95 ERA.

Andy Anderson
Pitcher; Height: 6'; Weight: 170

He was a left-handed pitcher who in 1947 pitched in the Class B New England League. In 1948 played for Kingston in the Class C Border League and St. Albans in a Vermont semi-pro league. He came to Minot with manager Lefty Levebvre, who had been his coach at Brown University and was the winner for Minot in its first home game, He pitched 4⅔ innings in relief of Satchel Paige, who had given up no runs in the three innings he had pitched. He finished the season with a 2–3 record and also appeared in five games as a fielder, batting .209 with no home runs and 3 RBI.

BILL ANDERSON

Pitcher

From Fargo, North Dakota, Anderson was a right-hander who pitched locally in Minnesota AA ball. He pitched briefly for Minot in 1950 and had a 1–0 record. In 1951 he pitched in one exhibition game for the Mallards.

ORENTHAL "ANDY" ANDERSON

Pitcher, Utility

Orenthal "Andy" Anderson, Carman Cardinals. Anderson was on the Carman roster briefly in 1951; he batted 14 times

He played one season in the Negro League with the Chicago American Giants in 1951 and played in the Class A Western League for Lincoln from 1952 to 1954. In 1955 he was 7–2 for Rochester in the semi-pro Southern Minny League. He joined the Minot Mallards in July of 1956 as an outfielder and also pitched and played catcher and third base. That season he batted .262. with seven home runs and 18 RBI and in a playoff game that season against Bismarck he hit a grand slam home run. He was back in 1957 and had a 1–0 record.

JOHN ANDRÉ

Pitcher; Bats—Left; Throws—Right; Height—6'4"; Weight 200 lbs.; Born—January 3, 1923 in Brockton, Massachusetts; Died—Centerville Massachusetts, November 25, 1976

In 1954, André led the Texas League with 21 wins while pitching for the pennant-winning Shreveport Sports and was named the league's most valuable player. In 1955 he appeared in 22 games for the Chicago Cubs and had a 0–1 record and a 5.80 ERA. He was 34 when he joined the Minot Mallards in 1957 and was expected to be their leading pitcher. He won his first three games, of which two were shutouts, then injured his arm and was released in early August. He finished with a record of 3–3 with a 5.37 ERA.

SONNY ANDREWS

Shortstop; Height — 5'7"; Weight — 175 lbs.; Born — 1926

Andrews had played for Carman in 1949 in the Manitoba Senior League (over 21 years of age) and had batted .366. Teammate Al McKerlie said that Andrews could get to balls most shortstops couldn't reach. Over his four seasons in the league he batted .333, 2 HR, 25 RBI in 1950; .264, 4 HR, 24 RBI in 1951; .280, 4 HR, 30 RBI in 1952; .268. 5 HR, 29 RBI in 1953. Many ManDak fans thought he was good enough to play in organized ball. In the off-season he worked at the Fisher Body Works in Detroit.

ORLANDO ANDUX

Shortstop

Andux was a player from Cuba who played for Drummondville in the Class C Provincial League in 1952 and batted .179. He joined the Brandon Greys in 1953 and batted .245 with 0 home runs and 17 RBI. That was his only season in the league.

CESAR ARGUDIN

Argudin came from Cuba and played briefly with the Brandon Greys in 1952. He then went into organized ball and signed with the St. Louis Cardinals. In 1956 he played with little success for the Winnipeg Goldeyes in the Class C Northern League.

DICK ASHLEY

Outfield

In 1948, Ashley played in organized ball. He briefly joined the Carman Cardinals in 1952 and was released.

JOE ATKINS

Outfield/Third Base; Bats — Right; Throws — Right; Height — 6'1"; Weight 190 lbs.; Born in Pittsburgh, Pennsylvania in 1922

Atkins could hit with power. He started his career in the Negro Leagues in 1947 with the Cleveland Buckeyes and in 1948 played in the Quebec Provincial League and batted .378. He played three seasons there until 1952, when he went into organized ball with Tampa in the Florida International League. He played there with little success, batting .210. He was 31 years old when he joined the Carman Cardinals in 1953. He played in 53 league games that season, batting .294 with seven home runs and 40 RBI. He played only that one season in the league. In 1954, he played eight games for Ottawa in the International League, and that was his last season in organized baseball. There is no record of him returning to the Negro Leagues. Over his career he also played in the winter leagues.

BOB BALL
Catcher/Utility

Ball started his career in 1941 with Moultrie in the Georgia-Florida League. Newspaper reports indicated that he had considerable amateur, semi-pro, and pro experience. His best season was in 1947, when he batted .358, with 10 home runs and 51 RBI with Fargo-Moorhead in the Northern League. He played for the Bismarck Barons in 1956 and batted .190 with 0 home runs and 3 RBI in 21 games. In 1957, he played again briefly for the Barons and batted .250, 0 HR, 0 RBI, and was released.

JIM BANKS
Pitcher/Outfield

In 1950, Banks saw limited action in the Negro Leagues while playing for the Baltimore Elite Giants. He joined the Brandon Greys in 1952 and played two seasons in the league. No records were available in 1952. In 1953, he batted .276 with 1 home run and 18 RBI.

QUINCY "BUD" BARBEE
Outfield/First Base; Bats: Right; Throws: Right; Height 6'0"; Weight 195 lbs.

Barbee played for both the Baltimore Elite Giants and the Kansas City Monarchs in the Negro Leagues. He had good power, but struck out a lot. In 1949, he played in the Quebec Provincial League and that season hit 23 home runs. He played three seasons in that league and hit well each season. He had 13 years of pro experience, mostly in the Negro Leagues and in Panama when he joined the Minot Mallards in 1952. He participated in a triple play against Brandon during a playoff game that year. With the bases loaded, second baseman John Kennedy fielded a ground ball, forced the runner at second and threw to Barbee at first. Barbee then threw home to catcher Joe Massaro, who tagged the runner coming home. Barbee finished the season with a .279 batting average with three home runs and 32 RBI. He completed his career in 1955 in the Class B Big State League, playing only 13 games and batting .233. By then he had lost much of his hitting skill.

ED BARR
Center field; Height — 6'1"; Weight — 180 lbs.; Born — 1926

Barr was 32 years old and had played 15 seasons of professional baseball. Barr played in the New York Yankees chain. He played four seasons in the

Double-A Texas League with Beaumont, Tulsa, Shreveport, and Austin. From 1949 to 1952, he played for Portland in the Pacific Coast League and averaged .250 while hitting with some power. In 1955, he played with Salt Lake City in the Pioneer League and batted .240. with six home runs and 66 RBI. He joined the Minot Mallards in 1956 and batted .324 with 12 HR and 62 RBI and led the Mallards in batting that season. Barr hit a grand slam home run in his second game, which was the Mallards' home opener.

Bill Barry

Second Base

Barry played the 1947 and 1948 seasons with Visalia in the Chicago Cubs chain and batted .220 and .227 those 2 years. In 1949 he batted .290, with 4 home runs and 93 RBI with Las Vegas in the Sunset League. Barry played briefly for the Winnipeg Royals in 1953 and was released.

Jack Barry

First Base

In 1944, Barry entered organized ball with Scranton in the Class A Eastern League. In 1946, he tried his hand at pitching for Visalia and had a 0–1 record. His best season was 1948, when he batted .264 in the Sunset League. He lacked power. Barry played briefly with the Winnipeg Royals in 1953 and batted .238. He was the brother of Bill Barry. Both brothers were considered to be light hitters

Lloyd "Pepper" Bassett

Catcher; Bats—Both; Throws—Right; Height—6'3"; Weight—220 lbs.; Born—August 5, 1919 Baton Rouge, LA.

Bassett played in the Negro Leagues from 1936 to 1950 and played for a number of Negro League teams. He never reached his full expectations as a player, but did have a long career and was a popular player. He played in four East-West All-Star games. He was 32 years old when he joined the Brandon Greys in 1951 and batted .252 with 2 home runs and 23 RBI. He returned to the Negro Leagues in 1954 and closed out his career with the Birmingham Black Barons. Early in his career, he was known as the rocking chair catcher. When he was with the Homestead Grays in 1936 and Pittsburgh Crawfords in 1937, he would catch a few innings while sitting in a rocking chair, much to the delight of the fans.

Dick Baxter

Pitcher; Height—5'11"; Weight—165 lbs.

Baxter played organized ball from 1947 to 1953 in the Cleveland Indians chain. In 1951 he was 12–3, with a 4.10 ERA with Raleigh in the Class B Carolina League. He joined the Williston Oilers in 1954 and batted .311 with no home runs and 11 RBI. He had less success on the mound, going 2–6. The next season he was with the Dickinson Packers, where he batted .231 and had a 3–6, 6.85 ERA pitching record.

Harvey Beaster
Centerfield

In 1939, Beaster was an All-Star in the Arkansas-Missouri League and that season led the league in hits with 171 and RBI with 106. He had a long career in organized baseball and played at Class C, B and A levels and hit well in every league he played. He joined the Minot Mallards in 1951 and batted .301 with five home runs and 30 RBI. During the season he had a 17-game hitting streak. That was his only season in the league.

Dick Beck
Pitcher

In 1947 he played in organized ball with little success. He was briefly with the Winnipeg Royals in 1953 and had no decisions when he was released.

Ed Benecke
Pitcher

Benecke was a local Bismarck player who had a successful amateur career. In 1955, he was signed when the Bismarck Barons had pitching injury problems. He was a tall pitcher who threw sidearm. He had a 4–1, 5.27 ERA record that season.

Bob Bennett
Pitcher

Bennett played in the Chicago White Sox chain. In the early 1950s, he pitched in the Western Canada Baseball League with success. In 1955, he played for the Superior Blues in the Northern League and led the league with a 2.31 ERA. He joined the Brandon Greys in 1957 and had a 7–10 record with a 3.62 ERA and led the league in strikeouts with 98. When his playing days were over, he coached at Fresno State University for many years.

Lorne "Boom Boom" Benson
Pitcher

Benson was a star pitcher in local baseball in Winnipeg. When the American import players had not arrived, he was called on to pitch for the Buffaloes and was the losing pitcher in his only game. He was an all-around athlete and was well known for his football ability with the Winnipeg Blue Bombers in the Canadian Football League.

DON BERG
Utility

Berg was from Oakes, North Dakota. He tried out for the Brooklyn Dodgers in 1946 and the Cleveland Indians in 1948. In 1949, he played 24 games for Madisonville in the Class D Kitty League and batted .263. He joined Minot in 1951 on the recommendation of Connie Juelke, who managed the Madisonville club. Berg hit a home run in his first at-bat for Minot and finished the season batting .310 with one home run and 12 RBI. In a Minot newspaper report, manager Otto Huber had high praise for Berg's versatility and value to the Mallards.

RAY BERNS
Outfield; Height — 5'10"; Weight — 175 lbs.; Born — 1928

Berns had 7 years of pro experience. He was with Sioux City in the Western league from 1951 to 1952 and the Minneapolis Millers in 1953. He joined the Williston Oilers in 1955 and batted .331 with seven home runs and 36 RBI. Back with the Oilers in 1956, Berns batted .253 with seven home runs and 48 RBI.

MIKE "RED" BERRY
Pitcher; Bats— Right; Throws— Right; Height — 5'11"; Weight —170 lbs.

Berry played the 1947 season with the Kansas City Monarchs and at best was just an average pitcher. He played very briefly, and with little success, for the Elmwood Giants in 1951 and was released.

BILL BEST
Pitcher; Height — 6'; Weight —170 lbs.

The *Williston Herald* reported that Best never had a losing season. He played in the Chicago White Sox chain. In 1949, he pitched for Superior in the Northern League. In 1952, he pitched for the Waterloo White Hawks in Class B and the Colorado Springs Sky Sox in Class A. From 1953 to 1955, he pitched for London, Ontario, in the Inter County League. In 1956, he played semi-pro ball. He joined the Williston Oilers in 1957 and had a 5–4 record and a 6.38 ERA.

JOE BESTUDIK
Outfield

Bestudik played for Indianapolis in the American Association in 1946 and batted .279. In 1947, he split the season between Milwaukee and St. Paul in the American Association and batted .281. He played very briefly for the Carman Cardinals in 1951 and was released. He then tried out with Minot, played briefly and again was released.

Bob Betz

Outfield; Height — 6'; Weight — 190 lbs.; Born — 1928

In 1949, Betz played for Youngstown in the Class C Mid-Atlantic League and led the league in batting with an average of .345, 181 hits and 135 RBI. In 1951, he played for the Savannah Indians in the Class A South Atlantic League and was selected to the All-Star team. He played in the Philadelphia A's and Brooklyn Dodgers organizations and played as high as Triple-A ball in the International League. He was 27 years old when he joined the Williston Oilers in 1955. He batted .343 with 8 home runs and 68 RBI.

Jack Bishop

Catcher

Bishop was from Minot, North Dakota. In June 1955, he was signed as a reserve catcher due to player injuries and appeared in only one game.

Willy Blackshire

Second Base

A member of Joe Legon's traveling team, Blackshire then left that club to join Saskatoon in the Western Canada Baseball League. In 1951 he played in one game for the Minot Mallards, then resigned.

Ralph Blinn

Outfield

Blinn played briefly with Tallahassee of the Florida International League in 1954, and was released after a few games. He then joined the Williston Oilers. He played only briefly and again was released.

Jim Bolden

Pitcher; Born — February 8, 1923

Bolden had the nickname of "Fire Ball." In 1946 and 1947 he pitched in the Negro Leagues for the Cleveland Buckeyes and Birmingham Black Barons. He then pitched semi-pro for various barnstorming Negro teams such as the Chattanooga Choo Choos and the New Orleans Creoles. He joined the last-place Elmwood Giants in 1951 when he was 28 years old and his pitching record for the Giants was 5–8. He did pitch with some success. After one season in the ManDak League he went back to the Negro Leagues in 1952 with the Birmingham Black Barons.

Marshall Boney

Catcher

Boney joined the Elmwood Giants in 1950 and batted .237

Lyman Bostock

First Base/Outfield; Bats—Left; Throws—Right; Height—6'1"; Weight—215 lbs.; Born—March 11, 1918, Birmingham, Alabama; Died—June 24, 2005, Birmingham, Alabama

Bostock played in the Negro Leagues for 11 seasons with four clubs, the Brooklyn Royal Giants, Birmingham Black Barons, Chicago American Giants, and New York Cubans. His Negro League career was interrupted by four years of military duty. He played in the 1941 Negro League All-Star game and was considered to be a good hitter. He also played in Mexico, and in 1948, toured with the Jackie Robinson All-Stars. He was 32 years old when he joined the Winnipeg Buffaloes in 1950. He batted .306 with one home run and 31 RBI. In 1951, he batted .288 with 34 RBI for the Buffaloes. When the Buffaloes folded, he finished his baseball career playing for the Carman Cardinals in 1952 and 1953. In 1952, he batted .328 with five home runs and 36 RBI, and in 1953, he batted .316 with two home runs and 55 RBI. He was a solid all-around player in his four seasons in the ManDak League, and was considered to be an excellent defensive player. He got many a timely hit. Lyman told me that when he played in Carman he was billeted by the Whiteside family. He said he remembered how well they treated the players and that he had fond memories of his stay in Carman. He retired from baseball in 1954.

Lyman Bostock, Carman Cardinals (courtesy of Dufferin Historical Museum of Carman, Manitoba).

Bob Bourbeau

Shortstop/Third base; Height—5'11"; Weight—185 lbs.; Born—1936

Bourbeau was a college player from Gonzaga University who batted .350

in college ball and was regarded as a good fielder. He joined the Williston Oilers in 1955 and batted .272 with six home runs and 26 RBI. In 1956 he played briefly for the Dickinson Packers.

ERNIE BOUSHY
First Base; Height — 6'; Weight — 190 lbs.; Born — 1933 in Gilbert Plains, Manitoba

Before joining the Carman Cardinals, Boushy played for the Dauphin Red Birds in Manitoba. He played in the Philadelphia A's organization and was 17 years old when he played for the Carman Cardinals in 1952. He batted .228 with no home runs and 28 RBI. The next year, he went into organized ball and in 1953 led the Appalachian League in hitting with a .349 average and led the league in hits with 169. In 1954, he batted .276 with five home runs and 50 RBI for Lancaster in the Piedmont League and closed out his organized baseball career in 1955 when he played briefly for Burlington in the Provincial League. He returned to his home in Swan River, Manitoba, and continued his sporting career in the game of curling. He skipped his rink to four provincial and two national mixed curling championships. Boushy was elected to the Manitoba Baseball Hall of Fame in 2000.

RON BOWEN
Second Base

Bowen was considered to be a good hitter and defensive player. He played in the New York Yankees organization. In 1948, he played with Albuquerque in the West Texas–New Mexico League and led the league in hits that year with 234. In 1950, he played for Muskegon, Michigan, and led the Class A Central League with 169 hits, 128 RBI and 28 home runs. In 1951, he again led that league in RBI with 114. He joined Williston in 1954 and midway through the season he wanted more money and was released. He then signed with Brandon and finished the season batting .366 with seven home runs and 28 RBI. In 1955, he became the playing manager for the Dickinson Packers and batted .318 with 18 home runs and 68 RBI.

JACK BOWES
Pitcher

Bowes was a Canadian who also played hockey for St. John, New Brunswick, in the Big Four Canadian Amateur Hockey League. He played in the Cleveland Indians chain and pitched as high as Double-A ball. In 1953 at Sherbrooke in the Provincial League, he had a 17–3 record with a 2.44 ERA. In 1954 he followed that with a 3–1 record with Sherbrooke, then joined Spartanburg in the Tri-State League, pitching well for them in recording a 13–7 record with a 3.88 ERA. In 1954 and 1955 he pitched with little success in the Eastern, Piedmont and Texas Leagues. He joined the Bismarck Barons in 1957 and had a 10–5 record with a 3.62 ERA and led the league with 98 strikeouts. His 10 wins tied for the league lead. He closed out his career in the Western Canada Baseball League.

DUKE BOWMAN

Third Base; Height — 5'11"; Weight — 160 lbs.

Bowman, from Oak Ridge, North Carolina, played in the Cleveland Indians organization. He played as high as Class B ball. In 1949, he was selected to the All-Star team with Burlington in the Class C Central Association. He joined the Minot Mallards in 1952 and played six seasons as their regular third baseman. Each year he would become a key member of the Mallards and could be counted on to do something outstanding. In the 1952 championship playoff series against Carman, he hit an inside-the-park home run to win the game 4–3. In 1953, he fashioned a 20-game hitting streak and had a big playoff series against the Winnipeg Royals. He hit two home runs in one game and had a triple and three doubles in another game. In game three of the 1954 playoffs against Carman, he had 7 RBI. July 1955 was a big month for Bowman, as he hit a home run and three singles, driving in five runs on July 24 against the Dickinson Packers. Then, on July 29, he went 5 for 5 with two doubles in a 9–8 Minot win. In 1956 in a series against Bismarck, Bowman had 13 hits in 20 at-bats. Over his six seasons in the league he had a batting average of .313, with 18 home runs and 261 RBI. Was the brother of Ed and Walt Bowman.

ED BOWMAN

Second Base; Height — 5'8"; Weight — 140 lbs.; Born — 1929

Ed was the younger brother of Duke Bowman. He was a light-hitting, good defensive player in the ManDak League. He had two seasons of pro experience with New Bern in the Class D Coastal League. In 1953 Bowman was signed by Minot when second baseman John Kennedy failed to report. He batted .243 with no home runs and 22 RBI. He did hit a home run in the championship series that year in a 6–4 Minot win. In 1954, he batted .247 and again had no home runs. He drove in 32 runs. Bowman led all second basemen in fielding his first two seasons in the league. In 1955, he had a .951 fielding average and was charged with just 17 errors and improved his batting average to .298, no HR, 29 RBI. He played in the Basin League in South Dakota with Huron in 1956, and in 1957 he was back in the ManDak League with Williston. He batted .303 with no home runs and seven RBI that season.

WALT BOWMAN

Infield

Walt was the oldest of the Bowman brothers. He played a number of seasons in the Basin League in South Dakota. He was added to the Minot Mallards roster late in the 1954 season and batted .130 with no home runs and two RBI. That would be his only season in the ManDak League.

FRED BRENZEL
Pitcher

In 1947 and 1948, Brenzel pitched for Clarksville in the Class C Kitty League. In 1947 he was 4–9, with a 6.06 ERA, and in 1948 had a record of 9-7, with a 7.06 ERA. He joined the Carman Cardinals in 1951 and had a 5–6 record and was back with Carman in 1952, with a 3–8 record. He returned to the ManDak League in 1955 with the Dickinson Packers and his record that season was 5–10 with a 6.98 ERA. In 1956 he signed with the Bismarck Barons and recorded a 5–8 record with a 5.23 ERA record. Brenzel returned to his home after each season to his high-school coaching job.

CHET BREWER

Manager/Pitcher; Bats— Both; Throws— Right; Height — 6'1"; Weight —187 lbs.; Born — Leavenworth, Kansas, January 14, 1907; Died — Whittier California, March 26, 1990

Brewer had a long and illustrious Negro League career from 1925 to 1948 and was one of the Negro Leagues' top pitchers. When he and Satchel Paige were teammates, they were tough to beat when they both played for the Bismarck Barons and with the Kansas City Monarchs. In many games Paige would start the game and Brewer would come in and finish it. On June 6th, 1935, Brewer and Paige hooked up in a pitching dual in Winnipeg. Not many baseball historians know about this game. Brewer was with Kansas City and Paige was with Bismarck. The game went nine innings and with the score tied 0–0, the game was called because of darkness. Paige struck out 17 batters and Brewer had 13 strikeouts. The *Winnipeg Evening Tribune* reported that the hitters were absolutely helpless. Brewer gave up only five hits and Paige gave up 7 hits. Both teams played well on the field and came up with some brilliant plays. The game was played in 1 hour 55 minutes. The teams played a three-game series that weekend. In 1938, Brewer was the first black American player to play in the Mexican League. He spent 11 seasons with the Kansas City Monarchs. In 1951, he played for the Sceptre Panthers in Saskatchewan, and in 1952, managed in organized baseball in the Southwest International League and joined the Carman Cardinals in 1953. Almer McKerlie, the Carman Cardinals catcher, was quoted as saying, "Brewer did not pitch that much for the Cardinals, but when he did he was untouchable for five or six innings." In later years, Brewer was a major league scout, and was an instructor for the Pittsburgh Pirates from 1957 to 1974. When his career was over he started a baseball program in the Watts area of L.A. for troubled boys. It was a huge success and the program sent several players to the major leagues. His Negro League and career record warrants his induction into baseball's Hall of Fame.

Johnny Britton

Third Base; Bats—Left; Throws—Right; Height—5'8"; Weight—160 lbs.; Born—Mt. Vernon, Georgia on April 21, 1919

Britton played in the Negro Leagues from 1943 to 1949, mostly with the Birmingham Black Barons. Britton was a spray-type hitter who could make contact. He did not hit with a lot of power and was just average defensively. His batting average over his Negro League career was .300. He toured one year with the Satchel Paige All-Stars and played one season in Mexico. He was 31 years old when he joined the Winnipeg Buffaloes in 1950 and batted .328 with one home run and 26 RBI. In 1951, he joined the Elmwood Giants and finished with a .310 average, three home runs, and 40 RBI. He was a star player in the ManDak League and after his ManDak days, he was one of the first black Americans to play in Japan, batting over .300 in his two seasons.

Dennis Brodeur

Shortstop

Brodeur briefly joined the Williston Oilers in 1957 and was a good fielder with a strong arm. He did not hit for a high average and this would lead to his release shortly into the season. He played hockey on the Canadian Olympic team.

Barney Brown

Pitcher/Outfield; Bats—Left; Throws—Left; Height—5'9"; Weight—165 lbs.; Born—Kimball, West Virginia

Brown played in the Negro Leagues from 1931 to 1949. He was one of the better hurlers in the Negro Leagues and pitched in five Negro League All-Star games. He also played in Mexico, and in 1950 led the Mexican League in strikeouts with 157. He played winter ball in Puerto Rico, with success. He was also a good hitter and would play the outfield when not pitching. It was said that Brown was over 40 years old when he played the 1952 and 1953 seasons for the Brandon Greys. It was proven later that this was correct. In those two seasons, he won 13 games and lost 5. He was regarded as one of the better Brandon pitchers. Before Brandon, he played for several teams in small towns in Western Canada. In 1955 he started the season with Minot and was released with a 0–3 record and a 9.00 ERA. After his release he joined the Lloydminster Meridians in the Western Canada Baseball League and appeared to get his pitching skill back as he posted a record of 5–5 with a 2.09 ERA. He was back again in 1956 and had a 4–6 record with a 6.31 ERA. In 1955, he listed his date of birth as October 23, 1912, but the United States Social Security Death Index listed him as being born on October 23, 1907. That would have made him 50 years old when he pitched for the Meridians.

Danny Brown
Outfield

Danny Brown played organized ball from 1948 to 1951 with limited success, and never advanced beyond Class C ball. He did not hit for a high average or with power. In 1953, he played briefly with the Winnipeg Royals and was released.

T. J. Brown
Second Base; Bats—Right; Throws—Right

T.J. Brown's Negro League career was from 1939 to 1950, mostly with the Memphis Red Sox. He was their regular shortstop for seven seasons. He played in the 1942 Negro League All-Star game and was considered a good fielder, but not a high average hitter. In 1951 he joined the Carman Cardinals, and midway through the season was traded to the Elmwood Giants. In 25 games, he batted .212 with 12 RBI. In 1952 and 1953 he played in organized ball with Danville in the Mississippi Valley League and he batted .241 and .163. After that season his career ended.

Willard Brown
Outfield; Bats—Right; Throws—Right; Height—5'11"; Weight—200 lbs.; Born—June 26, 1911 Shreveport, Louisiana; Died—August 8, 1996 Houston, Texas

In 1947, Willard Brown was the second former Negro League player in the American League. He played for the St. Louis Browns, batting .179. He was the first former Negro League player to hit a home run in the American League. He was released after 21 games. He played 11 of his 16 seasons for the Kansas City Monarchs and had six Negro League All-Star game appearances. He was one of the Negro Leagues' top home run hitters was considered by some to be the very best of all time. He averaged over .300 for his career in the Negro League. He played winter ball in Puerto Rico and still holds the record for the most home runs in a season with 27. Some baseball people didn't like his casual approach to the game. He joined the Minot Mallards in 1957 and batted .307 with nine home runs and 29 RBI.

Louis Bruni
Pitcher/Outfield

Bruni played in Mexico in the late 1940s with limited success. In 1952, he joined the Brandon Greys and had a 0–1 record when he was released.

Jack Bruton
Pitcher/Outfield

Jack Bruton was a right-handed pitcher who had a long career in the

Negro Leagues with many teams. He pitched very little for the Mallards but was a versatile player in the field. Reports at the time indicated that he had good power and was known to hit well in the clutch. He joined Minot in early July 1950 and batted .304 in 15 games with no home runs and 15 RBI. On August 10, 1951, he was released by Estevan of the Western Canada Baseball League and signed again with the Mallards. He batted only .156 with one home run and 8 RBI in 14 games. He played only the two seasons in the league.

NIP BRUTON

Pitcher

Nip Bruton was a right-handed pitcher who had pitched for the Negro League San Francisco Cubs in 1950 and the Denver Bears in 1951. He joined Minot in late June 1951 and recorded a 1-0 record. He was the brother of major leaguer Bill Bruton.

AL "LEFTY" BRYANT

Pitcher; Bat — Left; Throws Left; Height — 5'11"; Weight — 160 lbs.; Born — March 29, 1919 in Chicago, Illinois; Died — March 22, 1992 in Kansas City, Missouri

Bryant had a 10-year Negro League career and pitched for the Kansas City Monarchs in the early 1940's. He pitched for the Minot Merchants in 1949. He was 34 years old when he joined the Minot Mallards in 1952. On June 22, he was released after pitching only $2^{2}/_{3}$ innings. His record at the time was 0-1. After his release he joined the Elmwood Giants and had a 3-1 record.

WALTER BRYJA

Pitcher

Bryja played in the Washington Senators organization. In 1951, he was an All-Star in the Class D Kitty League and led the league with 24 victories. He joined the Dickinson Packers in 1956 and had a 3-3 record and 5.07 ERA.

NORM BUDZ

Pitcher; Throws— Left

Budz called Chicago, Illinois home. He was a 20-year-old when he asked for a tryout with Minot in 1957. He played very briefly with Minot and had a 0-0 record.

Earl Bumpus

Pitcher/Outfield; Bats — Left; Throws — Left; Height — 6'1"; Weight — 215 lbs.

Bumpus' Negro League career was from 1944 to 1948. He played for the Kansas City Monarchs, Birmingham Barons, and Chicago American Giants. He had a good season in 1945 with Birmingham, going 4–3 with a 3.63 ERA. He was regarded as a good pitcher in the Negro Leagues. He played very briefly for the Carman Cardinals in 1951, pitching with little success, and was released with no decisions.

Carl Bush

First Base; Height — 6'3"; Weight — 180 lbs.

Bush played organized baseball from 1949 to 1955, starting his career as a pitcher for Hornell of the Class D Pony League. He played in the Philadelphia Phillies organization. In 1949, he batted .349 with Union City in the Kitty League and in 1951 and 1952 he batted .279 and .273 with Schenectady in the Eastern League. He demonstrated some power, hitting 12 home runs each season. His best season was 1954 with Mattoon in the Mississippi-Ohio Valley League, where he batted .337 with six home runs and 47 RBI. He was considered to be one of the best fielding first baseman ever to play in Minot. In 1956, after joining Minot from Portsmouth in the Class B Piedmont League, he led all ManDak League first basemen with a .902 fielding average, and batted .256 with 11 home runs and 38 RBI. He was back in 1957 with Minot and hit .338, with 11 home runs and 55 RBI.

Bernard Busse

Manager

Busse was from Minot. He coached the Minot American Legion team. Along with his coaching, he was a school teacher in Minot. He joined the Mallards in 1955 as a non-playing manager, replacing Zoonie McLean, who wanted to concentrate on playing. Busse led the Mallards to a 19–12 record and the league championship.

Dick Butcher

Outfield

Butcher played four seasons in organized ball. In 1949, with Sweetwater in the Longhorn League, he batted .314 with 22 home runs and 78 RBI. In 1950, he was back with Las Vegas in the Sunset League, hitting .296 with 22 home runs and 97 RBI. In 1951, again with Las Vegas, he batted .306, with 11 home runs and 118 RBI. He joined the Winnipeg Royals in 1953 and batted .222 with seven home runs and 33 RBI.

Harry Butts

Pitcher; Bats—Right; Throws—Left

From 1949 to 1951, Harry Butts played for the Indianapolis Clowns. Midway through the 1951 season, he jumped to the Brandon Greys and finished the season with a 5–0 record and pitched very well for Brandon. In 1952, the hitters caught up to him as his record fell to 5–9. Midway through that season, he jumped the Greys and went into organized baseball with Vancouver of the Western International League. His last season was in the Piedmont League, where he pitched with little success.

Thomas "Pee Wee" Butts

Shortstop; Bats—Right; Throws—Right; Height—5'7"; Weight—145 lbs.; Born—1919 in Sparta, Ga.; Died—January 1973 in Atlanta, Ga.

Pee Wee Butts played 12 years in the Negro Leagues and was a six-time Negro League All-Star who was a good defensive player but did not hit with much power. His batting average was in the high .280's to low .300's. Along with Junior Gilliam, he formed one of the best-double play combinations in the Negro Leagues. He was 32 years old when he joined the Winnipeg Buffaloes in 1951 and batted .286 with one home run and 26 RBI. Major League scouts came to Winnipeg in 1951 with the thought of signing him, but it did not come to pass. In 1952, he followed his friend and manager, Willie Wells, to Brandon where he hit .215 with no home runs and eight RBI. Following his play in the ManDak League, he had one season of organized ball with Lincoln in the Western League, batting a poor .170. After that season he returned to the Negro Leagues. He retired after the 1955 season.

Jerry Cabana

Infield; Height—5'8"; Weight—165 lbs.; Born—Granby, Quebec

Cabana was from Granby, Quebec. He played in the Pittsburgh Pirates chain. He started his career in 1946 in the Border League with Granby and batted .270 with one home run and 17 RBI. He was with Geneva in 1947, batting 254, with no HR, 9 RBI. He then played three more seasons in the Quebec Provincial League with Granby and St. Jean. His best season was 1954, when he batted .303, with one home run and 12 RBI. In 1956, he played for North Bay in the Inter County League. He played very briefly with Minot in 1957 but was error-prone and was released.

Rafe Cabrera

Pitcher/Outfield; Bats—Right; Throws—Right; Born—Cuba

Cabrera started his career in 1944 with the Indianapolis Clowns and also played for the New York Cubans that year. Cabrera continued to play with the Cubans until the end of the 1948 season. In 1949, he played for the Brandon

Greys when the team was in the Manitoba Senior League (over 21 years of age). That season, he batted .292 and also had a 2–0 record as a pitcher. He remained with the Greys in their first ManDak season and batted .374 with six home runs and 33 RBI. This was second-best in the league. He started the 1953 season with Brandon and then joined the Elmwood Giants and finished the season batting .222 with four home runs and 27 RBI.

MARLON "SUGAR" CAIN

Pitcher/Outfield; Bats—Right; Throws—Right; Height—5'11"; Weight—188 lbs.; Born—February 14, 1914 in Macon, Georgia

Although he was born in Macon, Georgia, he called Philadelphia home. In 1957, the Williston newspaper said that Cain had received his nickname from the great Satchel Paige. He pitched for such teams as the Pittsburgh Crawfords and Indianapolis Clowns. His Negro League career lasted from 1937 to 1949. He also played in Mexico and Venezuela. He had a chance to go into organized ball with the Chicago White Sox and Pittsburgh Pirates, but refused as he only wanted to pitch in Triple A. Cain was listed as 37 years old when he joined the Minot Mallards in 1951. Many fans thought he was older than that, but because he was so effective on the mound no one questioned his age. For seven seasons he was their best pitcher and a recognized star in the ManDak League. Every season he would lead the league in various pitching statistics. He was also a very good hitter. In 1953 Cain led the league with 12 wins and 123 strikeouts. In 1954, he was ranked as one of the league's best pitchers and that season he had a streak of 11 straight victories and a minuscule 1.87 ERA. During the streak, he pitched one shutout, a two-hitter and two three-hitters. Up to 1954 he had completed 40 of his 45 starts, and from 1951 to 1953, he won all seven of the playoff games he pitched. In 1956, he completed all 15 games that he started and led the league with a 2.33 ERA. Sugar Cain was one of the most talented and popular players to ever play in Minot.

Rafe Cabrera, Brandon Greys (courtesy of Lillian Lowe).

	Pitching Record			Batting Record		
	W	L	ERA	Average	HR	RBI
1951	7	8		.268	1	10
1952	7	3		.279	3	14
1953	12	5		.316	2	18
1954	11	1		.451	2	20
1955	8	4	2.94	.254	1	6
1956	10	5	2.33	.325	1	10
1957	7	5	3.94	.318	0	8
Total	62	31		.319	10	86

Tony Campos

Second base; Height — 5'10"; Weight — 170 lbs.; Born — Cuba

Campos played 5 seasons in organized ball and played as high as Class C in the Philadelphia Phillies chain. He started his career with St. Petersburg in the Florida International League in 1947, and that season he batted .208, with one HR, 18 RBI. In 1948 and 1949 he played for Martinsville in the Carolina League. In 1948 he batted .213, with three HR, 32 RBI. In 1949 improved his batting average to .254 and showed some power with five home runs and 23 RBI. His last season in organized ball was with Granite Falls in the Western Carolina League, where he batted .267 with three home runs and nine RBI. He joined the Williston Oilers in 1954 and batted .289 with six home runs and 39 RBI and closed out his career in 1957 in the Mexican League. He returned to Cuba when his playing days were over.

Ernie Canada

Pitcher

Canada was a right-handed pitcher who played four years of ball at North Carolina A&T College in Greensboro. He pitched briefly in 1951 for the Philadelphia Stars and for a Greensboro semi-pro team. In 1954, he was released by Winston-Salem of the Class B Carolina League, then joined the Minot Mallards, for whom he had a 1–1 record and then left for military duty.

Wyman Carey

Pitcher

Carey played in the New York Yankees organization. He pitched briefly for the Minot Mallards in 1956 and had no decisions, then went back to organized baseball. In 1959, he played for the Birmingham Barons in the Double-A Southern League and was selected to the All-Star team.

Pee Wee Carlisle

Second Base

Carlisle had no Negro League experience. He was a light hitter but good defensively. He joined the Carman Cardinals in 1952 and batted .211.

Chuck Carroll
Outfield

Carroll played nine years in organized ball and played in the Chicago Cubs, Chicago White Sox, and Pittsburgh Pirate chains. In 1945, he played briefly for Milwaukee in the Triple-A American Association and batted .182. From 1948 to 1950, he played for Saginaw in the Central League and batted .260, with one HR, 66 RBI; .276, 7 HR, 44 RBI; .289, 9 HR, 74 RBI over the three seasons. In 1953, he was one of a number of players from the Class A Saginaw Bears to join the Minot Mallards. He finished that season with a .286 batting average, three home runs, and 38 RBI, and was considered to be a good defensive outfielder with a strong arm.

Ernest "Spoon" Carter

Pitcher; Bats—Left; Throws—Right; Height—6'; Weight—185 lbs.; Born—December 8, 1902 in Harpersville, Alabama; Died—January 23, 1974

Carter played in the Negro Leagues for 18 years for a number of teams. He started his career in 1932 with the Louisville Black Caps. Over his career, he pitched for two of the best Negro League teams—the Pittsburgh Crawfords and the Homestead Grays. He also played in Santo Domingo, Cuba, and Mexico during his career. In his prime, he had a good command of all his pitches. He was 48 years old when he joined the Winnipeg Buffaloes in 1950, and pitched with limited success in recording a 2–4 record. By then he was well past his prime, and his skills as a pitcher were eroded. That was his last season in baseball.

Robbie Cartledge
Pitcher

Cartledge's Negro League career was from 1951 to 1954. He pitched for the Philadelphia Stars and Birmingham Black Barons. He joined the Minot Mallards in 1955 as a late-season addition and had a 1–3 record with a 3.89 ERA.

Bill "Ready" Cash

Catcher; Bats—Right; Throws—Right; Height—6'2"; Weight—198 lbs.; Born—February 21, 1919 in Round Oak, Georgia

Cash's Negro League career lasted from 1943 to 1950. He was a durable receiver who had a strong throwing arm when he played for the Philadelphia Stars. He was chosen to play for the Satchel Paige barnstorming team in 1946, but an injury prevented him from playing. He was a Negro League All-Star in 1948 and 1949. He also played in the Mexican League, Latin American leagues, and briefly in the White Sox chain. In 1951, he played for Granby in the Quebec Provincial League, batting .296 and hitting 16 home runs. In 1952 he played in the White Sox minor league system at Waterloo in the Three-I League and Superior in the Northern League. He joined the Brandon Greys in 1953 at age 34 and left after a short time. He returned to the ManDak League in 1955 with the Bismarck Barons and batted .357, with 15 home runs and 61 RBI. He was regarded as one of the best catchers to play in the league.

Jerry Cashill
Pitcher

In 1954 and 1955, Cashill pitched with little success in the Kitty and Northern Leagues. His overall record in organized ball was 1–2, and in 1957 he arrived in Brandon and asked for a tryout. He played briefly in August and then returned home to get ready for college. At the time he had a 0–1 record.

Irvan "Chuck" Castille
Third Base

Castille's Negro League career was 1950 to 1951 and 1953. He played when the Negro Leagues were of lesser quality. He played for the Brandon Greys in 1952 and batted .309 with one home run and 22 RBI.

Willie Cathey

Pitcher; Bats—Left; Throws—Left; Height—5'10"; Weight—170 lbs.

Cathey was from Cincinnati, Ohio, and had good control. His Negro League career was from 1948 to 1950, and he pitched for the Atlanta Brown Bombers, Cincinnati Crescents, and Cincinnati Red Sox semi-pro ball clubs. He joined the Minot Mallards in 1950 as a replacement player after pitcher Steve Wylie jumped the club. For the next two seasons he was Minot's leading pitcher, recording 16 wins. He signed with Minot in 1952 but failed to report, and returned to the Negro League's with the Indianapolis Clowns.

Mario Chacon
Pitcher

Chacon was from Cuba. He pitched in the Mexican League in 1949 and had a 0–4 record. He briefly joined the Brandon Greys in 1950 and had no decisions.

John Chalfont
Catcher/Outfield

Chalfont played four seasons in the Cleveland Indians chain and advanced as high as Class B ball. He started in organized ball in 1948 with Batavia in the Pony League, batting .319, with five home runs and 72 RBI. In 1949, again with Batavia, he batted .289 with six home runs and 53 RBI and in 1950 batted .275, with no HR, 26 RBI. His last season in organized ball was in 1953 with Spartanburg. He batted .260 with 1 home run and 6 RBI. He joined the Williston Oilers in 1954 and batted .280 with 4 home runs and 33 RBI. Midway through that season he suffered a knee injury which finished his career.

Roy Chapman
Pitcher

Chapman was a left-handed pitcher who played for the New York Black Yankees in 1949 and 1950 and did not see much playing time in the Negro Leagues. He started the 1953 season in the Big State League, then briefly joined the Minot Mallards, pitching with little success in recording a 0–1 record.

Dan Chepkauskas
Outfield; Height — 5'10"; Weight —175 lbs.

Chepkauskas broke into organized baseball with Niagara Falls in the Class C Middle Atlantic League and played in the New York Giants chain. He played in 1953 and 1954 with Muskogee in the Western Association. In 1953, he batted .280 with 13 home runs and 78 RBI, and followed that by batting .252, 11 HR, 66 RBI. He joined the Williston Oilers in 1955 and batted .280 with 2 home runs and 10 RBI. He played for Dickinson in 1956 and batted .292 with 6 home runs and 45 RBI.

Luke Chojnowski
Infield

Chojnowski played in organized ball in 1947 with little success. He briefly joined the Carman Cardinals in 1950 and batted .170 with no home runs and 2 RBI, and was released.

Thad Christopher
Outfield/First Base/Catcher; Bats— Left; Throws— Right; Height — 6'1"; Weight —185 lbs.

Christopher's Negro League career lasted from 1935 to 1947 and 1949, for a number of teams. In 1948, he played for Brandon when they were in the Manitoba Senior League (over 21 years of age). That season he hit .333 and was runnerup for the batting championship. He was considered to be a very good hitter. In 1949 he returned to the Negro Leagues with the New York Black Yankees. He joined Brandon again in 1950, but played only briefly and then left the team.

Al Cihocki
Second Base; Bat — Right; Throws— Right; Height — 5'11"; Weight — 185 lbs.; Born — May 7, 1924 in Nanticoke, Pennsylvania

Cihocki played the 1945 season for the Cleveland Indians, appearing in 92 games and batting .212. He played second base, shortstop, and third base that season for the Tribe. He started his career in 1942 with Batavia in the Pony League, batting .342, with 7 HR, 64 RBI, then was in the military service in 1943 and 1944. From 1946 to 1952, he played for Baltimore in the International League. Over those seven seasons he averaged .256 and hit 66 home runs. In 1955, he was 32 years old when he joined the Bismarck Barons as their playing manager and batted .288 with 11 home runs and 36 RBI. He returned to Bismarck in 1956 and batted .306 with five home runs and 51 RBI. Cihocki holds the ManDak League record for the most doubles in a season with 30. He played for Albuquerque in 1957, batting .204, with no HR and 40 RBI, and closed out his career in 1958 with Allentown in the Eastern League, batting .200, with 1 HR, 3 RBI.

Lou Ciola

Bat — Right; Throws— Right; Height — 5'9"; Weight —165 lbs.; Born — June 6, 1922 in Norfolk, Virginia; Died — October 18, 1981 in Austin, Minnesota

Ciola attended the University of Richmond and had five years of Class A experience with the Philadelphia A's organization. In 1943, Ciola made it to the big club and appeared in 12 games. His record was 1–3 with a 5.56 ERA. He was a right-handed knuckleball pitcher who wore number 7 with the A's. In 1945, he joined the United States Navy and when he was finished with his service time, he resumed his baseball career. He was playing for Austin in the Southern Minny League in 1955, and on August 31, he signed with Minot as a league-sanctioned replacement player. There were some complaints as he was signed after the close of the final rosters, but the league executive made the ruling stand. He won his only start, against Dickinson in the playoffs.

Bill Cleveland

Outfield; Height — 5'10"; Weight —175 lbs.

In 1946, Cleveland played with Daytona Beach in the Class D Florida State League. He played in the Brooklyn Dodgers organization. In 1950, he batted .299, with 16 HR and 111 RBI, and in 1951 batted .306, with eight HR, 67 RBI for Tucson in the Southwest International League. Cleveland joined the Winnipeg Royals in 1953 and batted .297 with one home run and 18 RBI. He finished his ManDak career in 1954 with the Williston Oilers and batted .270 with three home runs and 38 RBI. He was considered a solid player in his two seasons in the league.

Luther Clifford

Catcher/Outfield; Bats— Right; Throws— Right; Height — 6'; Weight 200 lbs.

Clifford's Negro League career was from 1948 to 1950. He played for the Homestead Grays and Kansas City Monarchs. For most of his Negro League career he was a backup catcher. Clifford joined the Brandon Greys briefly in 1952. In 1953 he returned to the Negro Leagues with the Indianapolis Clowns. In 1956 he played for the Brantford, Ontario, Red Sox in the Inter County League and batted .377.

Lillard Cobb

Pitcher

Cobb, from the Detroit area, had played for Carman in 1949, in the Manitoba Senior League. He worked in the auto industry in Detroit and would get a leave of absence to play ball. In 1950, his first season in the ManDak League, he had a 5-4 record and along with Gentry Jessup, was considered to be Carmen's best pitcher. He joined Carman briefly in 1951 and had a 0-1 record when he returned to Detroit.

Jose Colas

Outfield Bats— Right; Throws— Right; Born — Cuba

Colas's Negro League career was from 1947 to 1950, with the Memphis Red Sox. He was an All-Star in 1947. He started the 1952 season with Scranton in the Eastern League and was unimpressive, batting .152. After his release he joined the Brandon Greys and batted .247 with three home runs and 21 RBI. In 1954 played organized ball with little success in the Mississippi-Ohio Valley League, where he batted .238.

Howard "Butch" Conley

Outfield

In 1951, Conley played for the Brooklyn Cuban Giants, a team that was not in the Negro Leagues. In 1952, he joined the Carman Cardinals and batted .185 with no home runs and seven RBI, and left the team.

Jack Cooper

Infield/Outfield

Cooper called Greensboro, North Carolina, home and had two years of pro experience. He then played semi-pro for three more seasons with Plessisville, Quebec, in the Laurentian League. In 1952, he batted .319. He joined Minot as an outfielder and was released on June 22 as Minot needed roster space for another player.

Bob Cope
Pitcher/Outfield

Cope was a right-handed pitcher. In college he played for the University of Montana and also was an outstanding basketball player. Newspaper reports indicated that he was looked at as a basketball player by the Boston Celtics. He also pitched for the Missoula Pirates of the semi-pro Montana State League. He joined the Minot Mallards in 1950 and pitched with little success. He also played a few games in the outfield and resigned on June 19th.

Don Corcoran
Center field; Height — 5'6"; Weight — 165; Born — 1926

Corcoran was from Minot. He was described as a short speedy outfielder who could hit with power. He had six years of pro experience and played as high as Class B in the Three-I League. In 1949, he was playing manager for the Moorhead, Minnesota, Red Sox semi-pro team. In 1951, he played with Springfield in the Western Minnesota League. He joined Minot in 1952 and played five seasons with the Mallards. Over that time he averaged .275, with 34 home runs and 175 RBI. In the 1954 playoffs with the Mallards, he batted .511 including two doubles, a triple and three home runs, and 11 RBI. He had the second-most home runs all time among Minot players.

John Cowan
Second Base/Third Base/Outfield; Bats — Right; Throws — Right; Height — 5'11"; Weight — 165 lbs.; Born — May 31, 1913 in Birmingham, Alabama; Died — October 24, 1993 in Birmingham, Alabama

Cowan was good defensively and a light hitter who could play a number of positions. Cowan had a long career in the Negro Leagues starting in 1934 with his hometown team in the Negro Southern League. In 1944, he started playing in the Negro National League with the Cleveland Buckeyes, and in his four seasons with the Buckeyes he averaged .229. Cowan then joined the Memphis Red Sox and played there in 1948 and 1949. His two-year batting average was .224. He joined the Elmwood Giants midway through the 1950 season and batted .249 with no home runs and 18 RBI. He was 37 years old at the time, and returned to his home town of Birmingham at season's end.

Bill Cox
Pitcher

Cox played 3 seasons of Class D ball in the St. Louis Cardinals chain. He played briefly with Phoenix in the Arizona-Texas League in 1948, saw limited action, and recorded a 0–0 record. In 1949 he was with Willows in the Far West League and had a 6–4 record with a 4.50 ERA. He was back with Willows in 1950 and was 6–7, with a 6.60 ERA. He joined the Winnipeg Giants briefly in 1952 and was released.

Marty Crue
Pitcher/Outfield

Crue's Negro League career was from 1942 to 1950, with the New York Cubans and Homestead Grays. He was 4–1 in 1947 for the New York Cubans. Crue played briefly for the Elmwood Giants in 1950 and played the outfield but did not pitch. He batted .267 with no home runs and eight RBI in 12 games, and returned to the Negro Leagues in 1951 with the New Orleans Eagles.

Bob "Slim" Cunningham
Pitcher

Cunningham pitched part of the 1950 season for the Cleveland Buckeyes, appearing in eight games, with a 0–2 record. After a short time, he left the Buckeyes to join the Elmwood Giants, where he had a 4–5 record. That was his only season in the ManDak League.

Nellie Daehn
Right Field

Daehn played in the Cotton States League in 1952 with the Monroe Sports and batted .296, with three HR and 31 RBI. He started the 1953 season with Monroe and was batting .304 when he was promoted to Shreveport in the Texas League. He finished the season batting .350. He was in Class B ball in 1954 with Temple, Texas, and batted .327, with eight HR and 94 RBI in the Big State League. In 1955, he was moved up to Shreveport again and batted .273, with three HR, 38 RBI. Daehn joined the Williston Oilers in 1956 and batted .304 with four home runs and 36 RBI. Daehn was a solid player for Williston and in 1957, he played Double-A ball in the Texas League, batting .233, with 2 HR, 29 RBI. Daehn closed out his career in 1958 with Pensacola in the Alabama-Florida League.

Dave Dana
Catcher

In 1951, Dana played briefly in the Class B Western International League, where he batted .270 with no home runs and three RBI. In 1957, he played very briefly for the Brandon Greys and was released.

Ray "Dandy" Dandridge

Third base; Bats—Right; Throws—Right; Height—5'7"; Weight—170 lbs; Born—August 31, 1913 in Richmond, Alabama; Died—February 12, 1994 in Palm Bay, Florida

Dandridge's Negro League career was from 1933 to 1949. He was a top hitter and known as well for his fielding. His lifetime batting average for the stats that are available in the Negro Leagues was .355. He played eight seasons in Mexico and 11 seasons in Cuba and played in a number of Negro League All-Star games. From 1949 to 1953, he played Triple-A for the Giants affiliate at Minneapolis. In 1949 he batted .362 and finished second in the batting race. Dandridge proved that his first season was no fluke as he batted .311 with 195 hits in 1950 and was voted the league's MVP and received the Silver Ball Award. He also was voted to the All-Star team. In 1951 he batted .324 and in 1952, his last season, he batted .291. He was considered too old for the major leagues but many fans think that Dandridge would have proved them wrong. He was 41 when he joined the Bismarck Barons in 1955. He batted .360 with eight home runs and 43 RBI and had 118 hits, which is the record for the most hits by a player in a ManDak season. In an interview, Williston pitcher Ed Williams stated that he considered Dandridge to be the "toughest out" in the league. When his career was over, Dandridge scouted for the San Francisco Giants for a few years. Dandridge was voted into baseball's Hall of Fame in 1987. Along with Leon Day and Willie Wells, he was the third ex–ManDak player in baseball's Hall of Fame.

Bob Danielson

Pitcher; Throws— Right

Danielson called Minneapolis, Minnesota, home. He played in the Washington Senators organization. He started his career in 1948 in the Southern Minny League and in 1949 pitched for Faribault, which was a better class of ball in Minnesota. He joined the Minot Mallards in 1950 and had a 6–4 record, then went into organized baseball. In 1952, he pitched for Charlotte in the Class B Tri-State League and that year pitched a no-hitter and led the league with a 2.62 ERA.

Ted Dargie

Outfield

Dargie was nicknamed "Tex." He played in the Cleveland Indians organization. In 1955, Dargie was an All-Star with the Fargo-Moorhead Twins in the Northern League. He joined the Bismarck Barons in 1956 and continued his good hitting, batting .346 with three home runs and 33 RBI. Dargie finished fifth in batting and had a number of key hits that season for the Barons.

Hal Daugherty

Second Base; Bats— Right; Throws— Right; Height — 6'; Weight —180 lbs.; Born — October 12, 1927 in Paris, Pennsylvania

Daugherty signed as a free agent with the Detroit Tigers in 1947. He started his career in 1948 with Williamsport in the Eastern League, batting .203 with seven home runs and 29 RBI. In 1951, he appeared in one game with the Detroit Tigers and struck out his only time at bat. He played in the International League in 1952 and 1953. In 1952 with Buffalo, he batted .225 with six home runs and 33 RBI and in 1953 he split the season between Buffalo and Springfield, batting .206 with three home runs and 40 RBI. He joined the Brandon Greys in 1954 and batted .257 with 11 home runs and 45 RBI. He also played for Minot in 1956 and batted .312, with 12 home runs and 56 RBI. He took over as manager of the Mallards midway through the season. After Minot, he closed out his career in the Basin League in South Dakota.

Lloyd "Ducky" Davenport

Outfield; Bats—Left; Throws—Left; Height — 5'4"; Weight —150 lbs.; Born — October 11, 1911 in New Orleans, Louisiana

Davenport's Negro League career was from 1935 to 1949, for several teams. Over his career he also played in Mexico and Cuba. He was considered to be an all-around player with speed. He might have been small in stature, but was big in ability. Was a five-time Negro League All-Star. Some of his recorded batting averages in the Negro Leagues were as follows .1936 — .313, 1937 — .313, 1942 — .360, 1944 — .304, 1945 — .345. He was 39 years old when he joined the Elmwood Giants in 1951 and batted .278 with one home run and 20 RBI. That was his only season in the league.

Lomax "Butch" Davis

Outfield; Bats—Left; Throws—Right; Height — 6'; Weight — 220 lbs.; Died —1990 in a traffic accident

Davis's Negro League career was from 1947 to 1949, with the Baltimore Elite Giants. He was a very good hitter with power and speed. As a rookie in 1947, he batted .340 and stole 27 bases. In 1949 with Baltimore, he batted .371. Davis joined the Winnipeg Buffaloes in 1950 and was the ManDak League batting champ the first two years he played. In 1950, he batted .456 with four home runs and 39 RBI, and in 1951, he batted .406 with seven home runs and 53 RBI. The 53 RBI led the league that year. His .456 average is the ManDak League record for batting. Midway through the 1951 season, he was signed by the Toronto Maple Leafs of the International League and sent to Albany in the Eastern League. Davis finished the season batting .350 with five home runs and 30 RBI. In 1952, he started the season with Scranton in the Eastern League, then early in the season he joined Toledo in Triple-A and batted .319 with four home runs and 35 RBI. He returned to the ManDak League in 1955 with the Minot Mallards and batted .369 with six home runs and 37 RBI. He lost the batting championship to Roy Weatherly of Williston on the last day of the season.

Leon Day

Pitcher/Outfield; Bats—Right; Throws Right; Height — 5'9"; Weight —170 lbs.; Born — October 16, 1916 in Alexandria, Virginia; Died — March 13, 1995 in Baltimore, Maryland

Day's Negro League career was from 1934 to 1949. He was an outstanding pitchers for the Newark Eagles. Day could pitch, hit, and play the infield and outfield with skill. Day had a 13–0 record for the Eagles in 1937. In 1940, he and Bill Byrd hooked up in an 18-inning marathon that ended in a 1–1 tie. The game had to be called because of darkness. Day struck out 19 batters that game. In 1946, Day tossed a no-hitter against the Philadelphia Stars. He was a many-time All-Star and over his career and in All-Star competition pitched 21 innings and had 23 strikeouts. Day also played winter ball in Cuba and Mexico. He joined the Winnipeg Buffaloes in 1950, had a 4–2 record pitching, and batted .324 with no home runs and 14 RBI. In the championship game, Day pitched all 17 innings to win 1–0 to give the Buffaloes the championship. Midway through the 1951 season, he was signed by the Toronto Maple Leafs of the International League. At the time he had a 4–1 record and was batting .339 with three home runs and 20 RBI. His record with Toronto was 1–1 with a 1.58 ERA and he batted .259. In 1952, he had a 13–9, 3.41 ERA record and batted .314 with Scranton in the Eastern League. In 1953, he played for Edmonton in the Western International League and had a 5–5 record. Day returned to the ManDak League in 1954 with the Brandon Greys and had a batting average of .314 with one home run and 17 RBI. He had a 0–2 record on the mound in limited action. His baseball ability can best be described as being "able to do it all." Day was elected to the Baseball Hall of Fame on March 7, 1995.

JACK DEAN

Pitcher

Dean played in the Chicago White Sox chain for a number of years. Dean started his career in 1936 with DeLand-Palatka in the Florida State League and had a 6–7 record with a 4.40 ERA. He bounced around playing for a number of semi-pro teams until 1949, and from 1949 to 1953 pitched for Topeka in the Class C Western Association. His record in 1949 was 13–7, 3.99; 1950 — 10–13, 5.73 ERA; 1951 — 19–8, 3.66 ERA; 1952 — 18–15, 2.78 ERA; and 1953 — 19–7, 2.80 ERA. He joined the Dickinson Packers in 1955 and had a 1–2 record with a 7.71 ERA. That was his only season in the league.

JOE DEGRAZIA

Shortstop; Height: 5'11"; Weight: 178 lbs.

DeGrazia played four years of pro ball before reporting to the Carman Cardinals in 1951. Midway through the season he was released and signed by the Minot Mallards. He finished the season batting .189, although he did hit better after joining the Mallards, batting .321 with 7 RBI. Before coming to the ManDak League, he had played in the Cotton States League and Northern League.

LARRY DEMPSEY
Pitcher; Throws— Right

Dempsey pitched from 1950 to 1952 in the Class D Coastal Plains League with New Bern and Wilson. In 1951 he recorded a 20-10, 3.39 ERA season and in 1952 his record was 13-14 with a 1.86 ERA. He joined the Minot Mallards in 1953 and had a 3-5 record. Dempsey pitched very well in the playoffs that year, winning four games, including the final game for the championship against Brandon. He also was the hitting star of that game, with a triple, double, and single, with 2 RBI in the 7-2 victory.

CARL DENT
Shortstop

Dent was listed on the Indianapolis Clowns' roster in 1950, but there is no record of him playing in any games in the Negro Leagues. He played briefly with little success for the Brandon Greys in 1950 and was released.

JACK DESKIN
Utility

Deskin started in organized ball in 1951 with Tucson-Las Vegas in the Southwest International League. He joined the Winnipeg Giants in 1952, and there were no statistical records on him available. On May 21, Deskin was involved in a fight at home plate with Carman's Joe Atkins. After teammates separated the players, both were ejected from the game. Midway through that season, Deskin jumped back to organized ball and played briefly for Hollywood in the Pacific Coast League.

GERALD DIDIER
Second Base

Didier played as high as Class B ball in the Brooklyn Dodgers chain, and also played in the Mexican League. Didier played for the Dickinson Packers in 1956 and batted .286 with three home runs and 33 RBI. In 1957, he closed out his career with Baton Rouge in the Evangeline League, batting .327, with no home runs and 19 RBI.

CHUCK DONLEY
Pitcher

Donley played organized ball from 1952 to 1955. In 1952 he pitched as high as Class A ball with Yakima. In 1954 he pitched for Channel Cities and had a 14-8 record with a 3.24 ERA. He joined the Williston Oilers in 1956 and had a record of 4-3 with a 4.43 ERA.

JESSE DOUGLAS

Catcher/Infield; Bats— Both; Throws— Right; Height — 5'10"; Weight —160 lbs.; Born — March 27, 1920 in Longview, Texas

Douglas's Negro League career was from 1937 to 1950. He was a versatile player who could play all positions. He toured with the Satchel Paige All-Stars in 1939 and over his career he played for several Negro League teams. He was 32 years old when he joined Winnipeg Giants in 1952 and batted .268 with two home runs and 25 RBI. He played in 1953 with the Winnipeg Royals and Brandon Greys, for whom he batted .252 and again had two home runs and 25 RBI. In 1954, he joined the Carman Cardinals and closed out his ManDak League career batting .286 with one home run and 44 RBI. He played organized ball in 1956 with Mexicali in the Arizona-Mexico League and batted .322. Douglas closed out his career in 1958 with Yakima in the Northwest League, batting .207.

SAMMY DRAKE

Outfield; Bats— Both; Throws— Right; Height — 5'11"; Weight —175 lbs.; Born — October 7, 1934 in Little Rock, Arkansas

Sammy Drake joined the Carman Cardinals in 1954 as a 19-year-old and batted .300 with two home runs and 21 RBI. After that season, he went into organized baseball with Macon in the South Atlantic League and batted .251, with one HR and 27 RBI. He was in the military service in 1957 and 1958. In 1959 he resumed his career with Burlington in the Three-I League, batting .292 with six HR and 26 RBI. Later that season, he was promoted to Double-A with San Antonio and batted .303, with 2 HR and 14 RBI. At 26 years old, he joined the Chicago Cubs in 1960 and batted .067 in 15 games. He was back in Triple-A with Houston in 1961 and had a good season, batting .306 with 10 HR, 45 RBI, but saw little action with the Cubs, as he appeared in 13 games, mostly in a defensive role. In 1962, he appeared briefly with the New York Mets and batted .192 with no home runs and seven RBI. In 1964 and 1965 he played Triple-A then retired. Sammy Drake was the brother of major leaguer and ManDak player Solly Drake. They were the first African-American brothers to play in the National League.

SOLLY DRAKE

Center Field; Bats— Both; Throws— Right; Height — 6'; Weight —170 lbs.; Born — October 23, 1930 in Little Rock, Arkansas

Solly Drake was 19 years old when he joined the Elmwood Giants in 1949 in the Manitoba Senior Baseball League and batted .260. He joined Elmwood for its first season in the ManDak league and batted .300 with two home runs and 25 RBI. Winnipeg baseball fans remember his many spectacular fielding plays. He had great speed and was an All-Star in 1951 with Topeka in the Class C Western Association. Drake batted .324, with 6 HR, 50 RBI.

He played for St. Paul in 1956 and batted .333, with nine HR, 27 RBI and that season was promoted to the Cubs. He batted .256 with two home runs and 15 RBI. In 1958, with Montreal in the International League, he was selected to the All-Star team and led the International League in runs with 105 and hits with 183. His batting average that season was .301 with nine HR, 68 RBI. He played briefly for the Dodgers and Phillies in 1959, batting .250 for the Dodgers and .150 for the Phillies. He played two more seasons in Triple-A with Buffalo, then retired.

Mel Duncan

Pitcher/Outfield; Bats — Right; Throws — Right; Height — 5'9"; Weight — 155 lbs.

Duncan's Negro League career was from 1949 to 1954. He played for the Kansas City Monarchs and Detroit Stars. Duncan threw a fastball and curve, but relied on his control. He joined the Minot Mallards in August 1955, and had a 3–1 record with a 4.50 ERA. When he played the outfield, he had a .321 batting average. In game two of the championship series that season against Dickinson, he hit a home run in the eighth inning to give Minot a 4–3 victory. In 1956 he was back with the Mallards and again had a 3–1 record. He closed out his career in 1957 in Mexico.

Bob Easterbrook

First Base

Easterbrook started his professional career as a pitcher in the New York Giants organization, and after an arm injury, was converted into a first baseman. This was because he was a good hitter, who hit with power. He was not a good defensive player. He played for the Trenton Giants before joining the Bismarck Barons in 1955, and that season batted .359 with 18 home runs and tied for the RBI lead with 68. He closed out his career in 1956 in the Northwest League, batting .297, with nine home runs and 61 RBI.

Howard Easterling

Infield; Bats — Both; Throws — Right; Height — 5'10"; Weight — 175 lbs.; Born — November 26, 1911 in Mount Olive, Mississippi; Died — September 6, 1993 in Collins, Mississippi

Easterling's Negro League career was from 1936 to 1949. He played most of his career with the Homestead Grays and was considered to be an all-around player. He was a switch-hitter with power. Easterling played in several Negro League All-Star games. He played in the Mexican League in 1951 and 1952, batting over .300 both years. He played briefly for the Brandon Greys in 1953 and left with a .238 batting average. By that time he was 42 years old, and his skills were slipping. He finished his career in 1954 in Mexico, batting .294 with one home run and eight RBI.

Valle Eaves

Pitcher; Bats— Right; Throws— Right; Height — 6'2½"; Weight —180 lbs.; Born — September 6, 1911 in Allen, Oklahoma; Died — April 19, 1950 in Norman, Oklahoma

Eaves had a 21-year pitching career. His motto could have been "Have arm will travel." He spent parts of five seasons in the major leagues. In 1935 he was with the Philadelphia A's and had a 1–2 record and a 5.14 ERA. From 1939 to 1942, he was with the Chicago White Sox and Chicago Cubs. His record for those years was 3–6 with a 4.87 ERA. In 1945, he led the Pacific Coast League in strikeouts with 187 and had a 21–15 record with a 3.00 ERA. In 1947, he pitched for Texarkana in the Big State League and led the league with 25 victories and lost only 5 games. He had 4.45 ERA. He pitched briefly for Minot in 1951 and was released at his own request. At the time had a 1–1 record. In 1953, he was an All-Star in the Gulf Coast League with Brownsville, where he had a 19–11 record with a 5.40 ERA. He closed out his career in 1957 with Hobbs in the Southwestern league, going 1–0 with a 4.50 ERA.

Bob Ebkor

Pitcher

Before joining the Minot Mallards in 1955, Ebkor pitched for Pierre, South Dakota, in the Basin League. He pitched in relief in one game for Minot, with no decision.

Ted Edmunds

Pitcher; Throws— Right

Edmunds had six years of pro experience. In 1953, his record was 9–6 with Yakima in the Class A Western International League. He was back with Yakima in 1954 and had a 19–9 record. He joined the Minot Mallards in 1955 and had a 4–3 record with a 6.82 ERA, and pitched a 1–0 shutout in his first game as a Mallard, giving up only two hits and driving in the winning run.

Chuck Eisemann

Pitcher

Eisemann started his career in 1939 with Henderson in the East Texas League and had a 4–4 record with a 4.44 ERA. He had a long minor-league career and played in the Chicago White Sox organization. In 1941, he pitched for Yakima in the Western International League, which was Class B at that time, and had a 12–13, 3.40 ERA record and led the league in strikeouts with 204. That earned him a callup to San Diego in the Pacific Coast League, where he had no decisions. In 1948, he played for Memphis in the Southern Association and was 16–11, with a 3.52 ERA and was selected to the All-Star team. In 1951 and 1952, he played for Ottawa and Syracuse in Triple-A going 4–7 with a 3.80 ERA and 2–2 with a 5.20 ERA. He joined the Bismarck Barons briefly in 1955 and had a 1–0 record. His other claim to fame was that he owned a German Shepherd named London that performed at various ballparks. He and the dog later appeared on the Johnny Carson show and in three movies.

PRESTON ELKINS
Pitcher/Outfield/Manager; Height — 6'2"; Weight — 170

Elkins played for a number of years in the Pittsburgh Pirate chain and pitched as high as Double-A. He broke into organized baseball as an infielder/outfielder in 1941 with Johnstown in the Penn State League. This made him a valuable player, as he could play the outfield when not pitching. In 1946, he had a 15–8 record with a 3.47 ERA with Albany in the Eastern League. He enjoyed another good season in 1949 with Albany, when his record was 15–8 with a 3.47 ERA. He played for the Williston Oilers in 1956 and had 15–4 record with a 2.71 ERA, and batted .300 with 14 home runs and 40 RBI. His 15 wins led the league that season. He was playing manager for Williston in 1957 and had a 6–6 record with a 7.03 ERA.

GORD ELLIOT
Second Base

Elliot was a Canadian whose parents moved to the Toledo area when he was young. His grandfather lived in Carman and while visiting him, Elliot asked for a tryout. He joined the Cardinals in 1950 and batted .214 with no home runs and 14 RBI. This was his only season in the league. He was a light-hitting player who tried hard and was popular with his teammates and Carman fans. On the eve of his marriage, the Cardinals held a party for him and he was presented with a check for $100 and a leather gladstone travel bag. It was reported that the Carman ladies served an attractive lunch, and there was dancing and singing by the more than 50 people in attendance.

AL ENDRISS
First Base

Endriss played in the Brooklyn Dodgers chain. He entered organized ball in 1948 in the Class D Eastern Shore League and batted .234 with one home run and 41 RBI. In 1950 he batted .263, with four home runs and 31 RBI for Bisbee-Douglas in the Arizona-Texas League. He played briefly for the Winnipeg Giants in 1952 and was released.

FRANK EVANS
Outfield; Born — 1922

Evans played in the Negro Leagues in 1949 and 1950 with the Cleveland

Buckeyes. Midway through 1951, he joined the Brandon Greys at the age of 29 and played only briefly. In later years he was a scout and manager in organized baseball.

GERVIS FAGAN

Infielder

Fagan's His Negro League career was from 1942 to 1943. He could play a number of positions. He played briefly with the Minot Mallards in 1950 and was released. The Minot newspaper reported that he had been a replacement player from the Indianapolis Clowns.

JERRY FAHR

Pitcher; Bats—Right; Throws—Right; Height—6'5"; Weight—185 lbs.; Born—December 9, 1924 in Marmaduke, Arkansas

In 1948 Fahr was an All-Star in the Longhorn League and led the league with a 1.96 ERA. He was drafted by the Cleveland Indians from Shreveport (Texas League) in the 1950 Rule V draft and broke in with the Indians in 1951. He appeared in five games for the Indians in 1951 and had no decisions and a 4.76 ERA. He was 31 when he joined the Dickinson Packers in 1956 and had a 7–10 record with a 4.31 ERA. He was one of the main pitchers for the Packers that season.

EV FAUNCE

Second Base/Outfield

Faunce was from Fergus Falls, Minnesota. He played briefly with the Minot Mallards at the start of the 1950 season and batted .207 in his brief stay. He had to quit the Mallards to begin his football coaching job. He had played football for the University of Minnesota and the Baltimore Colts, but his NFL career had been cut short by injury.

NORM FELDE

First Base/Outfield

Felde was a local player from Fargo, North Dakota, and had played amateur ball for the Moorhead Red Sox in the Minnesota Class AA North Central League and for Moorhead Teachers College. In 1949, he joined the Minot Merchants late in the season and then joined the Minot Mallards for their first season in 1950, batting .257 with two home runs and 30 RBI. His RBI total led the league. Felde was elected to the Moorhead State University Hall of Fame.

CHARLES FERGUSON
Second Base

Ferguson played six seasons in organized baseball and played as high as Class B ball. He played briefly for Williston in 1954.

AMANCIO FERRO
Pitcher Born — Cuba

Ferro played for the Brandon Greys in 1951 and pitched with little success in recording a 0–6 record. That was his only year in the ManDak League. He went into organized ball in 1952 and played for Hannibal in the Class D Mississippi-Ohio League. He led the league in strikeouts with 183 and was selected to the All-Star team

WILMER FIELDS

Outfield; Bats Right; Throws— Right; Height — 6'3"; Weight — 215 lbs; Born — August 2, 1922 in Manassas, Virginia; Died — June 4, 2004 in Manassas, Virginia

Fields was a good pitcher and hitter in the Negro Leagues and was a versatile player who could play several positions well. Fields played 11 seasons with the Homestead Grays and played on eight championship teams. In 1948, his last year in the Negro Leagues, he hit .311. In 1951, he was playing for the Brantford Red Sox in the Inter County League and was voted the MVP. He led the league with 70 hits and 10 home runs and was also outstanding on the mound with a record of 9–1. In 1952, he went into organized baseball with the Toronto Maple Leafs of the International League and hit .299. Over his career he played in Mexico, Panama, and the Dominican Republic. He played very briefly with the Brandon Greys in 1953 and was batting .411 with two home runs and six RBI when he left for South America for more money. Fields returned to Brantford in 1954 and batted .379 to win the league's batting championship and also led the league with 87 hits. He closed out his career in 1958 in Mexico.

RAY FINCH
Pitcher

Finch played the 1949 season in the Negro National League with the Cleveland Buckeyes. In 1950, he joined the Elmwood Giants and had a 2–6 record. In 1951 his record was 10–11, and many baseball fans thought he was overworked that season. In 1952, he was ineffective and he closed out his Man-Dak career with a 0–3 record. He then went to organized baseball with Danville in the Mississippi-Ohio Valley League, where he had a 1–2 record.

Ed Finney

Third Base; Bats—Right; Throws—Right; Height—5'8"; Weight—188 lbs.; Born—November 4, 1924 in Akron, Ohio

Finney played for the Baltimore Elite Giants from 1948 to 1950 and batted .278, .320 and .333. He was 27 years old when he joined the Brandon Greys in 1951. He batted .239 with one home run and nine RBI in 18 games. That was his only season in the league.

John Fitzgerald

Pitcher

Fitzgerald played organized ball from 1946 to 1954, reaching the Double-A level in the New York Yankees chain. He started his career in 1946 with Leaksville in the Carolina League and had a 10–15 record with a 6.93 ERA. His best season was 1949, when he was 17–10 with a 3.13 ERA and led the league in strikeouts with 166. In 1953 and 1954, he appeared briefly with Toledo in the American Association and had no decisions. Fitzgerald played the 1956 and 1957 seasons with the Bismarck Barons. In 1956, his record was 4–6 with a 5.46 ERA and in 1957 had a 6–4 record with a 4.75 ERA. Teammate Roger Higgins said that Fitzgerald would joke in the Bismarck clubhouse that the Yankees had called up the wrong left-hander. He was referring to Yankee ace Whitey Ford.

Ted Fowler

First Base/Third Base/Outfield

Fowler had attended the University of Arizona. In 1949 he played semi-pro ball in Santa Rita, Arizona and hit .409. He played briefly with the Minot Mallards in 1950, batting .192.

Charlie Frey

Outfield

Frey played with the Chicago Cubs, St. Louis Cardinals, and New York Yankees organizations. He was in the Cardinals system for six seasons, then was sold to the Yankees. He had a good minor-league career. In 1946, he set the Ohio State League record for triples with 20, and in 1947 he led the Appalachian League with 176 hits. In 1954, he batted .294 for Binghamton. In 1955, Frey joined the Minot Mallards late in the season as a replacement player and had some key hits in the playoffs.

Ed Funai

Pitcher

Funai played three seasons in organized ball in the Chicago Cubs chain and played as high as Class A. His best season was 1954, when his record was 8–5, with a 4.90 ERA. He played briefly for the Brandon Greys at the start of the 1957 season and had a 0–1 record.

Bill Furlong
Pitcher

In 1949, Furlong led the Class D Pony League in winning percentage, going 16–5, and also had the best ERA at 1.89, which was good enough to be selected to the All-Star team. In 1954, with Wilkes-Barre in the Eastern league, he had a record of 6–6 with a 3.87 ERA. He joined the Williston Oilers in 1955 and posted a 0–3 record, then left the club. He went back to organized ball with Augusta in the South Atlantic League and finished that season with a 7–2 record and a 4.76 ERA.

Jonas "Lefty" Gaines
Pitcher; Bats— Right; Throws— Left; Height — 5'9"; Weight —158 lbs.; Born — January 9, 1914 in New Roads, Louisiana

Gaines's Negro League career spanned 14 years. He had good control and a wide range of pitches. He started in the Negro Leagues in 1937 with the Newark Eagles and pitched in five Negro League All-Star games, 1943–1946, and 1950. Over his career he pitched with success in Mexico and Cuba. Gaines was 37 years old in 1951 when he joined the Minot Mallards. He was regarded as one of Minot's better pitchers with a 7–4 record. In 1952, his record was 4–3, and in 1953 he went to Japan for one season. In 1954, he was an All-Star in the West Texas–New Mexico League and had a 16–7 record with a 5.12 ERA. Gaines played for the Bismarck Barons in 1955 and fashioned an 8–3 record with a 3.27 ERA. He continued to play organized baseball until 1957 with Carlsbad in Southwestern League.

Tony Garcia
Pitcher

Garcia pitched 9 seasons in organized ball and pitched as high as Class B in the Washington Senators chain. He played for Lakeland in the Florida International league from 1947 to 1949. In 1947 he had a 10–14 record with a 4.13 ERA, 22–14 with a 3.47 ERA in 1948, 9–17 with a 3.05 ERA in 1949, and 10–12 with a 3.89 ERA in 1950. In 1954 he went 11–9 with a 4.77 ERA with Hagerstown in the Piedmont League and played there again in 1955. He then joined the Bismarck Barons in 1956 and had a 4–7 record with a 6.30 ERA.

Tom Gatts
Utility

Gatts played four seasons in organized ball, in the Chicago Cubs and

Milwaukee Braves chains. He played as high as Class A ball. He started in the ManDak League with Williston, then joined the Minot Mallards in 1955 and batted .297 with no home runs and eight RBI.

Lloyd Gearhart

Outfield; Bats—Right; Throws—Left; Height—5'11"; Weight—180 lbs; Born—August 10, 1923 in New Lebanon, Ohio; Died—April 2, 2001 in Dayton, Ohio

After 3 years with Atlanta in the Southern League, Gearhart's contract was purchased by the New York Giants. He was 24 years old when he joined the New York Giants in 1947. He batted .246 with six home runs and 17 RBI. That was his only year in the major leagues. He was a Southern League All-Star in 1945. Gearhart joined the Williston Oilers as playing manager in 1954 when he was 31 years old and batted .331, with 17 home runs and 61 RBI. His home run total led the ManDak League. He signed with Bismarck in 1955 and batted .319 with eight home runs and 28 RBI. Throughout his career he was always a very good hitter at the minor-league level. In his hometown he had a sports field named in his honor.

Bob Geels

Geels played in organized ball for four seasons, as high as Class C ball. In 1954, he started his career with Visalia in the California League and batted .233, with no HR and 2 RBI. He joined the Dickinson Packers in 1955 and was hitting .297 with one home run and 20 RBI when he jumped to the Provincial League. The following year, he played for Thompson in the Georgia State League and Aberdeen in the Northern League. He closed out his career in 1957 with Phoenix in the Arizona-Mexico League and batted .319, with two HR and 36 RBI.

Kent Geisler

Pitcher Height—6'3"; Weight—185 lbs.

Geisler joined the Williston Oilers in 1954 and pitched with little success, going 0–3. He then went into organized baseball and pitched in the California League in 1956 and 1957. He had a record of 5–11 with a 6.68 ERA.

Al Gettel

Pitcher; Bats—Right; Throws—Right; Height—6'3½"; Weight—200 lbs.; Born—September 17, 1917 in Norfolk, Virginia; Died—April 8, 2005 in Norfolk, Virginia

Gettel was 28 years old when he broke in with the Yankees in 1945. He finished that season with a record of 9–8 and a 2.45 ERA. He played eight seasons in the major leagues with the New York Yankees, Cleveland Indians,

Chicago White Sox, and St. Louis Cardinals, and had a career record of 38–45 with a 4.28 ERA. In 1946, the Yankees traded him to the Indians with Gene Bearden and Hal Price for Sherman Lollar and Ray Mack. Gettel had his best season in 1947 with the Indians. His record was 11–10, with a 3.20 ERA. In 1953, he pitched for Oakland in the Pacific Coast League and led the league with 24 victories and was selected to the All-Star team. His last appearance in the major leagues was in 1955, when he had a brief appearance with the Cardinals and had a 1–0 record in eight games. In the off-season, he acted in the movies and on television. He acted in the movie *Tin Star* with Henry Fonda, Betsy Palmer, and Anthony Perkins, and played in two television series, *The Western Marshal* and *Cheyenne*. He joined the Williston Oilers in 1957 and pitched with little success, recording a 1–4 record with a 7.82 ERA.

Yogi Giammarco
Right Field

Giammarco was signed by the New York Yankees and also played for New York Giants and Philadelphia Phillies farm clubs. He played seven pro seasons and advanced as high as Triple-A, in the International League. He was an exciting player and always a long-ball threat. In 1951 he was an All-Star with Saginaw in the Class A Central League. That season he batted .312 and had 21 home runs and 113 RBI. In 1954 he played for the Utica Blue Sox. Many of his teammates went on to play for the Phillies. Even though he didn't make the major leagues, he was Utica's most popular player. He was 30 years old when he joined the Minot Mallards in 1952. He batted .318 with 11 home runs and 47 RBI and hit three more home runs in the playoffs. He was back with Minot in 1954 and batted .344 with nine home runs and 30 RBI. With Minot he was again a very popular player. Like many a player at that time, he appeared to be stuck in the minors by baseball's reserve clause.

Dirk "Bubble Gum" Gibbons
Pitcher; Height — 5'10"; Weight — 195 lbs.

Gibbons started in the Negro Leagues in 1941 with the Philadelphia Stars and New York Black Yankees and saw limited pitching time. In 1948, he played for the Indianapolis Clowns. In 1949, he joined the Brandon Greys when the team was in the Manitoba Senior League. His record in league, tournament, and playoff games was 19–5 and he batted .272. In 1953, he started the season with the Brandon Greys, but they had a lot of pitchers, so he signed on with the Winnipeg Royals. He was a good pickup for the Royals as he finished the season with a 10–6 record. He was back in Brandon in 1954, and his record was 11–7. He joined the Minot Mallards in 1955 and pitched for them until the end of 1957. His record in 1955 was 5–7 with a 5.33 ERA; 1956 — 6–7, 4.95 ERA; and 1957 — 3–9, 4.33 ERA.

Tom Giuliano
Second Base

In 1954, Giuliano played in the Class B Piedmont League with Lancaster and was selected to the All-Star team. He joined the Brandon Greys in 1957 and batted .309 with one home run and 24 RBI.

Manuel Godinez

Pitcher; Bats—Right; Throws—Right; Born—Cuba

Godinez played for the Indianapolis Clowns from 1946 to 1949. He had a good fastball and curve. He joined the Brandon Greys in 1950 and had a 4–2 record. That was his only season in the league.

Preston Gomez

Shortstop; Bats—Right; Throws—Right; Height—5'11"; Weight—170 lbs; Born—April 20, 1923, in Preston, Cuba

In 1944, Gomez played eight games for the Washington Senators as a 21-year-old and batted .286 with no home runs and 2 RBI. He was sent down to the minors the next spring. In 1947, he was an All-Star in the Class B Colonial League. He was 32 years old when he joined the Bismarck Barons in 1955 and batted .251 with five home runs and 30 RBI. He returned to the major leagues as the first manager of the San Diego Padres and piloted them from 1969 to 1972. He also managed the Houston Astros (1974–1975) and Chicago Cubs (1980). As a major league manager he twice pinch-hit for pitchers who were throwing no-hitters. In 1970 with the Padres, he pulled Clay Kirby and in 1974 with the Astros he yanked Don Wilson.

Jack Gore
Outfield

Gore played organized ball in 1951, 1952, and 1955 with little success. He joined Dickinson Packers in 1956 and had no record.

Chuck Gowett
Pitcher

In 1950, Gowett was with El Centro and was selected to the All-Star team in the Sunset League. He joined the Winnipeg Giants in 1953. He pitched in six games and had a 2–0 record, then went back into organized baseball.

Jimmy Grant

Third Base; Bats—Left; Throws—Right; Height—5'8"; Weight—166 lbs; Born—October 6, 1918 in Racine, Wisconsin; Died—July 8, 1970 in Rochester, Minnesota

Grant started his career in the Northern League in 1937 and played four seasons. In 1941 with Grand Forks he batted .331, with 13 HR and 77 RBI. In 1942 he batted .313, with 6 HR and 70 RBI with St. Paul in the American Association and received a callup to the White Sox. In 12 games he batted .167 with no HR and one RBI. Grant started the 1943 season with the White Sox and was traded to the Cleveland Indians. He finished that season batting .247 with four home runs and 23 RBI. In 1944, his last season in the major leagues, he batted .273 with one home run and 12 RBI. His three-year career major league batting average was .246. He bounced around the minor leagues after that, and in 1951 he played briefly with the Minot Mallards until he was hurt. He finished that season batting .306 with one home run and 17 RBI in 14 games.

WHIT GRAVES

Pitcher; Bats—Right; Throws—Right

Graves's Negro League career was from 1950 to 1951, for the Indianapolis Clowns, for whom he had a 7–8 record with a 3.62 ERA. He joined the Minot Mallards in 1952 and had a 2–0 record. Midway through the season he jumped to organized ball. In 1953, with Richmond in the Piedmont League, he had a record of 6–12 and a 6.34 ERA. In 1954, with Petersburg, also in the Piedmont League, his record was 9–6 with a 4.62 ERA. The 1955 season found him in the Western League with Sioux City, and he also pitched in four games with the Minneapolis Millers. Over his career he played winter ball in the Dominican Republic.

JOE GREENE

Catcher Bats; Right; Throws—Right; Height—6'1"; Weight—200 lbs; Born—October 17, 1911 in Stone Mountain, Georgia

Joe Greene started his career in 1932 with the Atlanta Black Crackers. He caught for the great Kansas City Monarchs pitching staffs of the 1940's and had good catching skills. He hit for high averages and with power. Greene batted .346 in 1946, .324 in 1947, and .257 in 1948 in the Negro Leagues. He was 39 years old when he joined the Elmwood Giants in 1951. He still had his batting skill, compiling an average of .301 with two home runs and 16 RBI. That was his last season in baseball.

WILLIE GREENE

Pitcher/Utility

Willie Greene was from Minot. He played for the Minot Merchants and Estevan, Saskatchewan, in the Western Canada Baseball League in 1949. Was regarded as a utility player. He was 2–1 as a pitcher in both 1952 and 1954. He only batted .133 in 1952 and .182 in 1954.

Charles Griffith

Pitcher; Height — 6'3"; Weight — 194; Born — 1925; Throws — Right

Charles Griffith had five years of pro experience, and played as high as Class B in the Boston Red Sox chain. In 1951 and 1952, he was with High Point-Thomasville in the North Carolina State League and had two good seasons. He was 12–5 with a 2.43 ERA in 1951, and in 1952 he had his best season when he won 16 and lost 4 with a 2.74 ERA. In 1955, he played in the semi-pro Southern Minny League with Faribault and had an 11–4 record. He played briefly for the Minot Mallards in 1956 and had no decisions. He was plagued with a sore arm, and at times could not pitch.

Robert Griffith

Pitcher; Bats — Right; Throws — Right; Height — 6'5"; Weight — 235 lbs.; Born — October 1, 1913 in Liberty, Tennessee; Died — November 8, 1977 in Indianapolis, Indiana

Robert Griffith was a hard thrower, and due to his stature he was an imposing figure on the mound. He spent 17 years in the Negro Leagues, starting his career in 1933 with the Nashville Elite Giants. He pitched in three All-Star games, one in 1935 with the Columbus Elite Giants and in the 1948 and 1949 games with the New York Black Yankees and Philadelphia Stars. He pitched for the Kansas City Monarchs in 1946 after serving two years in the military. Griffith joined the Philadelphia Stars from 1949 to 1951, then signed with the Indianapolis Clowns for the 1952 season. He was 39 years old when he joined the Brandon Greys in 1953. His record that season was 8–6. Brandon's starters that season were Griffith, Pee Wee Jenkins, Barney Brown, Gread McKinnis, and Tom Parker, and that was not too shabby a group of starting pitchers.

Morrell Groves

Second Base; Born — 1929

Newspaper reports stated that Groves was 21 years old and had played Class A ball in 1948. He was from the Detroit area and had played for the semi-pro Detroit Wolves in 1949. The report stated that his batting power was well known in the Detroit area. In 1950, he came north with Red House, who started the season as the Carman Cardinals manager. The newspaper report appeared to be erroneous as Groves played only briefly and batted .200. He was released after a short time and returned to Detroit.

Tom Guderian

Pitcher; Throws — Right

Guderian started his organized ball career in 1952 in the Chicago Cubs chain. In 1955, in the Class C Pioneer League, he had a 3–2 record with a 5.46 ERA. In 1956, he split the season with Des Moines in the Class A Western

League and the Minot Mallards. He won his first game with the Mallards and finished with a 3–1 record and a 4.50 ERA.

LEN GZEBB
Shortstop

Gzebb was a Manitoba Senior Baseball League player who filled in on Opening Day in 1950 for the Elmwood Giants. The Giants were short of players because the American imports had not yet arrived. Gzebb went 1 for 5 and played well defensively. That was his only ManDak League game. He had been a star player in junior (under 21 years of age) and senior ball in Winnipeg. He came from a baseball playing family.

CURLY HAAS
Manager; Born — November 21, 1909; Died — February 19, 1977

In the 1920's, Haas started the Columbus Club baseball team in Winnipeg. In 1946, he and Eddie Cass organized the Elmwood Giants club, and Haas was on the committee that started the first Manitoba Junior Baseball All-Star game. He managed the North Division Junior League All-Stars to victory in 1947 and 1948. He became the manager of the Elmwood Giants in 1949 and was their manager the first season in the ManDak League. He was general manager for the Brandon Greys in 1954. Haas was elected to the Manitoba Baseball Hall of Fame in 2001.

ELWIN HAHN
Pitcher

Hahn played college baseball for Washington State University. The Williston newspaper reported that when Hahn was in college he pitched in games where he had 23 and 19 strikeouts. He joined the Williston Oilers midway through the 1957 season and had a 3–1 record with a 7.47 ERA.

JACK HALE
Pitcher; Throws — Left; Height — 6'1"; Weight — 185 lbs.

Hale played in the Kansas City A's organization. In 1955, he played with Burlington in the Class C Provincial League. That season he led the league with 17 wins and was selected to the All-Star team. In 1956 he went 6–3 with Abilene in the Class B Big State League. He joined the Minot Mallards in 1957 and posted a 6–6 record with a 5.49 ERA.

BRUCE HAROLDSON
Pitcher; Throws — Right

Haroldson was from Williston. He pitched as high as Class B ball in the

St. Louis Cardinals chain. He played briefly for Minot in 1956 and had no record, then went into organized ball and pitched until 1961. His best season was 1959 with Billings in the Pioneer League, where his record was 12–11 with a 5.17 ERA. In 1960 he was 1–5 with a 4.89 ERA with the Winnipeg Goldeyes in the Northern League.

Bob Harvey

Outfield; Bats—Left; Throws—Right; Height—6'1"; Weight—220 lbs; Born—May 28, 1918 in St. Michaels, Maryland; Died—June 27, 1992 in Montclair, New Jersey

Harvey's Negro League career was from 1943 to 1950. He played for the Newark Eagles and Houston Eagles. He batted over .300 for six straight seasons with the Eagles and played in two Negro League All-Star games. Harvey was 33 years old when he joined the Elmwood Giants in 1951. He batted .306 with nine home runs and 44 RBI.

Phil Haugstad

Pitcher; Bats—Right; Throws—Right; Height—6'2"; Weight—165 lbs.; Born—February 24, 1924 in Black River Falls, Wisconsin

Haugstad started his career in 1946 with Grand Forks in the Northern league and had a 15–13 record with a 3.34 ERA. In 1947, he was with St. Paul in the American Association, and after recording a 16–6 record with a 3.80 ERA, he was a late callup to the Brooklyn Dodgers. He finished that season with a 1–0 record and a 2.84 ERA. He was 24 years old when he broke in with the Dodgers. He pitched again briefly with the Dodgers in 1948 (0–0) and in 1951 (0–1, 6.46 ERA). In 1952 he pitched briefly with the Cincinnati Reds and had a 0–0 record and a 6.75 ERA. His best season was in 1949 at St. Paul in the American Association, when he led the league with 22 wins. He pitched briefly with the Williston Oilers in 1955 and had a 0–1 record with a 6.92 ERA.

Terry Hayes

Catcher; Born—1936; Height—5'10"; Weight—180 lbs.

Hayes was a 19-year-old from Villanova University who played the 1954 season with Mankato in the Southern Minnesota League. Newspaper reports indicated that the Cleveland Indians rated him as a top prospect. He joined the Williston Oilers in 1955, and batted .308 with one home run and one RBI.

Dennis Healy

Utility

Healy was considered to be one of the best utility players in the ManDak League. Before joining the ManDak League, he had played on five straight championship teams in organized baseball. In 1951, he was with Oneonta, N.Y., when they were crowned champs in the Canadian-American League. In 1952 and 1953 he played for Binghamton, winners in the Eastern League. In 1955, he played on championship teams with the Bismarck Barons, batting .297 with no home runs and nine RBI, and in 1957, he joined the Williston Oilers and batted .238 with no home runs and 18 RBI.

MEL HEIM
Pitcher

Heim played in the Cleveland Indians organization. In 1953, he led the Class D Wisconsin State League with 19 wins and a 2.14 ERA. In 1954 he was selected to the All-Star team with Omaha in the Class A Western League. He joined the Dickinson Packers in 1956 and posted a 6–10 record with a 5.18 ERA and moved over to the Brandon Greys for the 1957 season. He had a 0–1 record.

KEN HEINTZELMAN

Pitcher; Bats—Right; Throws—Left; Height—5'11½"; Weight—185 lbs.; Born—October 14, 1915 in Peruque, Missouri; Died—August 14, 2000 in St. Peters Missouri

Heintzelman played 13 seasons in the major leagues for the Pittsburgh Pirates and Philadelphia Phillies. His major league career record was 77–98 with a 3.93 ERA. His best season was 1949, when he finished with a 17–10 record and a 3.02 ERA in 250 innings. That season he pitched five shutouts and had a nine-game winning streak. He was a member of the 1950 Philadelphia pennant winning team called the "Whiz Kids." His record was 3–9 with a 4.09 ERA. In 1950, he appeared in one World Series game. He started in game three, and although he pitched well, still lost to the Yankees. He last pitched in the major league in 1952 with the Phillies. He was 39 years old when he joined the Bismarck Barons in 1955 and had a record of 5–4 with a 4.50 ERA.

JERRY HENDRICK
Second Base

Hendrick was from Lansford, North Dakota. He played three games at the start of the 1957 season for Minot. He had two hits on opening day. He was released after regular second baseman Buddy Messina arrived.

LEO HENRY

Pitcher; Bats—Right; Throws—Right; Height—5'4"; Weight—135 lbs.

Henry's Negro League career was from 1938 to 1947. He pitched on several Negro League teams, and was an effective hurler who pitched in the 1941 Negro

League All-Star game. He was picked up by Minot from the Indianapolis Clowns as a replacement player in 1950, pitched only briefly, and had a 0–0 record.

DON HERMAN
Pitcher

Herman started his career in the New York Yankees chain and had little success in organized ball from 1954 to 1956. In 1956, he started the season with San Jose in the California League, had a 1–1 record, and was released. He then signed with the Williston Oilers and finished the season with a 1–3 record with a 4.98 ERA.

ROGER HIGGINS
Pitcher

Higgins from the New England area, played several years in Boston Red Sox and Detroit Tigers chains and pitched as high as Double-A ball. He joined Bismarck in 1955 and for two years was one of the league's leading pitchers. In 1955 he was 8–3 with a 3.68 ERA and was even better in 1956, going 12–1 with a 4.91 ERA. A June 2, 1956 article in the *Bismarck Tribune* described him as a "local pitching legend." In 1957, he joined Las Vegas as a playing coach. That season he had a 16–12 record with a 3.96 ERA. With his pitching career over, he returned to Bismarck and became a sportscaster, and was president of the Bismarck team in the Northern League from 1963 to 1964.

SAM HILL

Outfield; Bats—Left; Throws—Right; Height—6'2"; Weight—180 lbs.; Born—1929 in Birmingham, Alabama

Hill's Negro League career was from 1946 to 1948 with the Chicago American Giants. He played in the 1948 Negro League All-Star game. He was said to be 21 years old when he joined the Winnipeg Buffaloes in 1950 and batted .209 with no home runs and 15 RBI. He batted .290 in 1951 with three home runs and 26 RBI, again with the Buffaloes. When the Buffaloes ceased operation in 1952, Hill signed with the Carman Cardinals and batted .288 with five home runs and 33 RBI. He played organized ball from 1954 in the Eastern League. In 1956, he returned to the ManDak League with Bismarck, batting .335 with 20 home runs and 73 RBI. Hill was an All-Star in 1957 with Superior in the Northern League.

JIM HINSON
Utility

In 1950, Hinson played briefly for El Centro in the Sunset League and was not a high-average hitter. He started the 1953 season with Visalia in the

California League and when released, joined the Winnipeg Royals. He was not around very long before the Royals released him.

BILL HOCKENBURY

Third Base

Hockenbury played in the Philadelphia A's organization. In 1947, with the Savannah Indians, he led the Class A South Atlantic League with 19 home runs. That season he also was selected to the All-Star team. He joined the Bismarck Barons in 1955 and batted .366 with 10 home runs and 30 RBI. In 1956, was again back with Bismarck and batted .307 with 18 home runs and 59 RBI. He was playing manager of the Barons in 1957 and batted .313 with 11 home runs and 52 RBI and closed out his career in 1959 with Williston, when the Oilers were in the Western Canada Baseball league.

BOBBY HOGUE

Pitcher; Bats—Right; Throws—Right; Height—5'10"; Weight—195 lbs.; Born—April 5, 1921 in Miami, Florida; Died—December 22, 1987 in Miami, Florida

Hogue played on the 1948 pennant-winning Boston Braves and that year had an 8–2 record and a 3.23 ERA as a reliever. He did not pitch in the World Series that year. He played five years in the major leagues. In 1951 he also pitched for the St. Louis Browns (1–1, 5.16 ERA) and the New York Yankees (1–1, 0.00 ERA) and pitched in the 1951 World Series for the Yankees in a relief role. He appeared in three games and gave up no earned runs. Hogue finished his big league career in 1952 with the Yankees and Browns, posting a 3–6 record with a 4.66 ERA. His career record in the major leagues was 18–16 with a 3.97 ERA. He was 34 years old in 1955 when he became the playing manager of the Williston Oilers. That season, he pitched in five games and had a 2–0 record with a 2.18 ERA.

BILLY HORNE

Second Base/Shortstop/Third Base; Bats—Right; Throws—Right; Height—5'10"; Weight—165 lbs.; Born—New Orleans, Louisiana

Horne's Negro league career was from 1938 to 1946. He played for the Chicago American Giants, Cincinnati Buckeyes, St. Louis Stars, and the Cleveland Buckeyes. He could play both shortstop and third base with equal skill. Horne, known as a clutch hitter, played in the 1939 Negro League All-Star game and again in 1944. He joined the Carman Cardinals in 1951 and batted .207 with no home runs and six RBI.

Tom Horton
Pitcher

Horton was a right handed pitcher who had seven years of pro experience and pitched as high as Class A ball in the Milwaukee Braves organization. In 1953, he played for Hagerstown in the Class B Piedmont League, had a record of 12–4 with a 2.11 ERA, and was selected to the All-Star team. He joined the Minot Mallards In 1955 and had a 3–0 record with a 5.34 ERA when he jumped back to organized ball. He finished that season with Portsmouth and was 5–4 with a 3.22 ERA in the Piedmont League.

Red House
Third Base/Manager

House's Negro League career was from 1937 to 1947. He played for the Detroit Stars and Homestead Grays. House also played for the Detroit Black Sox and other teams of lesser quality in Detroit. In the off-season he trained boxers at the Brewster Center in Detroit. In 1949, he managed the semi-pro Detroit Wolves. He joined the Carman Cardinals in 1950 as playing manager, and after his release he returned to Detroit.

Percy Howard
Catcher/Outfield

Howard played the 1950 season with the Winnipeg Buffaloes and batted .194. He played for the Detroit Stars and Indianapolis Clowns in 1954 and 1955, when the Negro Leagues were closing down.

Otto Huber
Second Base/Manager; Bats — Right; Throws — Right; Height — 5'10"; Weight — 165 lbs.; Born — March 12, 1914 in Garfield, New Jersey; Died — April 9, 1989 in Passaic, New Jersey

Huber played for the Boston Braves in 1939 at age 25 and appeared in 11 games, batting .273 with no home runs and three RBI. Huber also played for Evansville in the Class B Three-I League and Indianapolis in the American Association. In 1947, he managed the Mt. Vernon Braves in the Class D Illinois League. He was playing manager for the Minot Mallards in 1951 and batted .254 with no home runs and 10 RBI. He and shortstop Zoonie McLean had 27 double plays in 35 games, before Huber resigned in a salary dispute with the Mallards executive.

Pete Hughes
Outfield

Hughes played for several years in the Cincinnati Reds organization and was an All-Star at many minor league levels. He had good power and a good eye at the plate and holds the minor league record for the most walks in a season with 210, set in 1949 in the Sunset League. In 1952, he won the triple crown in the Southwest International League. That year he batted .366 with 28 home runs and 131 RBI. He is 15th on the all-time career list for batting average in the minor leagues and has a .350 lifetime average. He is fourth on the all-time list for RBI seasons, with nine. It was said that a broken leg early in his career hurt his chance to play in big leagues. He joined the Winnipeg Royals in 1953 and he batted .324 and led the league with 13 home runs and 66 RBI. Hughes was one of the best and most dangerous hitters to ever play in the ManDak League.

ART HUNT
Pitcher

Hunt joined the Brandon Greys in 1950, and that season was one of the top pitchers in the league with a 9–0 record. He was back in 1951 and had a 4–2 record and was a big-game pitcher for the Greys.

WILLIE "ACE" HUTCHINSON

Pitcher/Outfield; Bats—Right; Throws—Right; Height—5'10"; Weight—165 lbs; Born—Dallas, Texas

Hutchinson's Negro League career was from 1939 to 1950. He began his career with the Kansas City Monarchs, although he spent most of his career with the Memphis Red Sox. He was considered to have average control. He played for the Carman Cardinals in 1951 and had a 5–8 record. In 1952 he was 5–5 and finished his ManDak career in 1953 with a 3–6 record. He then went into organized ball with Danville in the Mississippi–Ohio Valley League where he had a 4–2 record and a 3.71 ERA.

COWAN HYDE

Outfield; Bats—Right; Throws—Right; Height—5'8"; Weight—150 lbs.; Born—April 10, 1908 in Pototoc, Mississippi; Died—November 20, 2003 in St. Louis, Missouri

Hyde's Negro League career was from 1927 to 1950, mostly with the Memphis Red Sox. He was 42 years old when he joined the Elmwood Giants in 1950. He batted .315 with no home runs and 5 RBI. He was back with the Giants in 1951 and batted .348 with two home runs and 10 RBI. He was with Brandon in 1952 and 1953 and batted .256, two HR, 26 RBI, and .292, no HR, 30 RBI. In 1953 he led the league in triples with 10. After that season he retired from baseball. As a young player he had exceptional speed and was a Negro League All-Star two times. He was a very popular player in the ManDak League. Even though he was at an advanced age it had little effect on his baseball skills. In 1997, his name was placed on a wall at Milwaukee's County Stadium that is dedicated in honor of the Negro League players.

AL JACOWSKI
Pitcher

Jacowski hailed from Gilbert Plains, Manitoba. In 1951, he won his only start for the Carman Cardinals. He was a very good pitcher at the local level and when the Cardinals found themselves short of pitching, they called on him.

WALLY JAKO (JAKOWCZYK)
Outfield

Jako played seven years in organized ball and played as high as Class A. He played three seasons with Utica in the Eastern League from 1944 to 1948 and batted .194, .289 and .294. His best season was 1947, with Terre Haute in the Three-I League, where he batted .333 with 14 home runs and 92 RBI. In 1951 he was hitting .280 with Chattanooga when he joined the Minot Mallards and batted .341 with seven home runs and 35 RBI. He continued his hot hitting in 1952 for the Mallards, batting .311 with seven home runs and 46 RBI.

BILL JANKOWSKI
Left Field/First Base

Jankowski played 10 seasons in the Philadelphia Phillies chain and advanced as high as Double-A ball. He was a good hitter and early in his career had success as a pitcher. His best season was in 1949 with Portland in the New England League, where he had a 13–4 record with a 3.96 ERA and batted .277 with two home runs and 20 RBI. He last pitched in 1951 with Schenectady, with little success. In 1952, he played for Tulsa in the Texas league and batted .226 with two HR, 24 RBI. He joined the Bismarck Barons in 1955 and batted .331 with three home runs and 38 RBI.

GIDEON JARVIS
Outfield; Height: 6'; Weight: 200 lbs.

Jarvis played in the Cincinnati Reds organization, starting his career with Wausau in the Northern League. He had several injuries early in his career. In 1956 he played for Topeka in the Western League and Tijuana in the Arizona-Mexico League, where he batted .291. He attended college in the off season. Jarvis joined the Minot Mallards in 1957 and batted .338 with five home runs and 26 RBI. He came to Minot on his own and requested a tryout. He was a good addition.

WILLIE JEFFERSON
Pitcher; Bats—Right; Throws—Right; Height—5'9"; Weight—165 lbs.; Born—July 16, 1904 in Clearview, Oklahoma; Died—1976 in Shreveport, Louisiana

Jefferson's Negro League career was from 1937 to 1946. He was considered a cagey pitcher with a good array of stuff. He played for several Negro League teams and also pitched in Mexico. He joined the Elmwood Giants in 1951 at the advanced age of 46, but he had lost much of his pitching skill. He finished the season with a 4–7 record and retired.

PEE WEE JENKINS

Pitcher; Bats—Right; Throws—Right; Height—5'8"; Weight—160 lbs.

Jenkins's Negro League career was from 1944 to 1950, mostly with the New York Cubans. He was a control pitcher. He joined the Winnipeg Buffaloes in 1951 and had a 8–5 record, and was a key member of their pitching staff. When the Buffaloes ceased operation, he joined his manager, Willie Wells, in Brandon with the Greys. He had a 3–3 record in 1952 and in 1953 had a 5–2 record and won many a key game for his team.

Gentry Jessup, Carman Cardinals (courtesy of Dufferin Historical Museum of Carman, Manitoba).

GENTRY JESSUP

Pitcher; Bats—Right; Throws—Right; Height—6'; Weight—180 lbs; Died—March 23, 1998

Jessup's Negro League career was from 1940 to 1949, with the Birmingham Black Barons and Chicago American Giants. He had much success in the Negro Leagues and was considered a great competitor. He pitched in five Negro League All-Star games. In 1944 and 1945, he led his league in victories. He joined the Carman Cardinals in 1950 and led the league with 10 wins and lost only 4 games. In 1951 he was 9–6. In 1952 he had an 8–8 record and after that season would retire. In his three seasons in the ManDak, he was considered a workhorse.

FELIPE JIMENEZ

Pitcher

Jimenez played in the Washington Senators organization. In 1946 he played Double-A for Chattanooga. He played three seasons in Class B for the Havana Cubanos in the Florida International League. He played for Carman in 1954 and batted .207.

MILT JOFFE

Center Field

Joffe had a nine-year career in organized ball and played in the Brooklyn Dodgers, New York Giants and Milwaukee Braves chains. He played as high as Double-A in the Texas League. From 1953 to 1955, he played with Beaumont in the Texas League. He batted .249, with 11 HR, 50 RBI in 1953; .146, no HR, four RBI in 1954, and .276, one HR, six RBI in 1955. He joined the Dickinson Packers in 1956 and batted .258 with eight home runs and 31 RBI.

BOB JOHNSON

First Base; Height — 6'1"

Bob Johnson was from the Detroit area and had played for the semi-pro Detroit Wolves in 1948. He joined the Carman Cardinals in 1949 when they were in the Manitoba Senior League and batted .340. He was back with Carman in the ManDak League in 1950 and 1951. He batted .269 with one home run and 26 RBI. In 1951 he batted .269 again, with two home runs and 32 RBI. He was a good-fielding first baseman and well liked by his teammates. The 1951 Carman souvenir book stated that Johnson was everyone's favorite player. You just had to ask any of the kids. In the off-season, he worked in the automotive industry in Detroit and later would become a church minister.

EARL JOHNSON

Catcher/Outfield

Earl Johnson entered organized ball in 1953 and played in the St. Louis Cardinals chain. In 1955, he split the season with Winnipeg in the Northern League (.199, nine HR, 45 RBI) and Columbus in the South Atlantic League (.133, 0 HR, 0 RBI). In 1955 he batted .258, 6 home runs and 42 RBI with the Dickinson Packers. He was the brother of Ev Johnson.

Ev Johnson
Catcher/Manager

Ev Johnson started in organized ball in 1936 as a pitcher and played in the Chicago Cubs and Cincinnati Reds chains. He played as high as Class C ball. Before joining Dickinson, his record in organized ball indicated that he was not a high-average hitter and lacked power. He joined the Dickinson Packers in 1955 and batted .298 with six home runs and 39 RBI.

Leonard Johnson
Pitcher; Throws—Right

Leonard Johnson's Negro League career was from 1947 to 1948 with the Chicago American Giants. He pitched briefly for the Minot Mallards from late July until August 15 in 1951 and had a 1–1 record.

Norm Johnson
Pitcher

Norm Johnson pitched in the Cleveland Indians, St. Louis Cardinals, and New York Giants organizations and pitched as high as Class B ball. He started his career in 1951 (7–4, 3.67 ERA) with Duluth in the Northern League. He had another good season in 1955 when his record was 5–3 with a 3.41 ERA with St. Cloud, again in the Northern League. He pitched for the Williston Oilers in 1956 and his record was 5–5 with a 4.45 ERA. In 1957 he was 7–10 with a 7.52 ERA.

Tom Johnson
Pitcher

Tom Johnson pitched briefly with the Indianapolis Clowns in 1950. Records indicate that he pitched very little for the Clowns. Midway through that season he jumped to the Brandon Greys and pitched with little success, recording a 0–2 record. He was released.

Dick Jok
Outfield

Jok entered organized baseball in 1947. His highest level of ball was Class A. His best season in organized ball was 1949 with Erie in the Mid-Atlantic League where he batted .300 with 16 home runs and 104 RBI. He played for the Dickinson Packers in 1955 and batted .302 with six home runs and 32 RBI.

Clarence "Lefty" Jones
Pitcher

Clarence Jones had no Negro League experience. He came from college ball straight to the Winnipeg Buffaloes in 1951. Newspaper reports indicated that the Buffaloes expected big things from him. He pitched briefly with little success in recording a 0–2 record.

Paul Jones

Pitcher; Bats—Right; Throws—Right; Height—6'3"; Weight—223 lbs.; Born—1929

Paul Jones's Negro League career was from 1949 to 1950. He was not very successful with the Louisville Buckeyes (2–11, 6.11 ERA) in 1949. He joined the Elmwood Giants in 1950 and had a 9–10 record. He then went into organized baseball from 1951 to 1954 and was unimpressive. Starting in 1951, his record was 3–19, 6.84 with Flint, and 4–6 with Vancouver in 1952. He continued pitching with little success until 1958.

Connie Juelke
Outfield

Juelke was from Kenmore, North Dakota. He played seven years of pro ball with six teams. He played in Grand Forks, St. Paul, Waterloo, Birmingham, Colorado Springs, and Muskegon. He hit .300 at every level. He was an All-Star in 1949 with Muskegon in the Class A Central League. He joined Minot in 1951 and was batting .280 with two home runs and 15 RBI when on July 1, he jumped the club. He returned to Minot in 1953 (.290, 11 HR, 49 RBI) and 1954 (.279, 7 HR, 46 RBI). He played for the Bismarck Barons in 1956 and batted .220 with four home runs and 12 RBI.

Ed Kalski

Pitcher; Throws—Right; Died—April 2, 2005 in Cohoes, New York

Kalski spent eight seasons in the minor leagues and pitched as high as Triple-A with Syracuse in the International League. In 1948 he was with Albany in the Eastern League and went 10–6, with a 3.21 ERA. His best season was 1949, when he was 14–6 with Albany in the Eastern League. After being out of baseball for three years, he attempted to come back with Albany in 1955 and pitched only three games, with little success. He pitched briefly with the Dickinson Packers in 1956 and was released, then joined Lloydminster in the Western Canada Baseball League.

Joe Kamis

Pitcher; Throws—Right

Kamis pitched four years in the Chicago White Sox chain, reaching Class

B ball. In 1949, he had a 10–6 record with a 3.02 ERA for Waterloo in the Three-I League. He joined the Minot Mallards in 1951 and on June 9, he broke his ankle. He stayed in Minot and came back late in the season to finish with a 1–1 record.

Mike Kanshin
Pitcher

Kanshin pitched in the New York Giants chain, reaching Class B ball. He started his pro career in 1948 with Las Vegas and had 4–4 record and a 6.04 ERA. His best season was in 1950 with Medford in the Far West League, where he had was 12–5 with a 3.71 ERA. He joined the Winnipeg Royals in 1953 and had a 4–0 record, then jumped to organized ball. Kanshin closed out his career in 1954 with Victoria in the Western International League, where he was 3–4 with an 8.45 ERA.

Stan Karpinski
Pitcher; Throws— Right; Height — 6'3"; Weight — 215; Born —1924

Karpinski broke into pro ball as an outfielder in 1946. In 1949, he turned to pitching and led the Class D Florida State League with 29 wins and a 1.56 ERA . That season he was selected to the All-Star team. He was again an All-Star in 1950 in the Class A South Atlantic League and led the league with 20 victories. He opened the 1955 season with Galveston in the Class B Big State League and had a 4–2 record when the team folded. He then signed with the Williston Oilers and had a record of 3–3 with a 5.12 ERA. In 1956, he was playing manager for Lloydminster in the Western Canada Baseball League.

Dick Kelly
Pitcher; Throws— Left

Dick Kelly played eight seasons in organized ball, in the Boston Braves chain. His highest level was Double-A ball. In 1950, he was 21–7 with a 2.85 ERA with Bluefield in the Appalachian League and had another good season in 1953 with Jacksonville, going 17–6 with a 3.16 ERA. He started the 1956 season with Austin in the Texas League and had 0–3 record when he was released. He then signed with the Minot Mallards and had a 6–5 record and a 3.50 ERA.

John Kelly
Pitcher; Throws— Left

In 1948, John Kelly signed with the Brooklyn Dodgers and was assigned to Abilene in the Class C West Texas–New Mexico League. He played in the Can-Am League with Three Rivers and had a 7–17 record. In 1950 he pitched for Fergus Falls in the Class AA amateur league in Minnesota and had a 22–2 record. He joined the Minot Mallards in 1952 and won his first six games en route to a 7–2 record that season. He started the 1953 season with the Mallards and hurt his arm. He finished the regular season with a 0–1 record. He came back ready to pitch again in the final championship series against Carman and was the winner in Minot's 6–2 win in game two.

Cliff Kempf

Catcher

Kempf played for the North Dakota State championship team in 1939 and the Montana State semi-pro champion in 1940. He came from Enderlin, North Dakota, and was considered a good receiver, but did not hit for a high average. In 1949, he played baseball with the Minot Oscars. He joined the Minot Mallards in 1950 and played for two seasons, batting .181 in 1950 and .193 in 1951.

John Kennedy

Second Base; Bats — Right; Throws — Right; Height — 5'10"; Weight — 175 lbs.; Born — October 12, 1926 in Jacksonville, Florida; Died — April 27, 1998 in Jacksonville, Florida

Kennedy had no Negro League experience when he joined the Winnipeg Buffaloes in 1950 and batted .256, with no HR and 22 RBI. In 1951 with the Buffaloes, he batted .324 with 2 HR, 15 RBI. He played for the Minot Mallards in 1952 and batted .286 with one home run and 26 RBI. He batted .270 with 19 HR and 81 RBI with High Point-Thomasville in 1957, and this earned him a callup to the Philadelphia Phillies. He played five games with the Phillies and had two at-bats with no hits. He was the first African American player for the Phillies. In 1961, he closed out his career in the South Atlantic League with Jacksonville.

Clarence King

Outfield

Clarence King's Negro League career was from 1947 to 1950 with the Birmingham Black Barons. With the Negro Leagues in decline, he came north to Canada and joined the Brandon Greys for one season, in 1951, and batted .274 with three home runs and 26 RBI. In 1958 he returned to play for the Detroit Stars.

Kevin King

Pitcher

Kevin King started his career as an outfielder in 1948. In 1949 he switched to pitching. He was with Vancouver in the Western International League in 1950 and 1951 and pitched with little success. He joined the Winnipeg Giants in 1952, had a 0–1 record, and was released.

Roy Klaudt
Pitcher

Klaudt hailed from Salem, North Dakota, and in 1953 went to the Pittsburgh Pirates farm camp and was assigned to Waco's Class B team of the Big State League. Instead of reporting, he joined the Mallards in 1953 and pitched only briefly, with a record of 0–1.

Pete Konyar
Third base

In 1951, Konyar led the Cotton States League in home runs with 27. That season he played for the Pine Bluff Judges, and was selected to the All-Star team. During his career, he played for the Aberdeen Pheasants in the Northern League and also played in Mexico, the Cotton States and Eastern Leagues. He joined the Williston Oilers in 1957 and was injured in a car accident with teammates Steve Molinari and Jack Sanoff. They were returning home from a game in Brandon. At the time he was batting .239 with one home run and eight RBI, and was being counted on to be a big hitter for the Oilers that season.

John Kropf
Outfield

Kropf played in the New York Giants organization. In 1949, he hit .315 for the St. Cloud Rox in the Northern League and was selected to the All-Star team. In 1950 played for the champion Minneapolis Millers in the American Association and batted .254, hitting 21 home runs and knocking in 97 runs. He was back with the Millers again in 1951. He was 29 years old when he joined the Bismarck Barons for the 1956 season and batted .316, with 13 HR, 43 RBI.

Rocky Krsnich

Third Base; Bats— Right; Throws— Right; Height — 5'10"; Weight — 174 lbs.; Born — August 5, 1927 in W. Allis, Wisconsin

Krsnich played for the Chicago White Sox in 1949 (.218, one HR, 9 RBI) and from 1952 (.231, 1 HR, 15 RBI) to 1953 (.202, 1 HR, 14 RBI). His career batting average in the major leagues was .215. He put up some good numbers in the minor leagues and was an All-Star in 1948 in the Piedmont League and again in 1950 in the Southern League. He joined the Dickinson Packers in 1956 at the age of 29 and batted .241 with two home runs and six RBI. He hit three home runs for Dickinson in a playoff game. He continued to play in the minor leagues and was an All-Star in 1962 in the National Baseball Congress Tournament while playing for the Wichita Transit. He played in that tournament again in 1964.

Gus Kyle
Catcher

In 1949, Kyle played for the Regina Caps in the Western Canada Baseball League and he was rated as a good hitter. He played three seasons in the National Hockey League with the New York Rangers and Boston Bruins. He played very briefly with the Brandon Greys in 1953.

Bob Landers
Pitcher; Throws—Left

Landers' Negro League career was from 1949 to 1952, with the Kansas City Monarchs. Landers joined the Minot Mallards in 1952, and before the start of the season pitched a no-hitter in a league tournament in Brandon. He had a 0–1 record when he was released on July 4th.

Mal Landry
Pitcher

Landry had four years of pro experience in the New York Giants organization. He reached Class A ball. In 1954, he pitched for the Muskogee Giants in the Class C Western Association and had a 17–8 record with a 3.27 ERA. In 1955 he pitched for Sioux City in the Western League and had a 3–5 record with a 6.13 ERA. He joined the Bismarck Barons in 1956 and had a 9–3 record with a 5.51 ERA. He played only one season in the league.

Whitey Landsen
Pitcher

Landsen, from Edmore, North Dakota, was a 19-year-old right hander who pitched very briefly for Minot in 1953 and had a 0–0 record.

Harvey Lapides
Outfield

Lapides had played at Brown University and was recommended to Minot by Lefty Lefebvre, his coach at Brown, He played several years of semi-pro ball in Fort Fairfield, Maine, and New Haven. He joined Minot in 1950 and batted .248 with two home runs and 12 RBI.

Bob Laskowski
Pitcher

In 1953, Laskowski was an All-Star in the Class D Wisconsin State League. He played for the Dickinson Packers in 1956 and had a 0–3 record with a 7.46 ERA when he was released.

Garland "Butch" Lawing

Outfield; Bats—Right; Throws—Right; Height—6'1"; Weight—180 lbs.; Born—August 29, 1919 in Gastonia, North Carolina; Died—September 27, 1996 in Murrells Inlet, South Carolina

In 1946, Lawing batted .133 playing in two games for the Cincinnati Reds and eight games for the New York Giants. In 1948, he led the Border League in batting (.379), hits (164), RBI (122), and runs scored (112). He played for the Quebec Braves in 1949 and 1950. He was an All-Star both years, and in 1950 won the Triple Crown, batting .346, with 19 home runs and 141 RBI. He holds the Canadian-American League record for the most walks in a season with 168, set in 1950. He joined the Dickinson Packers in 1956 at 36 years of age and batted .307, with 19 home runs. He tied for the lead in RBI with 73. He played for the Brandon Greys in 1957 and batted .288 with six home runs and 39 RBI.

Al Leap

Shortstop

Leap played many years in the Brooklyn Dodgers system and was a talented player who hit with power. His progress was blocked by the reserve clause, and he quit organized baseball. He played one season in the Basin League in 1955. In 1956, the company he worked for transferred him to North Dakota. The Bismarck Barons got permission from his company for him to play and he proved to be a good pickup. He played two seasons for the Barons and batted .285 with 23 home runs and 61 RBI in 1956 and .319 with 14 home runs and 53 RBI in 1957. He closed out his career with Williston in 1958 and 1959 in the Western Canada Baseball League. He played briefly each season and batted .389, with 2 HR, 20 RBI in 1958, and .296 in 1959.

Jim Leavitt

Catcher

Leavitt played organized ball from 1951 to 1955 in the Pittsburgh Pirates chain and reached Class A ball. Minor league stats indicated he was not a high-average hitter and lacked power. In 1955, he was with Channel Cities in the California League and batted .273, with 4 HR, 51 RBI. He joined Williston in 1956 and batted .272 with 5 home runs and 30 RBI.

Don Lee

Pitcher; Bats—Right; Throws—Right; Height—6'4"; Weight—205 lbs.; Born—February 26, 1934 in Globe, Arizona

Lee was 20 years old when he pitched for the Williston Oilers in 1955. He had a 5–2 record and 3.65 ERA. He had been the top hurler that season for the University of Arizona. Lee went on to pitch nine seasons in the major leagues, starting in 1957 and ending in 1966. He pitched for the Detroit Tigers, Washington Senators, Minnesota Twins, California Angels, Houston Astros, and Chicago Cubs. His best season was 1962, with the Twins and Angels, when his record was 11–11 with a 3.46 ERA. Over his career he appeared in 244 games with a 40–44 record and a 3.61 ERA. He was the son of Thornton Lee, a former major league hurler.

Bill "Lefty" Lefebvre

Pitcher; Bats—Left; Throws—Left; Height—6'; Weight—180 lbs.; Born—November 11, 1911 in Natick, Rhode Island

Lefebvre was 23 years old when he joined the Red Sox for the 1938 and 1939 seasons. In 1938, in his first major league at-bat, he hit a home run. He pitched for the Washington Senators in 1943 (2–0, 4.45 ERA) and 1944 (2–4, 4.52 ERA). Over his major league career he appeared in 36 games and had a 5–5 record and a 5.08 ERA. He also played Triple-A with the Minneapolis Millers in the American Association. He was 39 when he joined the Minot Mallards in 1950 as playing manager. He pitched very little that season and batted .241 with no home runs and 4 RBI.

Ed Leier

Outfield; Born—1927

Leier played baseball in Winnipeg for Morse Place in the Manitoba Junior League and the Elmwood Giants in the Manitoba Senior League. He was an All-Star in the Junior League in 1946 and 1947. He played in 19 games for the Elmwood Giants in 1950 and batted .197 with no home runs and eight RBI. That was his only season in the ManDak league. He also played in the National Hockey League with the Chicago Black Hawks. Leier was elected to the Manitoba Baseball Hall of Fame in 2000.

Cliff Lemme

Pitcher

Lemme was a right-handed pitcher with many years of pro baseball experience. In 1953 he pitched for North Battleford, Saskatchewan, in the Western Canada Baseball League. He joined the Minot Mallards in 1954 and had a 1–2 record.

Neal Lettau

Pitcher; Throws—Left; Height—6'1"; Weight—195 lbs.

Lettau played in the New York Yankees organization. In 1949, he pitched for Grand Forks in the Northern League and had a 15–10 record and was voted to the Northern League All-Star team. In 1952, he pitched Double-A ball in the Southern Association. He started the 1953 season with Binghamton and left to join the Minot Mallards. In his first game, he fired a two-hitter and finished the season with a 4–1 record. He was back in Minot in 1954 and had a 13–2 record. His 13 wins led the league. In 1955 his record fell to 3–6 with an 8.29 ERA, and he was released on July 25.

DAN LEWANDOWSKI

Pitcher; Bats—Right; Throws—Right; Height—6'; Weight—180 lbs.; Born—January 6, 1928 in Buffalo, New York; Died—July 19, 1996 in Hamilton, Ontario, Canada

Lewandowski was an All-Star with Allentown in the Class B Interstate League in 1951 and led the league with 24 wins. He was called up to the St. Louis Cardinals in September and appeared in two games. He had a 0–1 record and a 9.00 ERA. He joined the Dickinson Packers briefly in 1955 at the age of 27.

DOUG LEWIS

First Base

In 1953, Doug Lewis was an All-Star with the Plainview Ponies in the Class C West Texas–New Mexico League. In 1954 he again was an All-Star in that league with the Pampa Oilers. He joined the Brandon Greys in 1957 and he batted .294 with two home runs and 37 RBI.

GLEN LEWIS

Catcher

Glen Lewis played four seasons in organized ball, reaching Class B. He was not a high-average hitter and had little power. He played briefly with the Brandon Greys in 1952.

JOHN LLOYD

Outfield

Lloyd played three seasons in organized ball, reaching Class C. His best season was 1950, when he batted .311 in the Canadian-American League. He played briefly for the Elmwood Giants in 1951. In 1954 he played in the Longhorn League with Midland and batted .227.

LESTER LOCKETT

Outfield; Bats—Right; Throws—Right; Height—6'; Weight—195 lbs.; Born—May 26, 1912 in Princeton, Indiana

Lockett played in the Negro League from 1938 to 1950. The good-hitting outfielder was a Negro League All-Star three times. Lockett was a versatile player who could hit with power and had speed on the bases. In 1948 he was the Negro National League batting champion. He was 40 years old when he joined the Carman Cardinals in 1952. He batted .390 with no home runs and 18 RBI, but didn't have enough at bats to qualify for the batting championship. In 1953 with Carman he batted .332 with one HR, 30 RBI and hit .248, with 3 HR, 31 RBI in 1954. Each season he was a key player for the Carman club. In 1998, his name was placed on a wall of honor at Milwaukee's County Stadium that is dedicated to the Negro League players.

Lou Lombardo

Pitcher; Bats—Left; Throws—Left; Height—6'2"; Weight—210 lbs.; Born—November 18, 1928 in Carlsadt, New Jersey; Died—June 11, 2001 in Rock Hill, South Carolina

Lombardo was 20 years old when he appeared in two games for the New York Giants in 1948. He pitched five innings and had a 6.75 ERA. In 1950, he pitched in Double-A with Little Rock in the Southern Association. In 1952 he was 11–3 for Montgomery in the Class A Sally League. In 1953, he was 25 years old when he joined the Minot Mallards from Rochester, Minnesota, of the Southern Minny League (semi-pro). He pitched six games with little success and had a 0–3 record when he was released on July 16.

Chick Longest

Second Base/Third Base; Bats—Left; Throws—Right; Height—6'; Weight—175 lbs.

Longest's Negro League career was from 1942 to 1947. He was the starting second baseman and leadoff hitter for the Chicago American Giants. He played the 1950 season with South Bend in the Michigan-Indiana semi-pro league. He joined the Carman Cardinals in 1951 and batted .370, with eight home runs and 28 RBI. In 1951 it was reported that Longest had received an offer to play in Mexico for $1,100 a month, but decided to remain with Carman. He batted .345 with 8 HR, 41 RBI with Carman in 1952, second best in the league. In 1953 he batted .321 with six HR and 40 RBI, and in 1954, his last season with Carman, he batted .276 with 4 HR, 37 RBI. He closed out his career in 1955 with Burlington in the Quebec Provincial League, hitting .276.

Wymon "Red" Longley

Infield/Outfield; Bats—Right; Throws—Right

Longley's Negro League career was from 1932 to 1951. He played for the Memphis Red Sox, Chicago American Giants, and New Orleans Eagles. He was a versatile player who could play all positions but pitcher and was not a strong hitter. He played the 1950 season for the Elmwood Giants and batted .230 with no home runs and 10 RBI. After that season he returned to the Negro Leagues with the New Orleans Eagles.

Benny Lott

Second Base/Shortstop/Third Base; Bats—Right; Throws—Right; Height—5'11"; Weight—167 lbs.; Born—1927

Lott played in the Negro Leagues in 1949 and 1950, and was a consistent .300 hitter with power. In 1953, he played in 12 games with Tulsa in the Texas League and batted .303. That same season he joined the Carman Cardinals and batted .301 with one home run and 21 RBI. He was 26 years old. He started the 1957 season with Lloydminster in the Western Canada Baseball League, then jumped to the Brandon Greys and batted .301 with two home runs and 21 RBI.

Mike Lotz

Pitcher

Lotz was signed as a "bonus baby" by the Detroit Tigers and played four years in organized ball. He reached the Class A level. He joined Bismarck in 1955 and hadn't told the Tigers where he was. His teammate, Roger Higgins, said that the Tigers looked for him to try and get some of their bonus money back and didn't realize he was in North Dakota. He pitched very well for Bismarck and had an 8–2 record with a 2.95 ERA. The Bismarck newspaper reported that after that season he would be leaving baseball to attend Oxford University.

Lou Louden

Catcher; Bats—Right; Throws—Right; Height—5'10"; Weight—172 lbs.; Born—August 19, 1919 in West Point, Virginia; Died—August 31, 1989 in Newark, New Jersey

Louden's Negro League career was from 1942 to 1950. He had a good arm and was a good hitter. He played in four Negro League All-Star games. He played with the Willie Mays All-Stars in 1948–49 and was the only non-major leaguer. He was 32 years old when he joined the Elmwood Giants in 1951 and batted .273 with two home runs and 22 RBI. In 1952, he was with the Winnipeg Giants and batted .328. with five home runs and 43 RBI. In 1953, the Giants became the Royals, and Louden batted .252 with two home runs and 32 RBI. On August 19 he was voted the Royals' most popular player. He started the 1957 season with El Paso in the Southwestern League, then jumped to the Brandon Greys midway through that season and batted .256 with three home runs and 24 RBI.

Ian Lowe

Third Base/Manager; Born—1917; Died—1977

Ian Lowe called Bradwardine, Manitoba, home and was considered by some to be the best third baseman in the ManDak League. In 1948 and 1949,

Brandon player-manager Ian Lowe, photographed while playing for Victoria. This is his wife's favorite picture (courtesy of Lillian Lowe).

he played for Brandon in the Manitoba Senior League. In 1949, he led Brandon to what many Manitoba baseball fans called "the greatest season a team ever had in Brandon." He led the Greys to 87 wins, 18 losses and 3 ties. This was in league and tournament play. In 1946 he played pro ball for Victoria in the Western Baseball League and in 1947 for Edmonton in a semi-pro league. He returned home to play for Brandon in 1948. In 1950 he became the playing manager for Brandon for the Greys' first season in the ManDak League, and batted .319. He tied for the RBI lead with Butch Davis with 39. In 1951, he batted .298 and managed Brandon to its only ManDak League championship. Lowe was elected to the Manitoba Baseball Hall of Fame in 1997 and also was selected to the Manitoba Sports Hall of Fame in 2004.

TOM LOWE

Pitcher

Tom Lowe was a right-handed pitcher who was signed by the Detroit Tigers in 1940. He pitched in Triple-A with the Jersey City Giants in the International League and with the Jacksonville Tars in the Class A South Atlantic League. He joined the Minot Mallards in 1953 and had a 1–3 record. He was released on July 16.

JOE LUTZ

First Base; Bats — Left; Throws — Left; Height — 6'; Weight — 195 lbs.; Born — February 18, 1925, in Keokuk, Iowa

In 1947, Lutz was selected to the All-Star team in the Central Association. He was 26 years old when he played briefly with the St. Louis Browns in 1951. He appeared in 14 games, batting .167 with no home runs and 2 RBI. In 1953, he played 76 games for the St. Paul Saints in the American Association and batted .238, with eight doubles, a triple and nine home runs. He joined the Williston Oilers in 1954 at the age of 29 and batted .292 with eight home runs and 20 RBI. Lutz coached the Cleveland Indians in 1972 and 1973.

BILL LYNN
Outfield

In 1954, Lynn led the Evangeline League in hits with 211 and was selected to the All-Star Team. In 1955, he joined the Lafayette Oilers in the same league, again was selected to the All-Star team, and led the league with 196 hits. In 1956, he batted .286 in the Texas League and struck out only 19 times in 300 at-bats. Minor league statistics indicated that he was a high-average hitter. He joined the Williston Oilers in 1957 and batted .459 with five home runs and 33 RBI in 122 at-bats. He closed out his career with Williston in 1958 and 1959 in the Western Canada Baseball League. He batted .321 with two HR, 26 RBI in 1958 and won the batting championship in 1959 with an average of .376. He had six HR and 38 RBI.

AL LYONS

Pitcher; Bats—Right; Throws—Right; Height—6'2"; Weight—195 lbs.; Born—July 18, 1918 in St. Joseph, Missouri; Died—December 20, 1965 in Inglewood, California

Lyons pitched briefly with the New York Yankees in 1944 (0–0, 4.54 ERA) and 1946 (0–1, 5.40 ERA). He started the 1947 season with the Yankees and was traded to the Pittsburgh Pirates midway through the season. He finished with a 1–2 record and a 7.31 ERA. In 1948, he pitched for the Boston Braves and was 1–0, with a 7.82 ERA. For his career, he appeared in 39 games and had a 3–3 record with a 6.30 ERA. He was 38 years old when he joined Williston in 1956 and had a 4–1 record with a 2.48 ERA. He pitched for the Brandon Greys in 1957. He was regarded as their best pitcher. He had a 9–4 record and led the league with a 3.08 ERA.

GERRY MACKAY
Outfield; Born—February 19, 1930

As a youngster living in Brandon, Gerry MacKay was called a sports prodigy. He played with the Brandon Greys in 1950. He started the 1951 season with Brandon and was released, then joined the Minot Mallards. He batted .177 in 1950 and .229 in 1951 for Brandon. He proved to be a valuable player for the Mallards, batting .264, with three HR and 13 RBI in 125 at-bats. He signed with the Chicago Cubs in 1952, and in 1953 was selected to the Northern League All-Star team with the Sioux Falls Canaries. In 1955, he played for El Paso in Class B ball. He returned again to the ManDak League in 1957 with the Brandon Greys and batted .264 with four home runs and 27 RBI. He later would become the first Canadian National Baseball Team coach, and was elected to the Manitoba Baseball Hall of Fame in 1998.

Rod MacKay

Pitcher

Rod MacKay pitched four years in organized ball in the New York Giants organization. His best season was 1951 with Idaho Falls in the Pioneer League. He won 10 and lost 6, with a 5.17 ERA. In 1953, he was with Vancouver in the Western International League and had a record of 3–3 with a 4.79 ERA. He joined the Brandon Greys in 1954 and had a 4–2 record. That was his only season in the league.

Frank McCollum

Pitcher; Throws—Right

McCollum played in the Negro Leagues from 1954 to 1956, when the leagues were in decline. He played for the Louisville Black Colonels and Birmingham Black Barons. He played briefly for the Minot Mallards in 1957 and was released on June 13 with a 0–0 record and a high ERA of 12.87.

Walter McCoy

Pitcher; Bats—Left; Throws—Left; Height—5'9"; Weight—170 lbs.; Born—1925

Walter McCoy's Negro League career was from 1945 to 1948. In 1950, he played for Sacramento in the Pacific Coast League, where he had a record of 0–4, with a 6.23 ERA. He joined the Winnipeg Giants in 1952 when he was 27 years old. His record that season was 4–4. In 1953 he pitched very well for Carman and was one of their starting pitchers with a 10–8 record. He played briefly in the Mexican League in 1955.

Roy McCoy

Pitcher

Roy McCoy had no Negro League experience when he joined the Carman Cardinals in 1953. He did not have the success of his brother Walt. He only pitched briefly, had a 0–1 record, and was released.

Tom McDevitt

Second Base

McDevitt played the 1955 season with the Williston Oilers and batted .279 with no home runs and six RBI. He played in the St. Louis Cardinals chain and in 1956 batted .328, with two home runs and 41 RBI in the Class A Eastern League. His last season was 1958, with Winnipeg in the Northern League. He batted .254, with one home run and 33 RBI.

Morley McFarlane

Pitcher; Throws— Right; Born — October 21, 1935

McFarlane had a great fastball. He played briefly in 1954 with the Brandon Greys and was 3–1 in the playoffs. He signed with the Detroit Tigers and played in the Georgia State League. He became a star pitcher with the Brandon Cloverleafs in the late 1950's. His best season was 21–3 in 1958. He was elected to the Manitoba Baseball Hall of Fame in 1999.

Gib McClothin

Pitcher/Infield

McClothin pitched as high as Class B ball. He had played previously in the Northern League with Superior in the Chicago White Sox chain and had a 6–8 record with a 3.00 ERA. He pitched with little success in the minors until he joined the Brandon Greys in 1957. He had a record of 7–4 with a 4.89 ERA.

Curtis McGowan

Pitcher

McGowan was listed on the Memphis Red Sox roster in 1950, but there is no record of him playing in any games. He joined the Elmwood Giants in 1951, had a 0–1 record, and was released.

Henry McHenry

Pitcher; Bats— Right; Throws— Right; Height — 6'; Weight -200 lbs.

McHenry had a long Negro League career with some success from 1930 to 1950 and pitched for several Negro League teams. He pitched briefly for the Minot Mallards in 1951, had a 0–1 record, and was released on June 25.

Harry McIlvain

Pitcher

McIlvain played in the Philadelphia Phillies organization. In 1956, he pitched for the Bakersfield Boosters in the California League, with limited success. He joined the Brandon Greys in 1957 and had no decisions.

Almer McKerlie

Catcher; Born —1926

Almer McKerlie lived in Miami, Manitoba. He played his early career in Ontario. He was at the St. Louis Cardinals' training camp in 1949. The Cardinals scout wanted him to sign and have him report to Rochester in the International League, but in a play at home plate, he tore up his shoulder. The injury did heal, and he resumed his career with the Carman Cardinals. He was a good receiver, had a strong throwing arm, and was a team leader. He played all five seasons that Carman was in the ManDak league and in 1950 batted .267, with no HR, 11 RBI. He was injured in 1951 and batted .138, with no HR, nine RBI. He batted .278 with no HR, 21 RBI in 1952; .342, two HR, four RBI in 1953 and .283, no HR, six RBI in 1954. He was a very good athlete in other sports and was elected to the Manitoba Baseball Hall of Fame in 1997.

CLINT MCKERLIE
Pitcher

Clint McKerlie, Almer's brother, played for Miami and Carman Senior League teams (over 21 years of age). He was a good pitcher at the local level and pitched briefly for the Carman Cardinals in 1950, with a 0–1 record.

GREAD MCKINNIS
Pitcher; Bats— Right; Throws— Left; Height — 6'2"; Weight —170 lbs.; Born — October 11, 1913 in Bullock County, Alabama

McKinnis pitched in the Negro Leagues from 1941 to 1949, for five teams. He appeared in two Negro League All-Star games. In 1947, he was the first African American to pitch in the Minnesota Class A Tournament. He won three games for Rochester, Minnesota, including the semifinal game, and hit a home run to win the game. He was 37 years old when he joined the Brandon Greys in 1951 and posted a 11–6 record. That season his 11 wins were the most in the league. He returned to Brandon for the 1953 season and had a 7–5 record. He closed out his ManDak League career with Minot in 1956, with a 0–2 record.

ZOONIE MCLEAN
Shortstop; Height — 6'1"; Weight —180 lbs.; Born —1924

McLean was from Rugby, North Dakota. He was a well-known all around athlete in North Dakota and was all-conference four straight years at Minot State University. In 1947, he turned down offers from the Philadelphia Athletics because he wanted to teach school. In 1948, he batted .389 and in 1949 hit .467 with the Minot Merchants. He joined the Minot Mallards in 1950 and was considered to be one of the league's best players. He was a steady performer for the Mallards and the only player to play in all eight ManDak seasons. His batting average was:

Year	Average	HR	RBI
1950	.267	0	26
1951	.299	2	33
1952	.369	7	46 (Was the league batting champion)
1953	.285	2	21
1954	.314	2	20
1955	.351	13	57
1956	.317	6	50
1957	.365	9	58

Over his eight seasons he averaged .322, hit 41 home runs, and drove in 311 runs. He led all shortstops in fielding in 1954. On June 19, 1955, he hit three home runs against Williston and went 5 for 5. That same season, he had an 11-game hitting streak in which he batted .538. He closed out his career as playing manager for Williston in the Western Canada Baseball League in 1958. He was elected to the North Dakota and Montana Sports Halls of Fame.

Clyde McNeal

Second Base; Bats— Right; Throws— Right; Height — 6'; Weight — 185 lbs.; Born — December 15, 1928 in San Antonio, Texas

McNeal played for the Chicago American Giants in the Negro American League from 1945 to 1950. In 1950, he played in the Negro League East-West game, then signed with the Brooklyn Dodgers. In 1953 he batted .275 with Elmira and in 1954, with Newport News in the Piedmont League, he batted .309. That season earned him a callup to the Montreal Royals. In 1956, he was with Cedar Rapids in the Class B Three-I League and batted .309, with 27 home runs and 89 RBI. He joined the Bismarck Barons in 1957 and batted .304 with 16 home runs and 61 RBI.

Roy McWorter

Pitcher

McWorter joined the Carman Cardinals in 1950 and pitched briefly, with little success. He had a 0–1 record and was released.

Joe Mack

Infield/Outfield; Bats— Both; Throws— Left; Height — 5'11"; Weight — 185 lbs.; Born — January 4, 1912 in Chicago, Illinois; Died — December 19, 1998 in Atlanta, Georgia

Mack was a switch hitting outfielder. In 1945 he played in 66 games for the Boston Braves as a 26-year old and batted .231 with three home runs and 44 RBI. He played for the Milwaukee Brewers in the American Association before joining Minot on July 4, 1951. With Minot, he batted .242 with two home runs and 22 RBI.

Bill Malone

Outfield; Born — 1922

Malone was from the Detroit area. He was 28 years old when he joined the Carman Cardinals in 1950. He had played semi-pro for the Detroit Wolves in 1949 and had come north with manager Red House. When House was fired, Malone left and returned to Detroit. At the time he was having little success on the field.

Bob Manning
Outfield; Born —1927

Manning was 23 years old in 1950. He was living in the Detroit area, but grew up in the Southern United States. He had learned his baseball while in the service. In 1949 it was reported that he had batted .386 playing semi-pro ball in Detroit. He played briefly for the Carman Cardinals in 1950. He was playing with little success and left when manager Red House was fired.

Enrique "Ricky" Maroto
Pitcher

Maroto played very briefly for the Brandon Greys in 1952. He played in the Negro Leagues in 1954 and 1955 with the Kansas City Monarchs.

Ron Martin
Third Base/Outfield; Height — 5'11"; Weight —180 lbs

Martin was a local Williston player who had played four seasons of Junior Legion baseball. He joined Williston in 1954 and batted .264 with no home runs and 17 RBI. He was back in 1955 and batted .302 with three home runs and 28 RBI.

Warren Martin
Pitcher; Throws— Left; Height — 6'1"; Weight —175 lbs.

In 1951, Martin pitched for the Saginaw Jacks, and before joining the Minot Mallards in 1952, he pitched in the Class A Central League for the Saginaw Bears. He was a good starting pitcher for the Mallards. In 1952 his record was 3–1. In 1953 he was 6–3 and followed that in 1954 with a 7–5 record. He closed out his ManDak League career in 1955 with a 2–2 record and a 13.28 ERA.

Frank Mascaro
Outfield

Mascaro played the 1948 and 1949 seasons with the San Bernardino Pioneers in the Sunset League. He batted .354 in 1948 and .319 in 1949. In 1950, he batted .348 for Yakima in the Class B Western International League. In 1953, he batted .290 with Vancouver in the Western International League. He played well for the Brandon Greys in 1954, batting .317 with six home runs and 60 RBI.

Joe Massaro
Catcher; Height — 5'11"; Weight — 220 lbs.; Born —1926

During his years in the ManDak League, Massaro was considered to be a good defensive catcher, who could hit. He was stocky in build and a durable catcher who rarely missed a game. In 1951 he played for Richmond in the Class B Piedmont League. He joined the Minot Mallards in 1952 and led the league with 55 RBI while batting .286 with two home runs. On June 12 against Winnipeg, he hit three home runs that led to a Minot victory. In 1953 he signed with the Philadelphia Phillies organization, then quit and returned to the Mallards. He finished the season batting .305 with two home runs and 41 RBI. In 1954, he led the league again in RBI with 66 and hits with 92 and batted .325 with seven home runs. His last season with Minot was 1955, when he hit .279 with two home runs and 37 RBI. In 1957 he signed with the Williston Oilers and batted .336 with two home runs and 55 RBI.

Mack Massingale

Outfield

In 1945, Massingale played briefly in the Negro Leagues with the Kansas City Monarchs. In 1950, he joined the Carman Cardinals as he attempted a comeback, but played only briefly and returned to the United States.

Roy Mathews

Pitcher

In 1952, Matthews played for the Salisbury Pirates in the Class D North Carolina State League and led the league in victories with 20. He played briefly for Williston in 1957, and had a 1–1 record and a 9.01 ERA.

Rudy Mayling

Outfield

In 1956, Mayling led the Class B Big State League in home runs with 32 and batted .280 with 106 RBI. He played in the Kansas City A's organization and had some power at the plate. He played briefly with the Minot Mallards in 1957 and was released, then joined the Williston Oilers for the remainder of the season. He batted .211 with 10 home runs and 22 RBI.

Ed Mazur

Pitcher; Born — 1929; Died — 1995

Mazur was a star player in the Manitoba Junior and Senior Leagues. He excelled as a player with the Rosedales and St. Boniface Native Sons ball clubs in Winnipeg. Over his career, he pitched for several rural Manitoba teams. At the start of the 1954 season he pitched briefly for Carman and had a 0–1 record. He played in the National Hockey League with the Montreal Canadians and Chicago Black Hawks, and was elected to the Manitoba Baseball Hall of Fame in 1997.

Winslow Means
Pitcher

Means had no Negro League experience. He was a pitching star for the Brandon Greys in 1949 when they were in the Manitoba Senior League (over 21 years of age) and was one of their top pitchers. In 1949 he had an 18–4 record, combining all the league, playoff, and tournament games. He came back briefly in 1950 and had a 1–0 record.

Rollie Merrill
Pitcher

Merrill played four years in organized ball, from 1949 to 1952. He pitched for the Las Vegas Wranglers in the Southwest International League from 1950 to 1952. His record was 9–10. 6.36 ERA in 1950; 13–14, 4.95 ERA in 1951, and 12–13, 5.01 ERA in 1952. He joined the Winnipeg Royals in 1953 and had a 5–13 record.

Buddy Messina
Second Base; Height — 5'11"; Weight — 185 lbs.

Messina played four seasons in organized ball in the Cincinnati Reds chain. His best season was in 1951 in Class A ball with Columbia, where he batted .263, with four home runs and 17 RBI. In 1955 he batted .198, with five HR, 20 RBI with Sunbury in the Piedmont League. He joined Minot in 1957 and batted .269 with 12 home runs and 33 RBI. He was highly rated as a infielder by the Mallards. Newspaper reports stated that Shortstop Zoonie McLean and Buddy were regarded as the best double-play combination to ever play in Minot.

Jim Michalec
Pitcher

Michalec pitched 10 years in organized ball in the St. Louis Cardinals, Cincinnati Reds, and Baltimore Orioles chains. He joined the Dickinson Packers in 1955 and had a 5–7 record with a 5.33 ERA . In 1956 he was on the inactive list. In 1958 he pitched in Double-A with San Antonio in the Texas League, and recorded a 3–0 record. His last season was 1960, when he recorded a 7–6 record and a 5.17 ERA in the Mexican League. He was the brother of Vic Michalec.

Vic Michalec
Pitcher; Height — 6'1"; Weight — 175 lbs.

Vic Michalec played seven seasons in organized ball in the Cincinnati Reds chain and reached the Class B level. His best season was 1949 in the Longhorn League, where he had a 15–10 record with a 5.70 ERA. He started the 1954 season with the Tallahassee Rebels in the Florida International League and had a 0–5 record and a 4.41 ERA when he was released. He then joined the Williston Oilers and had a 6–8 record. He was back in the ManDak League in 1956 with the Dickinson Packers and had an 8–9 record and a 3.78 ERA.

STAN MILANKOVICH
Pitcher; Throws—Right

Milankovich had seven years of pro experience. In 1954 he played for St. Petersburg Saints in the Class B Florida International League and led the league with 18 victories. He then pitched for Dallas in the Texas League. He joined the Minot Mallards in 1955 and had a record of 4–2 and a 5.23 ERA.

ROLAND "ROLLIE" MILES
Infield

Rollie Miles had played with the Regina Caps in the Western Canada Baseball League and joined Minot briefly in 1951. He signed a football contract with the Green Bay Packers and then played in the Canadian Football League with the Edmonton Eskimos. He became a star in that league.

ZELL MILES
Third Base/Outfield

Zell Miles Negro League career was from 1946 to 1949. He played for the Harlem Globetrotters and the Chicago American Giants. He spent the 1947 season with the traveling Harlem Globetrotters team. He could play all outfield positions. He joined the Winnipeg Buffaloes in 1951 when the team lost players to organized ball and batted .286 with four home runs and 25 RBI. That was his only season in the league.

DON MILLER
Catcher/Outfield

Don Miller was from Bottineau, North Dakota. He attended the University of North Dakota. As a youngster, he started out as a pitcher, then switched to a position player. He played briefly in 1956 for the Minot Mallards. There were no statistics available.

BOB MILLER
Pitcher

Bob Miller played in the Cincinnati Reds organization and played in the Northern League with the Duluth Dukes. He joined the Carman Cardinals in 1954 and had a 3–6 record.

Herald Millon
Utility

In 1947, Millon was listed on the Chicago American Giants roster, but there are no records of him playing. He joined the Carman Cardinals in 1950, batted .182, and was released.

Steve Molinari

Outfield; Bats— Right; Throws— Right; Height — 5'10"; Weight —190; Born — August 13, 1931 in Boston, Massachusetts

In 1950, Molinari played for the Ada Herefords in the Sooner State League. He led the league with 39 home runs and 162 RBI and was selected to the All-Star team. Both are still league records. In 1951, he played for the Pine Bluff Judges and led the Cotton States League in RBI with 106. He was on the Baltimore Orioles roster for two years while in the service, and he joined the Williston Oilers in 1957. Early that season he was involved in a car accident when the team was returning from a game in Brandon. At the time he was batting .292 with four home runs and 17 RBI. The Oilers were counting on him to be one of their big hitters. In midseason, he tried to play, but the injury finished his career. Later that year he umpired games in the Man-Dak League and became a good umpire at the college and amateur level.

Joe Monteiro
Left Field

In 1951, Monteiro was an All-Star with Superior in the Northern League and led the league in hits with 154. In 1953 he was an All-Star again with the Richmond Colts in the Class B Piedmont League. He joined the Minot Mallards in 1955. Midway through that season he was batting .313, with 14 home runs and 51 RBI, when he jumped the club and signed with the Philadelphia organization.

Dee Moore

Catcher/Pitcher/Manager; Bats— Right; Throws— Right; Height — 5'11"; Weight —190 lbs; Born — April 6, 1914 in Hedley, Texas; Died — July 2, 1997 in Williston, North Dakota

Moore played in 96 major league games over a four-year period as a catcher. He was with the Cincinnati Reds in 1936 and 1937, and in 1936 he also pitched in two games for the Reds. In 1943 he was with the Brooklyn Dodgers and then was traded to the Philadelphia Phillies. He was up again with the Phillies in 1946. His career major league average was .232, with one home run and 22 RBI. In 1949, he was selected to the All-Star team in the Central League. In 1953, he was 39 years old when he joined the Winnipeg Royals and batted .281 with no home runs and 15 RBI. He was playing manager for Brandon in 1954 and batted .259 with three home runs and 19 RBI. He managed Williston to its only championship in 1956, and batted .250 with no home runs and three RBI in limited action. In 1957, he signed on again as playing manager for Brandon and batted .268, with no HR, eight RBI and had a 1–0 record with a 1.10 ERA on the mound. When he was in the minor leagues he was the only player to have pitched a no-hitter and caught a no-hitter. He pitched his no-hitter for Macon in the South Atlantic League on August 11, 1937. When his career was over he returned to live in Williston.

DICK MORGAN
Left Field

Morgan played seven seasons in the St. Louis Cardinals chain. In 1948 he batted .302, with 13 HR, and 79 RBI with the Willows Cardinals of the Far West League. His best season was 1949, when he batted .303, with 11 home runs and 79 RBI for the Pocatello Cardinals in the Pioneer League. He played the 1951 and 1952 seasons with the Columbus Redbirds in the American Association. He joined the Dickinson Packers in 1955 and batted .280, with six home runs and 42 RBI.

HOWARD MORGANSTERN
Outfield

Morganstern started his career in 1953 as a pitcher and had little success. He then switched to the outfield and in 1957 played briefly for the Minot Mallards after he had come to Minot and requested a tryout. He made only nine plate appearances, batting .222, and was released.

BARNEY MORRIS

Pitcher; Bats— Right; Throws— Right; Height — 6'; Weight —170 lbs; Born —1915

Morris's Negro League career was from 1932 to 1948. He pitched for several years with the New York Cubans and pitched in two Negro League All-Star games. He also played in Cuba and Mexico. He pitched briefly for the Elmwood Giants in 1951 and had a 0–2 record and was released. By that time he was at an advanced age and had lost much of his pitching skills.

CY MORTON

Shortstop; Bats— Right; Throws— Right; Height — 5'9"; Weight —165 lbs.; Died —1993 in Philadelphia, Pennsylvania

Morton's Negro League career was from 1940 to 1948. He played for the Philadelphia Stars during the 1940s and was considered an average player in all facets of the game. He played in the 1943 Negro League All-Star game. He was 28 years old when he joined the Elmwood Giants in 1950. He started the

1951 season with Elmwood, and when the Buffaloes lost players to organized ball, he joined them and batted .193. In 1953 he pitched for Grandview, Manitoba, in the Manitoba-Saskatchewan League. In 1954, he was with Rosetown in the Saskatchewan League and posted a 2–2 record.

Tom Mulcahy

Pitcher; Height — 6'2"; Weight — 180 lbs.

Mulcahy was a pitcher from the University of Washington, where he had a 10–1 record, with five shutouts, and batted .433. He played for the Lloydminster Meridians in the Western Canada League in 1954 and in one game recorded 15 strikeouts. He finished the season with a 2–4 record. He joined the Williston Oilers in 1955 and had a 7–5 record with a 5.26 ERA.

Billy Munyer

Catcher

Munyer played college ball for Jamestown (North Dakota), and was pressed into service with the Williston Oilers for one game in 1957. Joe Massaro, the Oilers' regular catcher, was injured and there was no backup. The newspaper reported that Munyer played well behind the plate, but had no hits in two appearances.

John Murray

Pitcher

John Murray, a left-hander, was a local Carman, Manitoba, player. He pitched in 1954 for the Carman Cardinals and had a 0–3 record. Following that year he continued to play with Carman in the local Manitoba Senior League.

Mal Murray

Pitcher

Murray was a 19-year-old right-handed pitcher when he joined Minot in 1952. He was recommended to the Minot Mallards by Ben Cain, Sugar Cain's brother. Ben was the manager of the Philadelphia Meteors in a semi-pro Negro League. Murray had an 8–1 record for the Meteors. His record for Minot in 1952 was 5–3 and in 1953 he was 2–1. In mid–June of 1953 he left the team to serve in the military.

Pedro Naranjo

Pitcher; Bats — Right; Throws — Left; Height — 5'10½"; Weight — 180 lbs.; Born — 1932

Naranjo played for the Indianapolis Clowns in 1950. Midway through the season he jumped to the Brandon Greys and had a 3–2 record. He was 20 years old when he came north. In 1951 he was back with Brandon and pitched well for the Greys, posting a 4–1 record. He went into organized ball in 1952 with Decatur in the Mississippi–Ohio Valley League and had his best season. His record was 13–10, with a 2.83 ERA. He played two more seasons in organized ball, with less success.

GENE NELSON
Pitcher

Nelson played five seasons in the Chicago Cubs organization. He reached Class B in the Three-I League with the Cedar Rapids Indians. In 1953, he had an 11–14 record with a 4.33 ERA with the Sioux Falls Canaries in the Northern League. He joined Bismarck in 1956 and had a 3–1 record and a 4.10 ERA.

FRANK NERI
Outfield

Neri started in organized ball in 1948 and played as high as Class B ball. He played in the Milwaukee Braves and Philadelphia Phillies chains and was a .240 hitter with little power. He joined the Bismarck Barons in 1957 and did the best hitting of his career, batting .283 with 11 HR, 30 RBI. He played the 1958 and 1959 seasons with the Saskatoon Gems and Moose Jaw in the Western Canada League. In 1958 he batted .272, four HR, 21 RBI and .288, one HR, 15 RBI in 1959. He played his last season in organized ball in 1960 in the Alabama-Florida League.

JIM NEWBERRY

Pitcher; Bats— Both; Throws— Right; Height — 5'7"; Weight —170 lbs.; Born —1922 in Birmingham, Alabama

Newberry's Negro League career was from 1942 to 1950. He had a good fastball and curve. In 1948 he had a 15–5 record for the Birmingham Black Barons. In 1950, at age 28, he joined the Winnipeg Buffaloes and had a 7–7 record. That year he was the pitching star for the Buffaloes in the playoffs, appearing in three winning games. In 1951 he was back with the Buffaloes and had a 6–3 record. In 1952, he pitched in Japan for the Hankyu Braves and had a 11–10 record and a 3.22 ERA, then came back to Carman for the 1953 season and had a 5–9 record. In 1955 he had his best season in organized ball with a record of 6–4 and a 5.01 ERA with the Port Arthur Sea Hawks in the Big State League. He closed out his career in 1959 in the Western Canada Baseball League where he pitched very briefly for Lloydminster and had a 0–0 record. That was his last season in baseball.

Chuck Orner
Catcher

Orner started in organized ball in 1950 and played five years in the Philadelphia A's organization. He played two years in Class A and two more in Class B. He was a good defensive catcher. His best season was in 1953 at Fayetteville, where he hit .316. He joined the Minot Mallards in midseason of 1956 and batted .265 with four home runs and 20 RBI and led all catchers with a .994 fielding average. He was back with the Mallards in 1957 and batted .275, with two home runs and 28 RBI.

Don Orwiler
Pitcher

Orwiler was a left-handed curveball specialist who played in the New York Yankees organization. He had a 1–6 record with an 8.17 ERA record with the Dickinson Packers in 1955, and left the team to pitch in the Big State League, where he set the record for the most complete games with 29. He was back in organized baseball in 1956 and was an All-Star in the Class C California League with the Modesto Reds. He returned briefly to the Brandon Greys in 1957 and left the team midway through the season to go back to organized baseball. In 1958 he was an All-Star in the Class C Pioneer League with the Missoula Timberjacks.

Bill Oster

Pitcher; Bats—Left; Throws—Left; Height—6'3"; Weight—198 lbs.; Born—January 2, 1933 in New York, New York

Oster appeared in eight games for the Philadelphia A's in 1954 and his record was 0–1, with a 6.32 ERA. He joined the Minot Mallards in 1956 at age 23 and had a 1–2 record with a 5.82 ERA. He won two games in the playoffs that year including a 3–1 four-hitter against Williston in the championship series. He was back with Minot in 1957 and pitched well, recording a 9–5 record with a 4.27 ERA.

Buddy Owens
Shortstop

Owens played third base for the Chicago American Giants in 1951 and after the season started, jumped to the Winnipeg Buffaloes and batted .244 with three home runs and 13 RBI. He returned to the Negro Leagues in 1952 with the Chicago American Giants.

Satchel Paige

Pitcher; Bats—Right; Throws—Right; Height—6'3½"; Weight—180 lbs.; Born—July 7, 1906 in Mobile, Alabama; Died—June 8, 1982 in Kansas City, Mo.

Paige pitched with success in the major leagues with the Cleveland Indians and St. Louis Browns. He did not commit an error in 179 major league games. He was signed by the Minot Mallards at the start of the 1950 season to pitch in parts of their first three games. This was done to increase fan interest. He didn't disappoint, as he pitched three innings in each game, giving up three hits and striking out 13. In the first game against Carman, he pitched three innings and gave up two doubles and struck out two and no runs. His second start was an exhibition game against Moorhead, Minnesota, and he struck out four in three scoreless innings. His last appearance was against Brandon, in which he gave up just one hit and struck out seven in three innings. The stadium was packed, and it was a good start for Minot and the ManDak League. Paige was 44 years old at the time.

In 1963 and 1964, Paige involved in a bit of a mystery. The Satchel Paige All-Stars and the Kansas City Monarchs barnstormed across the United Sates and Canada. The Paige name could still draw fans to the ballparks. The July 9, 1963, *Williston Herald* newspaper headlines read, "Paige And Paige Combine To Stop the Headliners, 5–1." The report stated that the second Paige was Satchel's son. In that game and at 57 years of age, the senior Paige pitched two shutout innings and Satchel Jr., pitched the last seven innings to record the victory for the All-Stars.

After reading the game report, this author wondered what kind of career Satchel Jr. had. I put the question out on the SABR bulletin board, with no results. Normally, SABR members are a good source of information, but even they were stumped. I then asked Negro League historian James A. Riley about Satchel Jr. He stated that it couldn't have been Satchel's son, as he was only 12 years old at the time. Then who was this mystery pitcher? The question was answered in a 1963 article in the Saskatoon, Saskatchewan, newspaper written by sports writer Dave Shurey. The article stated, "In 1963 Satchel pitched one inning and the remainder of the game was pitched by a lanky right hander who Satchel passed off as his son, Satchel Jr. In reality it was Sherman Cottingham."

In 1964, Paige joined the Monarchs as they closed out their barnstorming days. Satchel was once again the drawing card with Satchel Jr. finishing up the games. Rex Jones, who played on that team, told me that first baseman Leroy Doster played the part of Satchel's son that season. From those two sources, the mystery of Satchel Paige's son was solved.

FRED PARKER
Pitcher; Height: 6'4"; Weight: 206 lbs.

Fred Parker was a right-handed pitcher who played in the Cleveland Indians and New York Giants chains. In 1951 he was 8–4 with Odessa in the Longhorn League and in 1952 he played for Grand Forks in the Northern League. Parker was given the name of "Fireman Fred" for his outstanding relief work during the 1955 season. He was 27 years old and pitched for Minot and the Williston Oilers in 1954, and finished the season with a 3–7 record. In 1956 he was with Williston again and had a 2–5 record with a 5.68 ERA.

TOM PARKER

Pitcher Bats—Right; Throws—Right; Height—6'1"; Weight—210 lbs.; Born—1911 in Alexandria, Louisiana

Tom Parker's Negro League career was from 1929 to 1949, mostly with the New York Black Yankees. Over his long career he had some pitching success in the Negro Leagues and could throw every pitch. He joined the Elmwood Giants in 1951 at age 40. In 1951, his record was 5–2 and he followed that with a 5–3 record in 1952. In 1953, he signed on with Brandon Greys, for whom his record was 6–4. Even at his advanced age he still threw well.

PAT PATTERSON

Infield; Bats—BothThrows—Right; Height—5'11"; Weight—185 lbs.; Born—December 19, 1911 in Chicago, Illinois

Pat Patterson's Negro League career was from 1934 to 1949. He played on several Negro League teams. He played in four Negro league All-Star games. He was a switch-hitter who hit over .300 most seasons, and was regarded as one of the best Negro League third basemen during the early 1940's. He played briefly for the Elmwood Giants in 1950 at 39 years of age, and batted .253 with one home run and six RBI.

WILLIE PATTERSON

Utility

Willie Patterson's Negro League career was from 1950 to 1953. He was a catcher for the Birmingham Black Barons when he joined the Minot Mallards in August of 1955 and batted .286, with one home run and 13 RBI.

CARL PAYLOR

Third Base

Paylor played seven years in organized baseball. In 1953, he was with the Ogden Reds and batted .315 with three HR, 76 RBI. In 1956 he toured with the Nellie Fox All-Stars. The team played seven exhibition games and won all of them. Some of the major leaguers on that team were, Elroy Face, Ronnie Kline, Dick Groat, and Chuck Tanner. Paylor played most of his career in the Pioneer League. He played two seasons for the Williston Oilers. In 1956 he batted .348 with 1 HR, 22 RBI, and in 1957 batted .298, with 10 HR, 39 RBI.

JIMMY PEET

Pitcher

Peet was a left hander who joined the Minot Mallards in 1950 at age 17.

He had a 2–2 record, quit the team in early July, and went into organized baseball. In 1955, he pitched for Tucson in the Arizona-Mexico League and led the league with 24 wins and 322 strikeouts. His strikeouts were a record for that league.

CHARLES PEETE

Outfield; Bats— Left; Throws— Right; Height — 5'9½"; Weight —190 lbs.; Born — February 22, 1926 in Franklin, Virginia; Died —1956 in Caracas, Venezuela

Peete started the 1950 season with the Indianapolis Clowns. Midway through the season he jumped to the Brandon Greys and batted .220 with two home runs and 14 RBI. He was 21 years old. In 1954, he was an All-Star with Portsmouth in the Piedmont League and led that league with 174 hits. In 1955 and 1956, he played two seasons of Triple-A with Rochester and Omaha. In 1956 at Omaha, he was an All-Star and batting champion with a .350 average. That led to a brief appearance at the end of the season with the St. Louis Cardinals. He appeared in 23 games and batted .192, with no HR and 6 RBI. The Cardinals were expecting him to make the club in 1957, but that winter he and his family died in a plane crash on his way to winter ball in Venezuela.

ART PENNINGTON

Infield/Outfield; Bats— Both; Throws— Right; Height — 5'11"; Weight —185 lbs.; Born — May 18, 1923 in Memphis, Tennessee

Pennington's Negro League career was from 1940 to 1950. He had the nickname of "Superman." He was a good hitter with power, and a two-time Negro League All-Star. He played in Mexico and Venezuela. He played organized baseball in 1952 for the Keokuk Kernels and led the Class B Three-I League with a .349 average. He also led the league in runs scored with 126 and was named to the All-Star team. He joined the Bismarck Barons in 1955 and batted .349 with 11 home runs and 46 RBI. In 1956, again with Bismarck, he finished second in batting at .357, with 10 HR and 51 RBI. Statistics indicate that he was successful no matter which league he played in. He retired in 1959.

MIKE PEREZ

Catcher Born — Cuba

Perez was rated as a good receiver. He would always return to Cuba when the season was over. In those years there were no restrictions placed on Cuban players. In 1956, he joined the Bismarck Barons and batted .275 with no home runs and 26 RBI. He was back with Bismarck in 1957 and batted .217 with no home runs and 14 RBI. In the early 1960s he was manager and catcher for the touring Havana Cuban Giants. The showpiece of that team was Satchel Paige.

Alonzo Perry

Pitcher/Outfield; Bats— Both; Throws— Right; Height — 6'3"; Weight —190 lbs.; Born — April 14, 1923 in Birmingham, Alabama

Perry's Negro League career was from 1946 to 1950. He was originally a pitcher, but because of his hitting he became an everyday player. In 1949 he played for Oakland in the Pacific Coast League. In 1951, he started the season with Syracuse in the International League, then jumped to the Brandon Greys. He was 28 years old when he joined the Greys. He was batting .397 with five home runs and 19 RBI, when midway through the season he left to go to the Dominican Republic for a reported $1500 a month. For several years he played in Mexico and led that league in many offensive departments. He was a three-time All-Star in the Dominican Republic, 1955–57. With so much success on the field, one has to wonder why he never made it to the major leagues, although it was said he had questionable off-field activities.

Don Petschow

First Base; Height — 6'1"; Weight —190 lbs.; Born —1928

In 1949, Petschow led the Class D Rio Grande Valley League with 146 RBI and 28 home runs while playing for the Corpus Christi Aces. He reached the Class B level and was regarded as a power hitter in every league he played. He played in Mankato, Minnesota, in the Southern Minnie League in 1953 and 1954, and batted .375 and .319. He joined the Minot Mallards in 1955, and after suffering a broken elbow in midseason, he was released. When he healed, he finished the season with the Dickinson Packers. He batted .310 with 15 home runs and 40 RBI for the Packers.

Dan Phalen

First base

In 1949 and 1950, Phalen was an All-Star in the Class C Cotton States League. In 1952, he was an All-Star in the Northern League and in 1953 in the Class B Three-I League. He played in the St. Louis Browns and Chicago White Sox organizations. He played briefly with Williston in 1956 and batted .118 with two home runs and 7 RBI.

Frank Pickens

Pitcher

Pickens had no Negro League experience. He had played for the Louisiana Travelers barnstorming team and was signed as a replacement player by the Minot Mallards in 1950. He had a 0–1 record.

JOE PIERCEY
Pitcher

Piercey, a left hander, was a 14-year minor league veteran. Before joining Minot in 1956, he pitched with Houston in the Texas League. He played in Triple-A with San Francisco. With Minot, he had a 1–2 record with a 4.02 ERA in 1956. While with Minot, he requested more money, which the executive of the Mallards refused, and Piercey was released and returned to organized ball. In 1957, he pitched in the semi-pro Basin League in South Dakota

LENNY PIGG

Catcher; Bats—Right; Throws—Right; Height—5'9"; Weight 230 lbs.; Born—September 18, 1919 in Grant, Oklahoma

Pigg's Negro League career was from 1947 to 1949, and 1951. He played in Havana in 1947, then joined the Indianapolis Clowns, for whom he was a good-hitting catcher. He was 31 years old when he joined the Brandon Greys in 1950. He batted .273 with no home runs and five RBI. The Chicago White Sox tried to sign him in 1951, but he opted to stay in the Negro Leagues. In 1953, he played for Bowsman, Manitoba, in the Manitoba-Saskatchewan League.

BILL PINCKARD
Outfield

Pinckard had an 11-year minor league career and played as high as Double-A ball, In 1952, he hit 35 home runs and drove in 108 runs in the Class A Western League. He played briefly for Minot in 1954 and batted .348 with one home run and 11 RBI. He then left the Mallards and went back to California in August due to sickness in his family and did not return. He closed out his career in organized ball in 1960.

FELIX PINE
Pitcher

In 1953, Pine pitched briefly during the season and playoffs for the Carman Cardinals. He had a 1–2 record and was not invited back for the next season. In 1954 he returned to the Negro Leagues with the Detroit Stars.

ANDY PORTER

Pitcher; Bats—Right; Throws—Right; Height—6'4"; Weight—190 lbs.; Born—March 7, 1911 in Little Rock, Arkansas

Porter's Negro League career was from 1932 to 1950, with several teams. He pitched with success in the Mexican League from 1939 to 1943. He joined the Winnipeg Buffaloes in 1950 at the age of 39 and had a 5–4 record. In 1952, he pitched in organized baseball with Porterville in the South West League and had a 3–5 record. He finished his career in 1953 with the Carman Cardinals and had a 4–4 record. In 1998, his name was placed on a wall of honor at Milwaukee's County Stadium dedicated to the Negro League players.

JERRY POWELL
Shortstop

Powell joined the Winnipeg Giants in 1952 and batted .211 with one home run and 4 RBI. In 1955, he bounced around organized ball between Visalia, Fargo-Moorhead and Yakima, and played with little success.

AL PRESTON

Pitcher; Bats—Right; Throws—Right; Height—6'1"; Weight—170 lbs.; Born—June 26, 1926 in New York, New York; Died—1979 in New York, New York

Preston pitched in the Negro leagues in 1943, 1946 and 1949. He pitched for the New York Black Yankees, Baltimore Elite Giants, and Chicago American Giants. In 1947, he played organized ball with Stamford in the Colonial League and had a 2–3 record with a 4.59 ERA. In 1949, he started the season with the New York Black Yankees, then left to finish the season in Canada with the Elmwood Giants in the Manitoba Senior League. He was 24 years old in 1950, when he joined the Elmwood Giants for their first ManDak League season. He had a 2–2 record. He closed out his career in 1953 with the Carman Cardinals, for whom his record was 4–5.

HAL PRICE
Pitcher

Price had no Negro League experience. He was an import with the Elmwood Giants in 1949 in the Manitoba Senior Baseball League, and was a very good pitcher. He was fondly known as "Prince Hal" and was a fierce competitor with a good pickoff move to first base. He was picked up by Brandon for the 1949 Indian Head, Saskatchewan, Tournament and won the first game. In 1950 and 1951, he played for the Sceptre Panthers in the Saskatchewan League. In a June 1950 tournament in Medicine Hat, Alberta, he was selected as the All-Star pitcher. He played for the Winnipeg Giants in 1952 and had a 10–5 record. His 10 wins and 130 strikeouts led the league. He was regarded as the Giants' best pitcher. He played with success for several teams in Western Canada.

TED "DOUBLE DUTY" RADCLFFE

Catcher/Pitcher/Manager; Bats—Right; Throws—Right; Height—5'10"; Weight—190 lbs.; Born—July 7, 1902 in Mobile, Alabama

Radcliffe was given his nickname by Damon Runyon for his ability to catch one game and pitch the next. His Negro League career was from 1928 to 1950. He was a colorful player and a star for many teams. He was a dangerous hitter and a good pitcher. He played in six Negro League All-Star games and was the Negro American League MVP in 1943. He joined the Elmwood Giants in 1951 as playing manager and saw limited action on the field. He did have a 2–0 record as a pitcher. He also managed the Giants briefly in 1952 and was let go when the team got off to a poor start. Radcliffe is another player who could warrant being chosen for Baseball's Hall of Fame.

BILL RAEHSE
First Base; Height — 6'4"; Weight — 195 lbs.; Born — 1931

The *Williston Herald* reported Raehse to be a great glove man, a terrific hitter, and a fierce competitor. He had played in the Cincinnati Reds organization and had reached Triple-A ball. He played organized ball from 1945 until joining Williston in 1955. In 1955 with the Oilers, he batted .323 with eight home runs and 59 RBI, and in 1956 batted .329, with 17 home runs and 60 RBI. When that season was over, he joined the Nellie Fox All-Stars made up of mostly major league players. In 1957 with Williston, he batted .326 and led the league with 19 home runs and 88 RBI. His RBI total was the all-time ManDak League record. He started the 1958 season with Louisville in the American Association and batted .071, and finished that season with Knoxville in the South Atlantic League, where he batted .293 with one home run and nine RBI.

JOE RANCHER
Pitcher

Rancher started his career in 1939 with Trenton in the Inter-State League and batted .275, with six HR and 45 RBI, and in 1941 pitched briefly for Trenton. In 1950, he was with Paris in the Mississippi–Ohio Valley League and had an 8–10 record with a 4.40 ERA. He played briefly with Dickinson in 1955 and was 0–1 with a 5.25 ERA.

HICKEY REDD
Infield

Redd played in the Negro Leagues in 1940 and 1941 with the Birmingham Black Barons. In 1949, he joined the Elmwood Giants as an import player when the Giants were in the Manitoba Senior League. He played for the Elmwood Giants in 1950 and batted .272. He returned to the Negro Leagues in 1951 and 1952 with the Chicago American Giants.

DOLPH REGELSKY
Shortstop; Height — 6'3"; Weight — 205 lbs.; Born — 1930

Regelsky played in the Chicago Cubs organization and was with Macon in the Sally League and Des Moines in the Western League in 1948. In 1953, he played for the Meridian Millers in the Class C Cotton States League and was voted to the All-Star team. He spent the 1954 season with Little Rock in the Southern Association, and hit .257 with 26 doubles, six triples and 15 home runs. He was considered to be a very good hitter with power and an outstanding defensive shortstop. He was always a home run threat. He joined Williston in 1956 and won the batting championship with a .362 average, with 19 home runs and 68 RBI.

Don Reid

Pitcher

Reid had been a star with the Winnipeg Rosedales junior team in Winnipeg. He pitched briefly for the Carman Cardinals in 1950, had a 0–3 record, and was released.

Othello Renfroe

Catcher/Shortstop/Second Base/Outfield; Bats—Right; Throws—Right; Height—5'11"; Weight—175 lbs.; Born—March 1, 1923 in Newark, New Jersey; Died—September 3, 1991 in Atlanta, Georgia

Renfroe was a versatile player who played for the Kansas City Monarchs and the Satchel Paige All-Stars. He played winter ball in Mexico and Venezuela. In 1950, he was the most valuable player in the Mexican League with Torreon, where he batted .327. He was 28 when he joined the Minot Mallards in 1951. He batted .298 with three home runs and 15 RBI. In 1952, Renfroe was back in the Negro Leagues with the Kansas City Monarchs. He returned to Minot in 1953 and batted .275, with three home runs and 44 RBI, and followed that by hitting .349, with three HR and 39 RBI in 1954. In later years, he was a scout for the Montreal Expos.

Harry Rhodes, Carman Cardinals (courtesy of Dufferin Historical Museum of Carman, Manitoba).

Harry "Lefty" Rhodes

Pitcher/Outfield; Height—5'9"; Weight—169 lbs.; Bats—Left; Throws—Left

Rhodes played in the Negro Leagues in 1942, and from 1946 to

1950 with the Chicago American Giants. He joined the Carman Cardinals in 1952 and had a 3–3 record. He was back with Carman again in 1953, and had a 8–4 record. He pitched with some success for the Cardinals.

MURRAY RICHARDSON

Pitcher; Throws— Left; Height — 6'½"; Weight —185 lbs.; Born —1927

Murray Richardson played in the Brooklyn Dodgers system. The Dodgers sent him to Vero Beach in 1948 and he had a 13–6 record with a 3.70 ERA. From 1949 to 1951, he played in Johnstown, Greenwood, Newport News, and Danville in the Dodgers' chain and pitched with success at each stop. In 1949, he was an All-Star with the Johnstown Johnnies in the Mid-Atlantic League. In 1952, he joined the Carman Cardinals and had a 4–4 record. He also played for the Minot Mallards in 1954 and 1955, and in both seasons he had a 1–0 record. One of the better Manitoba-born pitchers, he was elected to the Manitoba Baseball Hall of Fame in 1997.

T.W. (TED) RICHARDSON

Pitcher

Ted Richardson's Negro League career was in 1951, and from 1953 to 1954. He played for the Indianapolis Clowns, Birmingham Black Barons, Memphis Red Sox, and Louisville Black Colonels, when the Negro Leagues were in decline. He played for the Brandon Greys in 1952 and had a 5–2 record. This was his only season in the league. He played organized ball from 1956 to 1958. In 1959 and 1960 he played for Lloydminster in the Western Canada Baseball League, where his record was 11–5 with a 2.93 ERA in his last season.

WELDON RIDLEY

Catcher/Second Base

From Morden, Manitoba, Ridley was a very versatile player who played briefly with the Carman Cardinals in 1952 and 1954. He batted .065 in 1952 and .222 with three home runs and 19 RBI in 1954.

BOB RITTENBERG

Third Base

Rittenberg played in the Philadelphia Phillies organization. In 1950, he batted .293 with the Klamath Falls Gems in the Class D Far West League. That earned him a promotion the next season to the Salt Lake City Bees in the Class C Pioneer League. He joined the Winnipeg Royals in 1953 and batted .260 with one home run and 40 RBI.

Frazier Robinson, Winnipeg Buffaloes. Note the Manitoba Parliament building in the background (courtesy of Winnie Robinson).

FRAZIER ROBINSON

Catcher; Bats—Right; Throws—Right; Height—5'11"; Weight—178 lbs.; Born—May 30, 1916 in Birmingham, Alabama; Died—1997 in Kings Mountain, North Carolina

Frazier Robinson's Negro League career was from 1942 to 1949. He was a good defensive catcher and a fair hitter with some pop in his bat. He played for several teams in the Negro Leagues. He started playing professionally with Satchel Paige, and Frazier's wife, Winnie, said that the two players remained lifelong friends. He was 34 years old when he joined the Winnipeg Buffaloes in 1950. He batted .278 with no home runs and 19 RBI. He followed that with an average of .318, with one home run and 37 RBI in 1951. In 1952, when the Buffaloes ceased operation, he joined his brother Norm Robinson with the Brandon Greys and batted .253 with no home runs and 13 RBI. He retired at the end of that season.

NORM ROBINSON
Outfield; Bats—Right; Throws—Right; Born—April 1, 1918 in Oklahoma City, Oklahoma

Norm Robinson's Negro League career was from 1939 to 1950 with the Baltimore Elite Giants and Birmingham Black Barons. He was a good defensive player with speed on the field. He played on the Satchel Paige All-Stars in 1939 with his brother Frazier and hit over .300 several times in the Negro Leagues. He was 34 years old in 1952 when he joined his brother with the Brandon Greys and batted .276, with one home run and 27 RBI. In 1953 he switched to the Carman Cardinals and batted .325 with one home run and 35 RBI. He retired from baseball after that season.

O. B. ROBISON
Pitcher

Robison had no Negro League experience. He joined the Winnipeg Buffaloes in 1951 and had a 4–2 record. He was considered to be a very good pitcher for the Buffaloes.

MICKEY ROCCO
First base; Bats—Left; Throws—Left; Height—5'11"; Weight—188 lbs.; Born—March 2, 1916 in St. Paul, Minnesota;

Rocco had a long minor league career from 1937 to 1950 and was one of the most feared sluggers in the Pacific Coast League with the Seattle Rainiers. He played 440 games over his four major league seasons with the Cleveland Indians during the war. He was a smooth fielder and in his four major league seasons he batted .240, 5 HR, 46 RBI in 1943; .266, 13 HR, 70 RBI in 1944; .264, 10 HR, 56 RBI in 1945, and .245, 2 HR, 14 RBI in 1946. In 1944 he led the Indians with 653 at-bats and also participated in 158 double plays. In 1943 he led the Indians with a .995 fielding percentage. In 1953, he was 37 years old and started the season with Minot, then was released and joined the Winnipeg Royals. He was making too much money for Minot to keep him. It was reported that he was making $1,000 a month and was one of the highest-paid players in the ManDak League. With the Royals he batted .298 and hit 12 home runs.

RAMON RODRIGUEZ
Catcher

Rodriguez was from Cuba. He played for the Brandon Greys in 1949 in the Manitoba Senior League and batted .293. He was back with Brandon in its first season in the ManDak League and batted .257, with one home run and 31 RBI. In 1951, he batted .269 with one home run and 23 RBI. After the 1951 season, he went into organized baseball. In 1959 he was selected to the All-Star team in the Mexican League.

FRANK ROELANDT
Catcher; Height — 5'10"; Weight — 180 lbs.

Roelandt played with Boise in the Pioneer League in 1951. In 1954 he played with the Oregon Elks semi-pro team, where he batted .340. During his career he played for several Oregon semi-pro teams. He was 30 years old when he joined the Williston Oilers in 1955. He batted .300 with three home runs and 30 RBI.

JESSIE ROGERS
Outfield

Rogers signed with the New York Giants in 1953 and was assigned to Oshkosh of the Class D Wisconsin League. He played as high as Class A ball. In 1954 he played for St. Cloud in the Northern League and batted .307 with 23 home runs. That earned him an All-Star selection. The following season, with Johnstown in the Eastern League, he batted .299 with 13 home runs. He joined the Minot Mallards in 1957 and led them with 14 home runs and 66 RBI. He batted .363. Three times he hit three home runs in a game and in one game he drove in six runs.

BILL "RED" ROSE
Pitcher

Rose played in the New York Yankees organization, and in 1946, with Fond du Lac in the Wisconsin State League, he set a league record with 16 wins in a row on his way to a 17–1 record. He joined the Brandon Greys in 1954 and had a 7–5 record. In 1955, he signed with the Dickinson Packers and had a 10–10 record and a 4.65 ERA. He was back with the Packers in 1956 as playing manager and had a record of 1–4 with a 6.09 ERA.

BOB ROUS
Outfield

Rous played six seasons in organized ball, in the Chicago White Sox chain. In 1955 he had his best season, with the Superior Blues in the Northern League where he batted .277, with 15 HR and 86 RBI. His statistics indicated that he did not hit for a high average at most of his minor league stops. He was on the inactive list in 1957 when he joined the Brandon Greys. In 1959, he was back in organized ball, and in 1960 played briefly for Sacramento in the Pacific Coast League.

Eldon Russell
Pitcher

Russell, a right hander, pitched for Lincoln in the Class A Western League in 1954. In 1955, he started the season with Wichita in the same league and had a 3–1 record. He jumped the club and signed with the Dickinson Packers, for whom he had a 1–0 record.

Norm Rynard
Pitcher

Rynard started his career in 1950 with St. Cloud in the Northern League and had a record of 3–3, with a 4.06 ERA. He pitched as high as Class A ball with Wichita in the Western League. His last season in organized baseball was in 1954. He then joined the Dickinson Packers in 1955 and had a 1–1 record with a 5.63 ERA.

Terry Sawchuk
First Base; Height — 5'11"; Weight —195; Born — December 28, 1929 in Winnipeg, Manitoba; Died — May 31, 1970

Sawchuk had been a star player in the local Winnipeg Senior League. In 1949 he batted .313 with the Elmwood Giants. He was a good hitter and fielder. He played briefly for the Elmwood Giants in 1950 when they were waiting for the import players to arrive from the United States. Sawchuk is best known as a star goaltender for many years in the National Hockey League. He is in the Hockey Hall of Fame.

Dean Scarborough
Outfield/First Base; Height — 5'11"; Weight —170 lbs.; Born —1923

Scarborough was signed by the New York Yankees, and in 1946 played at Binghamton in the Eastern League. In 1947, he played in the Pacific Coast League with the Hollywood Stars. He played Double-A ball with Little Rock in the Southern League. He was the Southern Minnesota League batting champion from 1950 to 1953 and batted .404 (1950), .419 (1951), .438 (1952). He joined the Minot Mallards in 1953 and was the batting champion with a .356 average. He hit 2 home runs and had 17 RBI. He batted .328 with two HR, 60 RBI in 1954, .289, 2 HR, 42 RBI in 1955, and .386, 1 HR, 6 RBI in 1956. He did a little pitching for the Mallards when they were short of arms and in 1954 had a 1–2 record.

Sam Scarpone

Catcher

Scarpone was from the same home town as Bismarck manager Al Cihocki, who brought Scarpone to Bismarck as his backup catcher in 1955. Scarpone saw limited action, batting .241 with no home runs and 17 RBI.

Hal Schacker

Pitcher; Bats—Right; Throws—Right; Height—6'; Weight—190 lbs.; Born—April 6, 1925 in Brooklyn, New York

In 1945, Schacker pitched in six games with the Boston Braves and had a 0–1 record, six strikeouts and nine walks, and a 5.28 ERA. That was his only season in the majors. In 1948, he was voted to the All-Star team in the Florida International League. He pitched in Triple-A with Indianapolis in the American Association. He was 26 when he joined the Minot Mallards in 1951 and had a 4–4 record.

Jack Schaefer

First Base/Outfield

Schaefer played with Grand Forks in the Northern League and Evansville and Quincy in the Three-I League. In 1949 with Grand Forks, he batted .296 with one home run and 68 RBI. He joined Carman in 1950 and batted .322 with one home run and 15 RBI. In 1951, he batted .321 with three home runs and 19 RBI. He was the Carman Cardinals manager in 1952, and batted .280 with one home run and 18 RBI. He was regarded as a very good defensive player.

Dick Schoonover

Pitcher; Height—6'1"; Weight—185; Born—1921

Schoonover played organized baseball from 1949 to 1953 and was in the Philadelphia A's and Cincinnati Reds chains. In 1953 he pitched in the Class A South Atlantic League for the Columbia Reds and had a 1–0 record. He joined the Williston Oilers in 1954 and had a 6–5 record. He had an 8–10 record in 1955 with a 3.67 ERA, which was sixth best in the league.

Mike Schultz

Pitcher

Schultz from Wells, Minnesota, reached Double-A with Little Rock in the Southern Association. During his career, he pitched for the Grand Forks Chiefs in the Northern League and played in the Class A Eastern League from 1953 to 1955. He joined the Minot Mallards in 1956 and had a 2–1 record with a 4.63 ERA.

Frank Schwartz
Pitcher

Schwartz started in organized ball in 1946 with Watertown in the Border League and had record of 3–7, with a 3.53 ERA. He played in the Border League again in 1949 and had a record of 10–5, with a 4.60 ERA. He pitched as high as Class C ball. He joined the Bismarck Barons in 1957 and had a 7–6 record and a 5.09 ERA.

Bill Sharp
Second Base; Height — 5'10"; Weight —170 lbs.

Sharp was considered to be a terrific fielder. He broke into pro ball in 1950 after coming out of the army and played Class A, B, and C ball. He joined the Williston Oilers in 1955 and batted .271 with five home runs and 31 RBI. He would bat .300, 0 HR, 18 RBI in 1956 and .347, 1 HR, 18 RBI in 1957. Over his three seasons he was a solid player for the Oilers.

Bert Shepard
Pitcher; Bats— Left; Throws— Left; Height — 5'11"; Weight —185 lbs.;
Born — June 28, 1920 in Dana, Indiana

Bert Shepard lost a foot in World War II while flying a P-38 fighter plane. In 1945, as a 25-year-old, he pitched one game for the Washington Senators. In five innings he gave up three hits and had a 1.69 ERA in a no-decision game. He was an inspiration to all wartime amputees. At several tournaments in North Dakota and Western Canada, he was a drawing card for barnstorming teams. He pitched very briefly for Williston at the start of the 1954 season and had no decisions.

Fred Shepard
Pitcher/Outfield; Bats— Right; Throws— Right

Fred Shepard's Negro League career was from 1945 to 1948, with the Atlanta Black Crackers, Birmingham Black Barons, and Chicago American Giants. He joined the Minot Mallards in 1950 as a replacement player from the Louisiana Travelers barnstorming team and batted .222 with no home runs and four RBI. That was his last season in baseball.

Jim Shupe
Infield

In 1954, Shupe was released early in the season by the Winnipeg Goldeyes in the Northern League. At the time, he was batting .167. He then signed with Brandon and played briefly, and again was released.

Ray Sisler

Catcher

In 1953, Sisler played with little success for Bakersfield of the California League, batting .114, with no HR, and six RBI. He joined Brandon in 1954 at the start of the season and was released.

Don Smith

Utility

Don Smith was from Minot, and played for Minot State Teacher's College. He played semi-pro ball with LaCrosse, Wisconsin, in the Western Wisconsin League. When injuries hit the Minot club in 1956, he joined the team. He had a 0–1 record with a 5.07 ERA as a pitcher, and batted .208 with two home runs and four RBI. In 1957, he again played briefly, batting .218 with one home run and 14 RBI. Following that season, he closed out his career with Williston when the Oilers were in the Western Canada Baseball League.

Gene Smith

Pitcher; Bats— Both; Throws— Right; Height — 6'1"; Weight —185 lbs.

Gene Smith's Negro League career was from 1939 to 1950, for several Negro League teams. Smith pitched three no-hitters in the Negro Leagues. He also played in Mexico and in Puerto Rico. He was very dangerous at the plate, and with Carman, he played the outfield when not pitching. He played for the Carman Cardinals in 1951 and had a 3–5 record on the mound and batted .325, with five home runs and 16 RBI.

Henry Smith

Second Base; Bats— Right; Throws— Right; Height — 5'9"; Weight — 161; Born —1914 in Houston, Texas

Henry Smith's Negro League career was from 1942 to 1947, for several Negro League teams. He was a .250 hitter at best. He was 36 years old when he joined the Minot Mallards in 1950 and batted .229 with no home runs and 6 RBI. That was his only season in the league.

Jay Smith

Pitcher/Outfield

Jay Smith played semi-pro ball in New Jersey before briefly joining the Williston Oilers in 1957 as an outfielder and pitcher. His pitching record was 0–1 with a 6.23 ERA.

Taylor Smith
Pitcher

Taylor Smith had a Negro League career from 1948 to 1949 and 1952 to 1953. He pitched for the Chicago American Giants and Birmingham Black Barons. He joined the Winnipeg Buffaloes in 1950 and had an 8–6 record. He returned to the Buffaloes in 1951, but did not pitch with the same success, recording a 3–10 record. In 1952 he returned to the Negro Leagues.

Cy Snead

Outfield/Shortstop, Second base; Bats—Right; Throws—Right; Height—5'10"; Weight—170 lbs.

Snead's Negro League career was from 1939 to 1946, with the Ethiopian Clowns, Kansas City Monarchs, Cincinnati Clowns, and New York Black Yankees. He was described as an average hitter and infielder. In 1949, he played for Elmwood in the Manitoba Senior League. In 1950, he joined the Giants for their first ManDak season and batted .253 with one home run and 15 RBI. During the season he helped Curly Haas manage the team that season. That was his only season in the league. He closed out his career in 1951 in the Provincial League and batted .174.

Larry Soffer
Right Field

In 1951, the Winnipeg Buffaloes lost five players to the St. Louis Browns. Soffer, who was visiting friends in Winnipeg, played one game for the Buffaloes during the player shortage.

Herb Souell

Third base/Outfield; Bats—Both; Throws—Right; Height—5'10"; Weight—170 lbs.; Born—February 5, 1913 in West Monroe, Louisiana

Souell's Negro League career was from 1940 to 1950. He played for the Ethiopian Clowns, Kansas City Monarchs, and Cincinnati Crescents. He was a solid third baseman with good speed, who played in four Negro League All-Star games. He was 38 years old when he joined the Carman Cardinals in 1951 and batted .306 with seven home runs and 39 RBI. In 1952, he played in organized ball. He returned to Carman in 1953 and batted .302 with five home runs and 39 RBI.

Bill Spaeter
Center Field

Spaeter played in the Boston Red Sox organization. In 1948, with Roanoke, he led the Class B Piedmont League in runs scored with 100. He joined the Winnipeg Royals in 1953 and batted .257 with five home runs and 41 RBI. He returned to organized ball until 1956, when he joined the Williston Oilers and batted .220 with no home runs and four RBI.

Pete Spatafore

Shortstop

Spatafore played in the Cleveland Indians and Brooklyn Dodgers organizations. In 1947, he was an All-Star with Meridian in the Class B South-Eastern League. In 1946, he walked seven times in a single game in the West Texas-New Mexico League. In 1953 he batted .301 and had 16 homers while in the Red Sox chain. In 1956, he started the season with Oklahoma City in the Texas League, and when the team went broke he signed with the Williston Oilers, for whom he batted .311 with 2 home runs and 15 RBI.

Al Spearman

Pitcher; Bats—Right; Throws—Right; Height—6'; Weight—185 lbs.

In 1950, Spearman played for the Chicago American Giants. In 1951 he joined the Carman Cardinals and had a 5–5 record. In 1952, he played for the Winnipeg Giants and had a 1–3 record. After that season he went into organized baseball. In 1956, with Stockton in the California League, he led the league with a 2.62 ERA and won 16 straight games. In 1958, he again led that league with a 2.60 ERA and both seasons he was selected to the All-Star team. In 1959, he pitched for Houston in the American Association and had a 3–9 record. Before May 1 of that year he had completed 33 consecutive starts.

Joe Spencer

Infield; Bats—Right; Throws—Right; Height—5'9"; Weight—150 lbs

Spencer's Negro League career was from 1942 to 1948, for several teams. He could best be described as an average player. In 1951, he joined the Elmwood Giants and batted .239 with three home runs and 32 RBI. That would be his only season in the league. Near the end of his career he played in organized ball in the Longhorn League.

Artis Stewart

Pitcher; Throws—Right

Artis Stewart pitched briefly in 1950 with the Cleveland Buckeyes and the Louisiana Travelers barnstorming teams. He signed with Minot in July and played only briefly, posting a 0–1 record before he was traded back to the Travelers for pitcher Frank Pickens.

DON STEWART
Outfield

Don Stewart played in the Brooklyn Dodgers organization. He hailed from Black Diamond, Alberta. He played in 1951 and 1952 for Ponca City, Oklahoma in the Kansas-Oklahoma-Missouri League. In 1952, he batted .318 and was selected to the All-Star team. He joined the Brandon Greys in 1954 and batted .333 with eight home runs and 41 RBI. In 1955, he closed out his career as playing manager for Lloydminster in the Western Canada Baseball League.

BOB STRADER
Shortstop

Strader was a 1950 All-Star in the Sunset League with El Centro. He joined the Winnipeg Giants in 1953 and batted .261 with eight home runs and 48 RBI. He led the ManDak League in doubles that season with 24.

MARLEY STRONG
Utility

Marley Strong was a native of Fargo, North Dakota. He played for the Fargo American Legion team in the early 1940s and in the mid 1940s for Moorhead State Teacher's College. In 1948, he played for Superior in the Northern League. In 1949, he played Class D ball in the Kitty League. That same season, he joined the Minot Merchants. He signed with the Minot Mallards in 1950 for their inaugural season and batted .236 with no home runs and seven RBI. After his playing days he was a scout for the New York Yankees.

OTHELLO STRONG
Pitcher; Bats—Both; Throws—Right

Othello Strong's Negro League career was from 1949 to 1950, for the Chicago American Giants. In 1951, he joined the Winnipeg Buffaloes and had a 2–1 record on the mound and batted .317 with four home runs and 16 RBI. He played briefly for the Winnipeg Giants in 1952. In 1953, he closed out his career with Danville in the Mississippi–Ohio Valley League, where he had a 3–2 record and a 1.93 ERA.

TED STRONG
Shortstop/Third base, Outfield; Bats—Both; Throws—Right; Height—6'6"; Weight—210 lbs.; Born—January 2, 1917 in South Bend, Indiana

Ted Strong's Negro League career lasted from 1937 to 1948. He was a versatile athlete and a good hitter and fielder. He was a switch-hitter with power and was a five-time Negro League All-Star. At 6'6", he was an imposing figure at the plate. He spent most of his career with the Kansas City Monarchs and the Indianapolis Clowns. He was an original member of the Harlem Globetrotters basketball team. In 1949, he batted .351 for the Minot Merchants. He joined the Minot Mallards in 1950 and even though he played the season, no statistics can be found. He hit one of the longest home runs ever hit in Minot on September 9 of that season in an exhibition game against the Fargo-Moorhead Twins of the Northern League. The ball went 60 feet over the right field wall. In 1951 he returned to the Negro Leagues to finish his career.

VIC STRYSKA
Pitcher

Stryska played in the Class D Sooner State League in 1948 and was selected to the All-Star team. He holds the league record for the most games pitched in a season, with 59. He continued his career in the minor leagues and in 1956 signed with the Bismarck Barons and had a 9–7 record, with a 3.86 ERA.

ARMANDO SUAREZ
Pitcher; Born — Cuba

Suarez joined the Brandon Greys in 1951 and had a 7–5 record. After that season he was signed by the Brooklyn Dodgers and was sent to Great Falls in the Pioneer League, where he had a 19–10 record and a 3.52 ERA. In 1955, he played briefly in Triple-A with St. Paul in the American Association and had a 0–2 record. He finished his career in 1957 in Mexico, going 1–3 with a 4.26 ERA.

ED SUDOL
First Base; Died — December 10, 2004 in Daytona Beach, Florida

Sudol was an All-Star for El Dorado in 1949, and led the Cotton States League that year in walks with 106. He joined the Minot Mallards in 1951 and batted .251 with four home runs and 34 RBI. He went on to become a major league umpire. He was a National League umpire from 1957 to 1977. On May 21, 1964 he umpired a National League game between the Giants and Mets that lasted a league record 7 hours and 23 minutes.

ROLAND SUMMERS
Pitcher; Throws — Left; Born — 1933

Summers played the 1951 season with the Philadelphia Meteors in a semi-pro Negro League. Newspaper reports indicated that in the spring of 1952 he had a tryout with the Milwaukee Brewers in the American Association. He was 19 years old when he joined the Minot Mallards on the recommendation of Ben Cain, brother of pitcher Sugar Cain. In 1952 he had a 0–2 record for Minot and was released.

Jim Swanton

Second Base; Height — 5'10"; Weight —155 lbs.

Swanton was a local Carman player who played most of his ball in the Manitoba Senior League. He saw action for the Carman Cardinals in one game in 1954 due to illness of regular player Jesse Douglas. That was his only appearance in the league.

Ray Tabacchi

Second Base

In 1960, Tabacchi played for Lewiston in the Northwest League and that season was selected to the All-Star team. He played briefly as an 18-year-old for the Carman Cardinals in 1952.

Frank Tanana

Outfield

Tanana played as high as Class A ball. In 1953, he played for the Peoria Chiefs in the Class B Three-I League and batted .310, with 18 HR, and 87 RBI and was selected to the All-Star team. He played five seasons in the Cleveland Indians organization and in 1956 he batted .244, with 12 HR, 45 RBI with Reading in the Eastern League. He joined the Williston Oilers midway through the 1957 season and batted .246 with four home runs and eight RBI.

Harry Taylor

Pitcher; Bats— Right; Throws— Right; Height — 6'1"; Weight —175 lbs.; Born — May 20, 1919 in East Glenn, Indiana

In 1946 at St. Paul, Harry Taylor led the American Association with 15 wins. He played for the Brooklyn Dodgers from 1946 to 1948. His pitching record was 0–0, 3.86 ERA in 1946; 10–5, 3.11 ERA in 1947, and 2–7, 5.36 ERA in 1948. From 1950 to 1952, he played for the Boston Braves. His record with the Braves was 2–0, 1.42 ERA in 1950; 4–9. 5.75 ERA in 1951, and 1–0, 4.10 in 1952. He appeared in one World Series game in 1947. He started game four and hurt his arm after pitching to only four batters. In 1954, he joined the Williston Oilers at the age of 35 and pitched well, recording a 9–4 record.

Joe Taylor

Outfield; Bats— Right; Throws— Right; Height — 6'1"; Weight —185 lbs.; Born — March 2, 1926 in Chapman, Alabama

Joe Taylor played the 1949 season in the Negro Leagues and had started his career as a catcher. He was 24 years old when he joined the Winnipeg Buffaloes for the 1950 season and batted .237 with three home runs and 15 RBI. In 1954, he was selected to the All-Star team with Ottawa in the International League. In 1957, he was an All-Star for Seattle in the Pacific Coast League and again in 1959 with Vancouver, also in the Pacific Coast League. In between he played in the majors with the Philadelphia A's, Cincinnati Reds, St. Louis Cardinals, and Baltimore Orioles. His major league batting averages over his four seasons were .224, 1 HR, 8 RBI in 1954; .262, 4 HR, 9 RBI in 1957; .289, 3 HR, 12 RBI in 1958, and .156, 2 HR, 11 RBI in 1959.

PETE TAYLOR

Pitcher; Bats — Right; Throws — Right; Height — 6'1"; Weight — 170 lbs.; Born — November 26, 1927 in Severn, Maryland; Died — November 17, 2003 in Annapolis, Maryland

In 1948, Pete Taylor pitched 250 innings and won 10 games for Wilkes-Barre in the Class A Eastern League. He pitched for San Antonio in the Texas League from 1950 to 1953. He pitched two innings for the St. Louis Browns in 1952 when he was called up from San Antonio and gave up four hits, walked three and had a 13.50 ERA. He played in the Texas League in 1954 with Oklahoma City. He was 29 years old when he joined Minot in 1956 and posted a record of 8–7 with a 2.86 ERA.

RON TEASLEY

Outfield; Bats — Right; Throws — Right; Height 5'11"; Weight —177 lbs.; Born — January 26, 1927 in Detroit, Michigan

Teasley played in the Negro Leagues in 1948 with the New York Cubans and that same season signed with the Brooklyn Dodgers. He was the eighth former Negro League player signed by the Dodgers. He joined the Carman Cardinals in 1949 when they were in the Manitoba Senior League. He played in 1950 for Carman in the ManDak League and batted .299 with three home runs and 19 RBI. He was a solid player for the Cardinals. In the off-season he attended Wayne State University in Detroit and received a degree in physical education. At Wayne State he was a two-sport star in baseball and basketball. He was elected to the Wayne State University Hall of Fame in 1986. Today he

Ron Teasley, Carman Cardinals (courtesy of Dufferin Historical Museum of Carman, Manitoba).

volunteers in Detroit with inner-city kids in a program sponsored by the Detroit Tigers, and teaches seniors how to golf.

WALT THOMAS

Outfield/Catcher; Bats — Left; Throws — Right; Height — 5'10"; Weight — 165 lbs

Thomas' Negro League career was from 1936 to 1947, for several teams. In 1948 he batted .268, playing in organized ball for Wilkes-Barre in the Class A Eastern League. He joined the Carman Cardinals in 1950 and batted .245 with one home run and 22 RBI. He was back in 1951, batting .238 with no home runs and 22 RBI.

RAY THONN

First Base

Thonn was a college player who had played the 1956 season for the University of Illinois and batted .340. Reports indicated he was one of their top hitters and could hit with power. He joined the Bismarck Barons in 1957 and batted .269 with three home runs and 26 RBI.

BOB TILLER

Catcher/Utility

Tiller was a Minot amateur player. He joined the Minot Mallards briefly as a backup catcher and utility player in 1952. He batted .250 in 12 at-bats and had no home runs and no RBI.

BRAD TOLSON

Pitcher; Throws — Right

Tolson was a star for the University of Arizona. In his four years of college ball he recorded a 20–4 record and at one time had a 17-game win streak. The Minot *Daily News* reported that he had chances to sign with the Red Sox, White Sox, Dodgers, and Phillies. In 1949, he pitched for the Minot Merchants. He joined the Minot Mallards in 1950 and 1951, but did not have the success he had had in college. His record was 1–6 in 1950 and 1–3 in 1951. There were games in which he pitched well enough to win, but received little help from his teammates.

PHIL TOMKINSON

Catcher

Tomkinson had six seasons of pro baseball. He was with the Minneapolis Millers in the American Association in 1950, and in 1951 was with Ottawa in the International League. He played briefly with Minot in 1953 and then left to go back into pro ball when he found out his contract had been sold to Oklahoma City of the AA Texas League.

Lou Tost

Pitcher; Bats—Left; Throws—Left; Height—6'; Weight—175 lbs.

Tost pitched for the Boston Braves from 1942 to 1943 and was 31 years old when he made his debut with the Braves. His best season was his rookie year in 1942, when his record was 10–10 with a 3.53 ERA. In 1947 he pitched in one game and had no decision with the Pittsburgh Pirates. He had several successful seasons in the Pacific Coast League with the Seattle Rainiers, Hollywood Stars, and Oakland Oaks. In 1951 he had a 10–6 record for Wenatchee in the Class B Western League. He pitched briefly for Brandon in 1952 and had a 0–1 record when he left the club. Having been an ex–major leaguer, Brandon had expected him to be an ace on their staff.

Del Triplett

Second Base/Right Field

Triplett was from Kenmore, North Dakota, and had played for the Minot Merchants in 1948 and 1949. He was a principal and coach at Lansford High School. He joined the Minot Mallards in 1950 and batted .216 with no home runs and 13 RBI. The Minot newspaper reported that he was popular with his teammates.

Bob Turner

Catcher; Bats—Right; Throws—Right; Born—1927

Turner played for the Kansas City Monarchs in 1946 and was not a high-average hitter. He played in the North Atlantic League in 1949. In 1951, he played in the Southwest International League and batted .265, then joined the Regina Caps of the Western Canada Baseball League. He wasn't there long when he jumped again to the Minot Mallards. He finished the season batting .182 with no home runs and 3 RBI. He joined the Carman Cardinals in 1953 and batted .204 with one home run and 33 RBI.

Whitney Ulrich

Pitcher

Ulrich played six years in organized ball, in the St. Louis Cardinals, Cincinnati Reds, and Milwaukee Braves chains. In 1952 he had his best season at 10–5 and a 2.75 ERA record with Columbus in the South Atlantic League. He started the 1956 season with Topeka and was released with a 1–1 record. He then signed with the Williston Oilers and had a record of 1–4 with a 6.00 ERA.

BILL UPTON

Pitcher; Bats— Right; Throws— Right; Height — 6'; Weight —167 lbs.;
Born — July 18, 1929 in Esther, Missouri

In 1952, Upton was an All-Star in the Class B Tri-State League and led the league with 21 victories. In 1954, he was 24 years old when he appeared in two games for the Philadelphia A's. His record was 0–0 with a 1.80 ERA in five innings of work. Over his career he pitched for Spartanburg in the Tri-State League and Indianapolis and Ottawa at the Triple-A level. He joined the Minot Mallards in 1957 at the age of 28 and had a record of 7–6 with a 3.96 ERA.

JIM VALENTINE
Second Base

Valentine played briefly in the 1952 season. In the 1953 season with the Brandon Greys, he batted .306 with one home run and 25 RBI. He then went to the Negro Leagues from 1954 to 1955 and played for the Louisville Colonels, Detroit Stars, and Memphis Red Sox. He finished his career in the Western Canada Baseball League with Lloydminster, batting .307 in 1955, and .249 in 1956. He played in one game in 1959.

LEN VAN DE HEY
Right Field

Van De Hey played in the New York Giants chain. In 1955, he played for the Texas City Texans in the Class B Big State League and led the league in batting with a .377 average. He also had the most hits with 195 and was selected to the All-Star team. In 1956, he batted .359 for the Albuquerque Dukes in the Class A Western League and led the league with 197 hits. He joined the Bismarck Barons in 1957 and won the batting championship with a .404 average with 10 home runs and 66 RBI. Ed Williams, who pitched for Williston at the time, said he couldn't understand why Van De Hey didn't play at a higher level, as he was such a good hitter.

BOB VAN EMAN
Outfield

Van Eman had ten years of organized baseball experience. In 1950, he was with the Salt Lake City Bees in the Class C Pioneer League. That season he led the league in batting with a .368 average and was selected to the All-Star team. In 1952, he was batting champion for Wichita Falls, Texas, in the Big State League. He played as high as Triple-A ball and in 1956, he joined the Minot Mallards and batted .313 with eight home runs and 46 RBI. He left the team on August 2 to play in Double-A in the Southern Association.

Armando Vasquez

Infield/Outfield; Bats—Left; Throws—Left; Height—5'8"; Weight—160 lbs.; Born—August 20, 1922 in Juines, Cuba

Vasquez's Negro League career was from 1944 to 1948 with the New York Cubans. He was an average hitter in the Negro Leagues, but was a very good fielder. He played in Cuba. He then came to Canada to play for Brandon in 1948 when the team was in the Manitoba Senior League. He used the name Bus Quinn, then later changed to his real name. He batted .324 in 1948 and .323 in 1949. He was 28 years old in 1950 when Brandon entered the ManDak League, and he batted .244 with one home run and 27 RBI. In 1951, he batted .279 with three home runs and 36 RBI and in 1952 hit .314 with one home run and 24 RBI. He sometimes would be used as a pitcher when Brandon was short of arms or in a mop-up role. He closed out his career in 1955 in the Mexican League.

Armando Vasquez, Brandon Greys (courtesy of Lillian Lowe).

Fred Vaughan

Second Base; Bats—Right; Throws—Right; Height—5'10"; Weight—185 lbs.; Born—October 18, 1918 in Coalinga, California; Died—March 2, 1964 in Near Lake Wales, Florida

Vaughn was 36 years old when he joined the Bismarck Barons in 1955. He batted .293 with seven home runs and 31 RBI. He had been working in the oil fields in the Williston area and was signed as a replacement player after playing manager Al Cihocki was injured. In 1944 and 1945, he played for the Washington Senators and he batted .257 with 1 HR, 25 RBI in 1944 and .235, with 1 HR, 25 RBI in 1945. He played five years in Triple-A ball and was considered a good hitter, with some power. In his off-seasons he was also a crooner with a big band.

Dick Vinson

Pitcher

Vinson was a 20-year-old pitcher when he briefly joined the Brandon Greys in 1950. He pitched with little success. He had pitched in semi-pro ball in Ohio with the Columbus Blues.

Jack Warwick

First Base; Born — March 29, 1927

Warwick played in the Manitoba Senior League with Norwood/St. Boniface. In that league he was a good hitter and a good defensive first baseman. In 1948, he played for Fulton, Kentucky, in the Washington Senators organization. In 1949, he batted .308 with Elmwood in the Manitoba Senior League. He joined the Elmwood Giants in 1950, their first season in the ManDak League, and batted .216. After that season he continued his career in the Senior League with Transcona and the St. Boniface Native Sons. He played in many tournaments in Manitoba and Saskatchewan and was elected to the Manitoba Baseball Hall of Fame in 1999.

Bill Washburn

Pitcher; Throws— Left; Height — 5'9"; Weight —150 lbs.; Born —1929

Washburn played in the Philadelphia Phillies organization, as high as Class A ball. In 1946, he pitched for the Salina Blue Jays in the Western Association and led the league in strikeouts with 242. He joined the Minot Mallards in 1953 and was released in mid–June along with Mickey Rocco, as both wanted more money. He then signed with the Winnipeg Royals and had a 10–7 record. After that season he pitched with Winston-Salem in the Class B Carolina League. He returned to Minot in 1954 and 1955. His record in 1954 was 7–2 and in 1955 it was 2–5 with a 6.06 ERA .

John Washington

First base/Third Base; Bats— Left; Throws— Right; Height — 6'2"; Weight —185 lbs.

Washington's Negro League career was from 1933 to 1950. He was a good hitter with power. He usually hit .300-plus in the Negro Leagues. He was a Negro League All-Star in 1936 and 1950. He joined the Elmwood Giants in 1951 and batted .359 with six home runs and 41 RBI. In 1952 he batted .265 with two home runs and 28 RBI for the Winnipeg Giants. In 1953 he joined the Brandon Greys and batted .327 with four home runs and 45 RBI. He finished his ManDak League career in 1954 with the Carman Cardinals, batting .277 with one home run and 36 RBI. He was considered to be a very good defensive player in the ManDak League.

Paul Wasseth

Third Base

Wasseth was attending Brown University in 1950 and playing semi-pro ball for Fort Fairfield, Maine. He was recommended to Minot, but played only briefly, with little success. He batted .168 with one home run and 10 RBI.

Frank Watkins
Pitcher

Watkins was a local player who called Reston, Manitoba, home. He played for the Riverside Canucks in the Manitoba Senior League before joining the Brandon Greys in 1949. In the final playoff game in 1949, he pitched and batted the Greys to a 15-inning victory and the championship. He joined the Greys in 1950 in their first ManDak season and had a 3–6 record. In 1951, he had an 8–1 record for the Dauphin Red Birds in the Senior League, then joined the Minot Mallards briefly and finished the season with a 2–4 record. He was considered one of the best pitchers Manitoba ever produced.

Murray Watkins

Third Base; Bats—Left; Throws—Right; Height—5'4"; Weight—135; Born—October 16, 1915 in Towson, Maryland.

Watkins' Negro League career was from 1941 to 1950. He batted leadoff, and because of his small stature, drew a lot of walks. He was a good fielder who played in two Negro League All-Star games. He toured with the Jackie Robinson All-Stars and joined the Brandon Greys in 1950 when he was 34 years old. He batted .222, 0 HR, 13 RBI in 1950, and .262, 1 HR, 26 RBI in 1951 and closed out his ManDak League career batting, .225, 0 HR, 13 RBI in 1952.

Amos Watson

Pitcher; Bats—Right; Throws—Right; Height—6'; Weight—170 lbs.; Born—Lake Alfred, Florida

Watson played in the Negro Leagues from 1945 to 1949. In 1950, at the age of 24, he joined the Elmwood Giants and had a 1-1 record. That was his only season in the league.

Roy "Stormy" Weatherly

Outfield; Bats—Left; Throws—Right; Height—5'6"; Weight—165 lbs.; Born—February 25, 1915 in Warren, Texas; Died—January 19, 1991 in Woodville, Texas

Weatherly had a 10-year career in the major leagues. He was 21 years old when he joined Cleveland in 1936. He spent seven years with the Indians, then two with the New York Yankees and one with the New York Giants. He appeared in 811 big league games, with a lifetime batting average of .286. His best years were in 1939 and 1940, when he batted .310 and .303. He appeared in the 1943 World Series with the New York Yankees. On April 28 and June 24 of 1943, while with the Yankees, he caught 10 fly balls in a game and became the first major league player in history to have 10 putouts twice in a major league season. He also starred in the minor leagues and was selected to the International League All-Star team in 1952. He joined the Williston Oilers in

1954 at age 39 and was batting champ that year, hitting .412 with 14 home runs and 58 RBI. He followed that with his second batting championship in 1955, with a .371 average, 21 home runs and 61 RBI. He split the 1956 season between Williston and Bismarck, batting .324 with nine home runs and 39 RBI. In 1957 he was back with Williston and batted .262 with two home runs and nine RBI.

Dan Webster

Pitcher/Catcher; Born—1916 in Louisville, Kentucky

Webster lived in the Detroit area and played semi-pro ball. He was 34 years old when he played briefly for the Carman Cardinals in 1950. He was brought to Carman by manager Red House. Webster had a 0–1 record before his release.

Willie "The Devil" Wells

Infield/Manager; Bats—Right; Throws—Right; Height—5'8"; Weight—160 lbs.; Born—August 19, 1905 in Austin, Texas; Died—January 22, 1989 in Austin, Texas

Wells's Negro League career lasted from 1924 to 1949. He was considered the best shortstop in Negro League baseball. He was outstanding in the field and at the plate. Wells was a member of the Newark Eagles' "Million Dollar Infield" and was a consistent .300 hitter with power. He came to Winnipeg in 1949 to play with the Elmwood Giants in the Manitoba Senior League, and batted .333. He became the playing manager of the Winnipeg Buffaloes in 1950 when he was 44 years old, and batted .304 with no home runs and 22 RBI. That season he managed the Buffaloes to the first ManDak League championship. In 1951 he batted .314 with three home runs and 40 RBI. After the Buffaloes ceased operation, he signed on to manage the Brandon Greys in 1952. He only batted six times that season and had four hits. In 1953, he batted .234 with no home runs and 4 RBI, then retired from baseball. At times when the Greys were short of arms or needed someone in a mopup role, he would pitch.

Mark Flynn, a friend of mine, told me an interesting story about Wells. Midway through the 1949 season, when Wells played for the Elmwood team and Mark was playing for the Giants (under 21-year-old team), the teams would play a practice game together. As was the custom in those days, when an inning was over, the players left their gloves on the playing field. When the practice was over, Mark picked up Wells's glove to give to him. Mark said the glove looked like it had been with Wells for many years. He also noticed what felt like small weights at the end of the fingers on Wells's glove. He asked Wells about it and Wells said he did that so he would keep his glove down on ground balls. Wells also said laughingly "that the glove came in handy sometimes when things got rough on the field, if you know what I mean." Willie Wells was elected to the Baseball Hall of Fame in 1997.

WILLIE WELLS JR.

Infield/Outfield; Born — October 23, 1922, in Austin, Texas; Bats — Right; Throws — Right; Height — 5'5"; Weight — 158 lbs.

Wells Jr.'s Negro League career was from 1940 to 1950, for the Memphis Red Sox. He had only average defensive skills and did not hit for a high average. He played in the shadow of his father. He was 27 in 1950 when he, along with his father, joined the Winnipeg Buffaloes. The younger Wells batted .214 with one home run and 15 RBI. He played only one season in the league.

BOB WHITCHER

Pitcher; Bats — Left; Throws — Left; Height — 5'8"; Weight — 165 lbs.; Born — April 29, 1917 in Berlin, New Hampshire; Died — May 8, 1997 in Akron, Ohio

In 1945, Whitcher saw action in six games with the Boston Braves. His record was 0–2 with a 2.87 ERA. He spent 13 seasons playing pro and semi-pro ball. He pitched well for Evansville in the Class B Three-I League from 1946 to 1948. His record for those years was 4–1, 13–11, and 14–11. In 1949, he managed Brantford in the semi-pro Ontario League. In 1951, he had a 5–5 record with Rochester in the Southern Minnie League. He was 36 years old and had been pitching in the Class A Western League when he joined the Minot Mallards in 1953. He had a 2–3 record when he was released.

CHARLEY WHITE

Catcher/Third Base; Bats — Left; Throws — Right; Height — 5'11"; Weight — 192 lbs.; Born — August 12, 1928 in Kinston, North Carolina; Died — May 26, 1998 in Sea-Tac, Washington

In 1950, White played one season for the Philadelphia Stars in the Negro American League. He started as a third baseman, but was switched to catcher because of his strong arm. He joined the Winnipeg Buffaloes in 1951 at age 23 and batted .330 with one home run and 19 RBI. Midway through that season, he was signed by the Toronto Maple Leafs. He played briefly with the Milwaukee Braves and batted .237 with 1 HR, 8 RBI in 1954 and .233, 0 HR, 4 RBI in 1955. He closed out his career in 1965 with Vancouver in the Pacific Coast League.

RALPH WILCOX

Third Base

Wilcox started in organized ball in 1946 and reached the Class B level in the Pittsburgh Pirates chain. In 1955, with Phoenix in the Arizona-Mexico League, he batted .330, with 37 home runs and 164 RBI. The next season, he hit .342 with 31 home runs and 133 RBI in the same league. In 1957, his club folded. He joined the Brandon Greys and batted .256 with nine home runs and 37 RBI.

BOB WILES
Pitcher

Bob Wiles signed with the Philadelphia Phillies organization in 1947. He pitched in Class A ball with Utica, New York, in the Eastern League and had a 3–2 record. He pitched briefly for Minot in 1951 and was released with no decisions. He was the brother of Charles Wiles.

CHARLES WILES
Catcher

Charles Wiles started in organized ball in 1945 and played in the Chicago Cubs organization. He signed with the Minot Mallards in 1951 and batted .202 with no home runs and 15 RBI. On July 7, he jumped the Mallards for Mankato in the semi-pro Southern Minnesota League. In 1952, he played for Superior in the Northern League, batting .309, with two home runs and 27 RBI.

JOE WILEY
Second Base/Third Base; Died — March 13, 1993

Wiley's Negro League career was from 1947 to 1950, for the Baltimore Elite Giants and the Memphis Red Sox. In the Negro Leagues he was mainly a utility player. He joined the Elmwood Giants in 1950. Midway through the 1951 season, he was traded from Elmwood to the Carman Cardinals and batted .249 with no home runs and 22 RBI. He walked five straight times in a game in 1952.

CURLY WILLIAMS
Infield/Outfield; Bats— Left; Throws— Right; Height — 5'10"; Weight —175 lbs.; Born —1923 in Holly Hill, South Carolina

Curley Willliams' Negro League career was from 1945 to 1950. He played for the Newark Eagles. His best season was 1949, when he batted .390. In 1952, he was with Toledo in Triple-A and Scranton in Class A. He played for the Carman Cardinals in 1953 at age 30 and batted .286 with 12 home runs and 40 RBI. That was his only season in the ManDak League, but he played a number of years in the Western Canada Baseball League and ended his career in 1960 in Lloydminster, Saskatchewan.

DEWEY WILLIAMS
Catcher; Bats— Right; Throws— Right; Height — 6'; Weight —160 lbs.; Born — February 5, 1916 in Durham, North Carolina; Died — March 19, 2000 in Williston, North Dakota

Before the 1944 season, Dewey Williams was listed as the starting catcher for the Chicago Cubs. He played for the Cubs from 1944 to 1948 and appeared in 193 games. His career batting average was .233. His best season was 1945, when in 59 games he batted .280. He was a good defensive catcher. In 1953, he caught 93 games for Toledo in the American Association and made only four errors on his way to a .992 fielding average. He joined the Williston Oilers in 1954 at age 38 and batted .246 with one home run and 10 RBI. In 1955 and 1956, he played for Minot and batted .230, with 5 HR, 23 RBI, and .227, 1 HR, 9 RBI. He was back with Williston in 1957 and batted .166 with no home runs and one RBI. He closed out his long career with Williston in 1958 and 1959 in the Western Canada Baseball League.

ED WILLIAMS

Pitcher; Height — 6'3"; Weight — 188 lbs; Born — 1930

In 1950, Ed Williams played for Olean in the Pony League and was selected to the All-Star team. He won 17 games that season and led his team to a first-place finish. He joined the Williston Oilers in 1954 and had a 2–3 record. His pitching records for the remaining seasons were 6–5, 4.22 ERA in 1955; 5–6, 3.37 ERA in 1956, and 2–6 and a 6.49 ERA in 1957. After he finished baseball, he continued his sports career as a long-distance runner. He completed a number of 100-mile runs and in 1999 was the first person of 70 years of age to complete the 100-mile run in Leadville, Colorado.

LEN WILLIAMS

Infield; Bats — Right; Throws — Right; Height — 5'10"; Weight — 185 lbs.

Len Williams started his career in the ManDak League with the Minot Mallards in 1950. He was batting .358 at midseason when he jumped to the Negro Leagues and played the remainder of the season with the Indianapolis Clowns. In the Mallards' first game, he got their first hit, a home run over the left field wall. After the 1951 season he went into organized baseball and played with some success. In 1957, he played for Topeka in the Western League and was an All-Star. He led the league with 43 home runs.

SAM WILLIAMS

Pitcher; Bats — Left; Throws — Right; Height — 6'1"; Weight 155 lbs.; Born — 1923

Sam Williams's Negro League career was from 1947 to 1950. In 1948, he was 6–3 with a 3.23 ERA for the pennant-winning Birmingham Black Barons. The next two seasons his record was 8–6, 3.21 ERA, and 13–7, 3.89 ERA. He was 28 when he pitched for the Brandon Greys in 1952, with a 1–2 record. That was his only season in the league. His last season in baseball was in the Mexican League in 1957.

AL WILMORE

Pitcher; Bats—Right; Throws—Right; Height—6'1"; Weight—180 lbs.; Born—November 15, 1924 in Philadelphia, Pennsylvania

Wilmore's Negro League career was from 1946 to 1950, with the Philadelphia Stars and Baltimore Elite Giants. He had a variety of pitches. In 1949, he was a Negro League All-Star, with a 10–6 record. He joined the Winnipeg Buffaloes in 1951 at 26 years of age and had a 5–4 record. That was his only season in the league. In 1952, he signed with the Philadelphia A's, but an arm injury ended his career.

Chuck Wilson, Brandon Greys (courtesy of Lillian Lowe).

CHUCK WILSON

Infield/Outfield

In 1948, Wilson played briefly for the Indianapolis Clowns. He joined the Brandon Greys in 1949 when the team played in the Manitoba Senior League, and batted .280. In 1950, he once again was with Brandon in the initial ManDak League season, and batted .306 with one home run and 21 RBI. He played very well for Brandon.

DANNY WILSON

Infield/Outfield; Bats—Both; Throws—Right; Height—5'10"; Weight—170 lbs.; Born—1913; Died—December 23, 1986 in St. Louis, Missouri

Danny Wilson's Negro League career was from 1937 to 1947, for several Negro League teams. He was considered a good hitter and was a two-time Negro League All-Star. In 1952, he was 39 years old when he played briefly for the Winnipeg Giants. He batted .238 with one home run and 16 RBI. At his advanced age he had lost much of his batting skill.

JACK WILSON

Outfield; Height—6'4"; Weight—195

Jack Wilson played four years of service ball while in the U.S. Navy and finished the 1954 season in the Class B Three-I League. He started the 1955 season with Colorado Springs in the Western League and was released early in the season. He joined the Williston Oilers and batted .269 with three home runs and 19 RBI.

John Wingo

Pitcher

Wingo played in the New York Yankees organization. He pitched for the Carman Cardinals in 1950 and had a 5–4 record, then went into organized ball. In 1952, he led the Provincial League with 16 wins. In 1955 and 1956, he was selected to the All-Star team with Birmingham in the Double-A Southern Association.

Harry Wise

Pitcher

Wise, a tall, lanky right hander, led the Class C Western Association with a 2.61 ERA in 1951. During his career he played for the Topeka Owls in the Chicago Cubs organization. Before joining the Barons, he played two seasons for Yankton, South Dakota, in the semi-pro Basin League. In 1956, he was a late-season addition to the Bismarck Barons, but had no decisions.

Lester Witherspoon

Outfield; Bats—Both; Throws—Right; Height—6'1"; Weight—190 lbs.

Witherspoon's Negro League career was from 1947 to 1949, for the Indianapolis Clowns and Homestead Grays. He played briefly with the Minot Mallards in 1950 and was batting .356 when he jumped to organized baseball. He played with some success, batting over .300 for three straight seasons. He played seven games for San Diego in the Pacific Coast League and batted .154.

Pius Wolf

Utility

Wolf was a successful amateur player in North Dakota, but never played organized ball. He was signed at a Bismarck tryout camp. He played several positions well, although he had trouble at the plate. In 1955, he batted .143 with no home runs and seven RBI and in 1956, .190 with no home runs and three RBI.

Buddy Woods

Pitcher; Bats—Right; Throws—Right; Height—6'2"; Weight—205 lbs.; Died—In Philadelphia, Pennsylvania

Woods's Negro League career was from 1946 to 1950, for the Cleveland

Buckeyes and Memphis Red Sox. In 1948, he had a 10–6 record and a 4.06 ERA with the Red Sox. He joined the Carman Cardinals in 1954 and had a 5–8 record. In 1955 and 1956, he pitched in the West Texas–New Mexico League. In 1956, his record was 10–6. His last year in ball was 1957.

GEORGE WOPINEK
Outfield

Wopinek played in the Pittsburgh Pirates organization. In 1954, he played for Williamsport in the Class A Eastern League and that season batted .284 and led the league in home runs with 16. He joined the Minot Mallards in 1955 as a late-season replacement for the injured Butch Davis and batted .381, with one home run and five RBI.

ART WORTH
Pitcher

Worth played three seasons in organized ball in the Class A Western International League and had a 11–6, 3.81 ERA with Spokane. He pitched for Bismarck in 1955 and had a record of 2–3 with a 4.78 ERA.

MORT WRIGHT
Pitcher; Born —1935 in Ninette, Manitoba

Wright was from Brandon. He played for the Greys in 1954 and had a 3–4 record. He attended the Washington Senators camp in Florida in 1953 and major league teams showed interest, but an arm injury hurt his career. He did play well for several years with the Brandon Cloverleafs in the Manitoba Senior League. He was playing manager of the Cloverleafs from 1958 to 1960, and they won three championships in the Central Manitoba Baseball Association. He was elected to the Manitoba Baseball Hall of Fame in 2000.

STEVE WYLIE
Pitcher; Bats— Right; Throws— Right; Height — 6'; Weight —180 lbs.; Born — May 7, 1911 in Crossville, Tennessee; Died — October 23, 1993 in Clarksville, Tennessee

Wylie began his Negro League career in 1944 with the Kansas City Monarchs. He was a hard thrower. His last season in the Negro Leagues was 1947. After that season he toured with the Satchel Paige All-Stars. He signed with the Brandon Greys in 1948 when they were in the Manitoba Senior League. He had an 8–2 record. He had a 15–6 record for the Minot Merchants in 1949. He returned to Minot in 1950, the Mallards' first season in the ManDak League, and his record that season was 3–0 when he jumped the club. Over his career he pitched with success for several semi-pro teams.

BOB YANEN
Pitcher

Yanen played in the Cleveland Indians organization. In 1955, he pitched for the Keokuk Kernals in the Class B Three-I League and led the league in strikeouts with 177. He joined the Williston Oilers in 1957 and had a 7–9 record with a 4.41 ERA.

Remaining Players

DON HUNTER
Outfield

JIM SLEVIN
Catcher

JERRY SMITH
Pitcher

When the Brandon Greys returned to the league in 1957, they were waiting for several regular players to arrive from the United States. All the above played in the Manitoba Senior League and were signed on a temporary basis. Hunter and Slevin were stars for the Brandon Cloverleafs and Jerry Smith played for Hamiota, Manitoba. They were released on July 10, 1957. Jim Slevin was voted to the Manitoba Baseball Hall of Fame in 2000. In 1950, Bill Antoniak (Winnipeg Reos) and in 1952, Lou Sabo (CUAC Blues) played one game for the Elmwood Giants when the team was short of players.

Appendix I
1950 Minot Mallards Team Rules

MINOT BASEBALL ASSOCIATION, INC.
MINOT MALLARDS

THE FOLLOWING RULES AND REGULATIONS WILL BE IN EFFECT FOR THE 1950 SEASON:
Night game with game scheduled following day player must have retired by 1:00 A.M.
Night game and no game next day player must have retired by 2:00 A.M.
Night game with game scheduled in afternoon of the following day, player must have retired by 12:00 midnight.
Night game with club scheduled to depart on road trip prior to 9:00 A.M. player must be retired by 12:00 midnight, if scheduled to leave prior to 12:00 noon, player must be retired by 1.00 A.M.
Partaking of alcoholic beverages so as to affect player's physical condition will absolutely not be tolerated.
Discipline will be administered as follows:
Fines: First offense — $10.00
Second offense — $25.00
Third offense — Suspension
It will be expected that all players will report two hours prior to each game at ball park.

BOARD OF DIRECTORS
MINOT BASEBALL ASSOCIATION, INC.
ROY R. REIMER, President

Appendix II
Batting and Pitching Records

BATTING STATISTICS—1950

	Team	G	AB	H	HR	RBI	AVE
Butch Davis	Winnipeg	42	171	78	4	39	.456
Rafe Cabrera	Brandon	37	131	49	6	33	.374
Len Williams	Minot	17	67	24	—	—	.358
Chuck Witherspoon	Minot	15	45	16	—	—	.356
Andy Phillips	Elmwood	15	47	16	0	8	.340
Sonny Andrews	Carman	45	180	60	2	25	.333
Joe Wiley	Elmwood	36	118	39	1	21	.331
John Britton	Winnipeg	47	198	65	1	26	.328
Leon Day	Winnipeg	31	108	35	0	14	.324
Jack Schaefer	Carman	38	152	49	1	15	.322
Ian Lowe	Brandon	46	188	60	1	39	.319
Cowan Hyde	Elmwood	33	143	45	0	5	.315
Chuck Wilson	Brandon	48	199	59	1	21	.306
Lyman Bostock	Winnipeg	47	180	55	1	31	.306
Willie Wells Sr.	Winnipeg	37	112	34	0	22	.304
Jack Bruton	Minot	15	46	14	0	5	.304
Solly Drake	Elmwood	47	210	63	2	21	.300
Ron Teasley	Carman	48	214	64	3	19	.299
Frazier Robinson	Winnipeg	21	79	22	0	19	.278
Gentry Jessup	Carman	23	54	15	1	8	.278
Len Pigg	Brandon	7	22	6	0	5	.273
Hickey Redd	Elmwood	30	81	22	0	7	.272
Bob Johnson	Carman	47	186	50	1	26	.269
Zoonie McLean	Minot	45	187	50	0	26	.267
Almer McKerlie	Carman	37	120	32	0	11	.267
Marty Crue	Elmwood	12	30	8	—	8	.267
Norm Felde	Minot	45	187	48	2	30	.257
Ramon Rodrigues	Brandon	45	167	43	1	31	.257
John Kennedy	Winnipeg	46	176	45	0	22	.256
Pat Patterson	Elmwood	22	79	20	1	6	.253
Cy Snead	Elmwood	47	162	41	1	15	.253
John Cowan	Elmwood	45	197	49	0	18	.249
Harvey Lapides	Minot	27	109	27	2	12	.248
Walt Thomas	Carman	46	192	47	1	22	.245
Armando Vasquez	Brandon	47	201	49	1	27	.244
Lefty Lefebrve	Minot	18	58	14	0	4	.241
Lillard Cobb	Carman	40	143	34	2	14	.238
Joe Taylor	Winnipeg	34	114	27	3	15	.237

Appendix II

	Team	G	AB	H	HR	RBI	AVE
Marshall Boney	Elmwood	44	152	36	1	28	.237
Marley Strong	Minot	23	72	17	0	7	.236
Red Longley	Elmwood	27	100	23	0	10	.230
Henry Smith	Minot	20	70	16	0	6	.229
Murray Watkins	Brandon	42	176	39	0	13	.222
Fred Shepard	Minot	13	54	12	0	4	.222
Charles Peete	Brandon	33	127	28	2	14	.220
Jack Warwick	Elmwood	30	116	25	1	18	.216
Del Triplett	Minot	44	162	35	0	13	.216
Gord Elliot	Carman	32	117	25	0	13	.214
Willie Wells Jr.	Winnipeg	35	112	24	1	15	.214
Dirk Gibbons	Brandon	17	57	12	0	5	.211
Andy Anderson	Minot	19	43	9	0	3	.209
Sam Hill	Winnipeg	43	163	34	0	15	.209
Manual Godinez	Brandon	28	77	16	0	15	.208
Taylor Smith	Winnipeg	15	49	11	9	5	.208
Ev Faunce	Minot	20	82	17	—	—	.207
Ray McWorter	Carman	8	10	2	0	0	.200
Bob Danielson	Minot	10	20	4	0	1	.200
Willie Cathey	Minot	12	35	7	0	9	.200
Frank Watkins	Brandon	13	25	5	0	2	.200
Morrell Groves	Carman	11	35	7	—	—	.200
Don Peerman	Brandon	3	5	1	0	0	.200
Len Gzebb	Elmwood	1	5	1	—	—	.200
Ed Leier	Elmwood	19	61	12	0	8	.197
Percy Howard	Winnipeg	31	98	19	0	8	.194
Andy Porter	Winnipeg	11	31	6	0	3	.194
Ted Fowler	Minot	8	26	5	—	—	.192
Ed Torner	Carman	11	37	7	—	—	.189
Herald Millon	Carman	6	11	2	0	0	.182
Cliff Kempf	Minot	38	127	23	0	14	.181
Gerry MacKay	Brandon	48	186	33	0	11	.177
Joe Adams	Carman	21	17	3	0	0	.176
Art Hunt	Brandon	14	41	7	0	1	.171
John Wingo	Carman	25	82	14	1	6	.171
Luke Chojnowski	Carman	17	53	9	0	2	.170
Paul Wasseth	Minot	32	113	19	1	10	.168
Bob Cunningham	Elmwood	19	36	6	1	4	.167
Paul Jones	Elmwood	27	52	8	0	1	.154
Tom Johnson	Brandon	7	13	2	0	2	.154
Spoon Carter	Winnipeg	7	28	5	0	2	.143
Amos Watson	Elmwood	4	7	1	0	3	.143
Ray Finch	Elmwood	25	56	8	0	5	.143
Jim Newberry	Winnipeg	19	45	6	0	5	.133
Pedro Naranjo	Brandon	11	20	2	0	2	.100
Brad Tolson	Minot	11	25	2	0	1	.080
Carl Dent	Brandon	No Record Available					
Gervis Fagan	Minot	No Record Available					
Red House	Carman	No Record Available					
Mac Massingale	Carman	No Record Available					
Bill Malone	Carman	No Record Available					
Victor Savingne	Brandon	No Record Available					

Pitching Statistics — 1950

	Team	W	L	PCT.
Art Hunt	Brandon	9	0	.1000
Steve Wylie	Minot	3	0	.1000
Don Peerman	Brandon	2	0	.1000
Bill Anderson	Minot	1	0	.1000
Dick Vinson	Brandon	1	0	.1000
Winslow Means	Brandon	1	0	.1000
Armando Vasquez	Brandon	1	0	.1000
Gentry Jessup	Carman	10	4	.761
Willie Cathey	Minot	9	3	.750
Dirk Gibbons	Brandon	8	4	.666
Manuel Godinez	Brandon	4	2	.666
Leon Day	Winnipeg	4	2	.666
Bob Danielson	Minot	6	4	.600
Pedro Naranjo	Brandon	3	2	.600
Taylor Smith	Winnipeg	8	6	.571
John Wingo	Carman	5	4	.555
Lillard Cobb	Carman	5	4	.555
Andy Porter	Winnipeg	5	4	.555
Jim Newberry	Winnipeg	7	7	.500
Jimmy Peet	Minot	2	2	.500
Al Preston	Elmwood	2	2	.500
Amos Watson	Elmwood	1	1	.500
Paul Jones	Elmwood	9	10	.473
Bob Cunningham	Elmwood	4	5	.444
Andy Anderson	Minot	2	3	.400
Frank Watkins	Brandon	3	6	.333
Joe Adams	Carman	2	4	.333
Spoon Carter	Elm/Winnipeg	2	4	400
Ray Finch	Elmwood	2	6	.244
Brad Tolson	Minot	1	6	.144
Jack Bruton	Minot	0	1	.000
Frank Pickens	Minot	0	1	.000
Roy Hughes	Minot	0	1	.000
Clint McKerlie	Carman	0	1	.000
Dan Webster	Carman	0	1	.000
Roy McWorter	Carman	0	1	.000
Lorne Benson	Winnipeg	0	1	.000
Artis Stewart	Minot	0	1	.000
Andy Phillips	Elmwood	0	1	.000
Bob Manning	Carman	0	2	.000
Tom Johnson	Brandon	0	2	.000
Cy Snead	Elmwood	0	2	.000
Don Reid	Carman	0	3	.000
Satchel Paige	Minot	0	0	.000
Mario Chacon	Brandon	0	0	.000
Leo Henry	Minot	0	0	.000

League Leaders — 1950

Batting	Butch Davis	Winnipeg	.456
Home Runs	Rafe Cabrera	Brandon	6
RBI	Ian Lowe Brandon, Butch Davis	Winnipeg	39
Most Wins	Gentry Jessup	Carman	10
Best Record — Pitcher	Art Hunt	Brandon	9–0

Batting Statistics — 1951

	Team	*G*	*AB*	*H*	*HR*	*RBI*	*AVE*
Tom Parker	Elmwood	19	42	18	4	11	.429
Butch Davis	Winnipeg	50	212	86	7	53	.406
Alonzo Perry	Brandon	16	63	25	5	19	.397
Johnny Lloyd	Elmwood	17	40	15	0	2	.375
Chick Longest	Carman	38	154	57	8	28	.370
John Washington	Elmwood	61	234	84	6	41	.359
Cowan Hyde	Elmwood	30	132	46	2	10	.348
Walter Jako	Minot	44	167	57	7	35	.341
Ted Radcliffe	Elmwood	15	47	16	0	13	.340
Leon Day	Winnipeg	22	59	20	3	20	.339
Charlie White	Winnipeg	26	103	34	1	19	.330
Gene Smith	Carman	26	80	26	5	16	.325
John Kennedy	Winnipeg	42	173	56	2	15	.324
Jack Schaefer	Carman	51	212	68	3	19	.321
Jimmy Grant	Minot	14	47	15	1	7	.319
Frazier Robinson	Winnipeg	56	223	71	1	37	.318
Othello Strong	Winnipeg	12	41	13	4	16	.317
O.B. Robison	Winnipeg	8	19	6	0	0	.316
Hal Schacker	Minot	11	19	6	0	4	.316
Willie Wells Sr.	Winnipeg	40	121	38	3	40	.314
John Britton	Elmwood	56	245	76	3	40	.310
Don Berg	Minot	19	71	22	1	12	.310
Roy Swanson	Elmwood	47	156	48	1	21	.308
Herb Souell	Carman	59	242	74	7	39	.306
Bob Harvey	Elmwood	44	173	53	9	43	.306
Joe Greene	Elmwood	31	113	34	2	16	.301
Harvey Beaster	Minot	62	259	78	5	30	.301
Zoonie McLean	Minot	62	271	81	2	33	.299
Othello Renfroe	Minot	27	94	28	3	15	.298
Ian Lowe	Brandon	60	215	64	5	52	.298
Gentry Jessup	Carman	37	121	36	1	25	.298
Joe Mitchell	Brandon	62	233	69	4	43	.296
Sam Hill	Winnipeg	55	217	63	3	26	.290
Willie Jefferson	Elmwood	22	52	15	0	6	.288
Lyman Bostock	Winnipeg	59	222	64	2	34	.288
Pee Wee Butts	Winnipeg	61	245	70	1	26	.286
Zell Miles	Winnipeg	25	105	30	4	25	.286
Connie Juelke	Minot	23	100	28	2	15	.280
Willie Cathey	Minot	30	61	17	1	7	.279
Armando Vasquez	Brandon	57	201	56	3	36	.279
Ducky Davinport	Elmwood	54	209	58	1	20	.278
Clarence King	Brandon	61	241	66	3	26	.274

Batting and Pitching Records

	Team	G	AB	H	HR	RBI	AVE
Lou Louden	Elmwood	37	139	38	2	22	.273
Andy Anderson	Carman	14	33	9	1	6	.273
Bob Johnson	Carman	62	242	65	2	32	.269
Ramon Rodriguez	Brandon	42	156	42	2	23	.269
Sugar Cain	Minot	36	97	26	1	9	.268
Jim Valentine	Brandon	10	34	9	0	2	.265
Sonny Andrews	Carman	53	182	48	4	24	.264
Fred Brenzell	Carman	18	61	16	0	4	.262
Murray Watkins	Brandon	61	275	72	1	26	.262
Otto Huber	Minot	21	71	18	0	10	.254
Pepper Bassett	Brandon	41	155	39	2	23	.252
Ed Sudol	Minot	60	235	59	4	34	.251
Joe Wiley	Carman	55	201	50	0	22	.249
Buddy Owens	Winnipeg	25	90	22	3	13	.244
Joe Mack	Minot	36	120	29	2	20	.242
Joe Spencer	Elmwood	53	201	48	3	32	.239
Ed Finney	Brandon	18	67	16	1	9	.239
Ray Finch	Elmwood	32	80	19	0	13	.238
Walt Thomas	Carman	48	172	41	0	16	.238
Jesse Douglas	Elmwood	15	49	13	—	6	.232
Gerry MacKay	Bran/Minot	55	192	44	3	20	.229
T.J. Brown	Carman	25	104	23	—	12	.212
Rafe Cabrera	Brandon	52	188	39	3	36	.207
Billy Horne	Carman	21	87	18	0	6	.207
Al Wilmore	Winnipeg	17	49	10	0	4	.204
Charles Wiles	Minot	22	84	17	0	15	.202
Taylor Smith	Winnipeg	15	30	6	0	3	.200
Willie Hutchinson	Carman	18	50	10	0	1	.200
Cy Morton	Elmwood/ Winnipeg	17	57	11	0	5	.193
Cliff Kempf	Minot	32	109	21	0	15	.193
Joe Degrazia	Minot	41	148	28	0	9	.189
Bob Turner	Minot	8	22	4	0	3	.182
Armando Suarez	Brandon	18	38	6	0	3	.158
Jack Bruton	Minot	14	32	5	1	8	.156
Gread McKinnis	Brandon	19	53	8	0	3	.151
Almer McKerlie	Carman	26	80	11	0	9	.138
Pedro Naranjo	Brandon	17	51	7	1	5	.137
Willbert Hammond	Winnipeg	15	58	7	0	2	.121
Pee Wee Jenkins	Winnipeg	20	43	5	1	2	.116
Jim Boldon	Elmwood	20	37	4	0	3	.108
Amacio Ferro	Brandon	10	16	1	0	0	.063
Earl Bumpas	Carman	5	5	0	0	0	.000
Larry Soffer	Winnipeg	1	3	0	0	0	.000
Albert Lombard	Elmwood	2	6	0	0	0	.000
Frank Evans	Brandon	No Record Available					
Joe Bestudick	Minot	No Record Available					
Norm Felde	Minot	No Record Available					
Willy Blackshire	Minot	No Record Available					

Pitching Statistics — 1951

	Team	W	L	PCT.
Harry Butts	Brandon	5	0	.1000
Ted Radcliffe	Elmwood	2	0	.1000
Willie Wells	Winnipeg	1	0	.1000
Al Jacowski	Carman	1	0	.1000
Nip Bruton	Minot	1	0	.1000
Pedro Naranjo	Brandon	4	1	.800
Leon Day	Winnipeg	4	1	.800
Tom Parker	Elmwood	5	2	.714
Jim Newberry	Winnipeg	6	3	.667
O.B. Robison	Winnipeg	4	2	.667
Bill Anderson	Brandon	2	1	.667
Othello Strong	Winnipeg	2	1	.667
Jim Valentine	Brandon	2	1	.667
Jack Bruton	Minot	2	1	.667
Art Hunt	Brandon	4	2	.667
Gread McKinnis	Brandon	11	6	.647
Jonas Gaines	Minot	7	4	.636
Pee Wee Jenkins	Winnipeg	8	5	.615
Gentry Jessup	Carman	9	6	.600
Armando Suarez	Brandon	7	5	.583
Al Wilmore	Winnipeg	5	4	.555
Willie Cathey	Minot	7	7	.500
Al Spearman	Carman	5	5	.500
Hal Schacker	Minot	4	4	.500
Leonard Johnson	Minot	1	1	.500
Vallie Eaves	Minot	1	1	.500
Jim Kamis	Minot	1	1	.500
Red Barnes	Winnipeg	1	1	.500
Ray Finch	Elmwood	10	11	.476
Sugar Cain	Minot	7	8	.467
Fred Brenzel	Carman	5	6	.455
Jim Bolden	Elmwood	5	8	.385
Willie Hutchinson	Carman	5	8	.385
Gene Smith	Carman	3	5	.375
Willie Jefferson	Elmwood	4	7	.364
Frank Watkins	Brandon/Minot	2	4	.428
Brad Tolson	Minot	1	3	.250
Taylor Smith	Winnipeg	3	10	.231
Henry McHenry	Minot	0	1	.000
John Bass	Carman	0	1	.000
Red Berry	Elmwood	0	1	.000
Armando Vasquez	Brandon	0	1	.000
Lillord Cobb	Carman	0	1	.000
Bob Hall	Elmwood	0	1	.000
Curtis McGowan	Elmwood	0	1	.000
Frank Thompson	Elmwood	0	1	.000
John Alexander	Elmwood	0	1	.000
Barney Morris	Elmwood	0	2	.000
Clarence Jones	Winnipeg	0	2	.000
Junior Williams	Elmwood	0	2	.000

Batting and Pitching Records

	Team	W	L	PCT.
Andy Anderson	Carman	0	2	.000
Amancio Ferro	Brandon	0	6	.000
Earl Bumpus	Carman	0	0	.000
Bob Wiles	Minot	0	0	.000

League Leaders—1951

Batting:	Butch Davis	Winnipeg	.406
Home Runs:	Bob Harvey	Elmwood	9
RBI:	Butch Davis	Winnipeg	53
Most Wins:	Gread McKinnes	Brandon	11

Batting Statistics—1952

	Team	AB	H	2B	3B	HR	RBI	AVE.
Willie Wells	Brandon	6	4	0	0	0	1	.667
Andy Porter	Carman	7	3	1	0	0	2	.429
Othello Strong	Winnipeg	51	20	1	1	2	11	.392
Lester Lockett	Winnipeg	100	39	6	0	0	18	.390
Zoonie McLean	Minot	195	72	12	6	7	46	.369
Chick Longest	Carman	220	76	10	3	8	41	.345
Luther Clifford	Brandon	112	37	10	1	3	23	.330
Lyman Bostock	Carman	195	64	11	1	5	36	.328
Lou Louden	Winnipeg	186	61	18	1	5	43	.328
Gentry Jessup	Carman	105	34	6	1	1	18	.324
Yogi Giammarco	Minot	188	56	15	4	11	47	.318
Clarence King	Brandon	143	45	7	3	2	19	.315
John Kelly	Minot	54	7	2	1	1	6	.315
Armando Vasquez	Brandon	159	50	9	6	1	24	.314
Wally Jako	Minot	222	69	18	2	7	46	.311
Chuck Castillo	Brandon	149	46	6	4	1	22	.309
Joe Mitchell	Brandon	205	62	11	13	0	28	.301
Duke Bowman	Minot	233	70	9	5	2	27	.300
Warren Martin	Minot	27	8	0	0	0	2	.296
Cesar Argudin	Brandon	41	12	—	—	—	2	.292
Sam Hill	Carman	222	64	9	3	5	33	.288
Joe Massaro	Minot	220	63	11	3	2	55	.286
John Kennedy	Minot	196	55	7	8	1	26	.286
Sonny Andrews	Carman	189	47	9	3	4	30	.280
Jack Schaefer	Carman	82	23	4	0	1	18	.280
Sugar Cain	Minot	61	17	2	0	3	14	.279
Quincy Barbee	Minot	172	48	6	3	3	32	.279
Almer McKerlie	Carman	126	35	2	1	0	21	.278
Norm Robinson	Brandon	196	54	9	5	1	27	.276
Jesse Douglas	Winnipeg	183	49	9	3	2	25	.268
John Washington	Winnipeg	181	48	7	0	2	28	.265
Tom Parker	Winnipeg	34	9	2	0	1	7	.265
Don Corcoran	Minot	190	50	4	1	9	33	.263
Fred Brenzel	Carman	90	23	3	0	0	8	.256
Cowan Hyde	Winnipeg	211	54	5	2	2	26	.256
Nick Canulli	Winnipeg	193	49	9	1	1	30	.254

	Team	AB	H	2B	3B	HR	RBI	AVE.
Frazier Robinson	Brandon	91	23	3	0	0	13	.253
Len Pigg	Brandon	40	10	1	0	0	6	.250
Bob Tiler	Minot	12	3	0	0	0	0	.250
Jose Colas	Brandon	147	36	4	0	3	21	.247
Hal Price	Winnipeg	77	19	2	0	1	10	.247
T.W. Richardson	Brandon	33	8	1	0	3	4	.242
Danny Wilson	Winnipeg	181	43	8	1	1	16	.238
Ray Finch	Winnipeg	13	3	1	0	0	1	.231
Ernie Boushy	Carman	202	46	3	2	0	24	.228
Murray Watkins	Brandon	213	48	6	3	0	13	.225
Pee Wee Butts	Brandon	50	11	1	0	0	8	.215
Harry Rhodes	Carman	65	14	1	0	4	2	.214
Murray Richardson	Carman	14	3	0	0	0	7	.214
Al Spearman	Winnipeg	42	9	0	0	0	12	.211
Jerry Powell	Winnipeg	147	31	7	2	1	4	.211
Pee Wee Carlisle	Carman	5	19	4	0	0	0	.211
Jonas Gaines	Minot	26	5	0	0	0	1	.192
Al Bryant	Winnipeg	21	4	0	0	0	3	.190
Barny Brown	Brandon	16	3	0	0	0	4	.188
Ed Albosta	Minot	16	3	0	0	0	1	.188
Ed Conley	Carman	65	12	1	0	0	7	.185
Mel Gallegos	Wpg/Carman	60	11	1	0	0	5	.183
Mal Murray	Minot	39	6	1	0	0	5	.176
Pee Wee Jenkins	Brandon	30	5	0	0	0	3	.167
Norman Banks	Brandon	34	5	1	0	0	3	.147
Ray Tabacchi	Carman	21	3	0	1	0	2	.143
Willie Greene	Minot	113	15	3	2	0	8	.133
Walt McCoy	Winnipeg	24	3	2	0	1	5	.125
Willie Hutchinson	Carman	30	3	0	0	0	1	.100
Bill Cox	Winnipeg	10	1	0	0	0	1	.100
Mario Amero	Brandon	21	2	0	0	0	0	.095
Weldon Ridley	Carman	18	1	—	—	—	0	.065
Sam Williams	Brandon	5	0	0	0	0	0	.000
Chuck Chohalas	Brandon	No Record Available						
Jack Deskin	Winnipeg	No Record Available						
Al Endriss	Winnipeg	No Record Available						
Cliff Gonzales	Winnipeg	No Record Available						
Bob Harvey	Winnipeg	No Record Available						
Don Loewen	Carman	No Record Available						
Herb Souell	Carman	No Record Available						
Al Tehero	Wpg/Bran.	No Record Available						
Jim Valentine	Brandon	No Record Available						
Emmett Wilson	Winnipeg	No Record Available						
Gus Kyle	Brandon	No Record Available						
Kyle Wilson	Brandon	No Record Available						
Ray White	Winnipeg	No Record Available						
Lou Sabo	Winnipeg	No Record Available						

Pitching Statistics—1952

	Team	W	L	PCT.
Andy Porter	Carman	2	0	1.000
Whit Graves	Minot	2	0	1.000
Almer McKerlie	Carman	1	0	1.000
Barney Brown	Brandon	4	1	.800
John Kelly	Minot	7	2	.778
Warren Martin	Minot	3	1	.750
T.W. Richardson	Brandon	5	2	.714
Sugar Cain	Minot	7	3	.700
Hal Price	Winnipeg	10	5	.667
Willie Greene	Minot	2	1	.667
Eddie Allen	Minot	2	1	.667
Tom Parker	Winnipeg	5	3	.625
Mario Amero	Brandon	5	3	.625
Mal Murray	Minot	5	3	.625
Al Bryant	Minot/Winnipeg	3	2	.600
Jonas Gaines	Minot	4	3	.571
Gentry Jessup	Carman	8	8	.500
Walt McCoy	Winnipeg	4	4	.500
Pee Wee Jenkins	Brandon	3	3	.500
Willie Hutchinson	Carman	5	5	.500
Murray Richardson	Carman	4	4	.500
Harry Rhodes	Carman	3	3	.500
Harry Butts	Brandon	5	9	.357
Armando Vasquez	Brandon	2	4	.333
Sam Williams	Brandon	1	2	.333
Fred Brenzel	Carman	3	8	.273
Al Spearman	Winnipeg	1	3	.250
Ed Albosta	Minot	1	6	.167
Ray Finch	Winnipeg	0	3	.000
Bob Landers	Minot	0	1	.000
Earl Christian	Winnipeg	0	1	.000
Hairfield	Winnipeg	0	1	.000
Arnie Fernandez	Winnipeg	0	1	.000
Bruni	Brandon	0	1	.000
Lou Tost	Brandon	0	1	.000
Kevin King	Winnipeg	0	1	.000
Roland Summers	Minot	0	2	.000
Quincy Barbee	Minot	0	0	.000
Willie Wells	Brandon	0	0	.000
Butch Buttgereit	Brandon	No Record Available		
Tony Maze	Brandon	No Record Available		

League Leaders—1952

Batting:	Zoonie Mclean	Minot	.369
Home Runs:	Yogi Giammarco	Minot	11
RBI:	Joe Massaro	Minot	55
Most Wins:	Hal Price	Winnipeg	10
Strikeouts:	Hal Price	Winnipeg	130

Batting Statistics—1953

	Team	G	AB	H	HR	RBI	AVE.
Wilmer Fields	Brandon	5	17	7	2	6	.411
Carlos Forten	Winnipeg	21	24	9	0	1	.375
Dean Scarborough	Minot	49	222	79	2	17	.356
Bob Griffith	Brandon	23	49	17	0	9	.347
Almer McKerlie	Carman	21	76	26	2	4	.342
Lester Lockett	Carman	56	232	77	1	30	.332
Duke Bowman	Minot	70	281	93	2	49	.331
John Washington	Brandon	71	300	98	4	45	.327
Norm Robinson	Carman	64	243	79	1	35	.325
Pete Hughes	Winnipeg	74	241	78	13	66	.324
Harry Rhodes	Carman	40	93	30	1	16	.323
Chick Longest	Carman	57	221	71	6	40	.321
Lyman Bostock	Carman	72	307	97	2	55	.316
Sugar Cain	Minot	—	117	37	2	18	.316
Jim Valentine	Brandon	55	216	66	1	25	.306
Barney Brown	Brandon	18	49	15	0	10	.306
Herb Souell	Carman	72	318	96	5	39	.302
Benny Lott	Carman	37	136	41	1	21	.301
Bill Cleveland	Winnipeg	52	165	49	1	18	.297
Warren Martin	Minot	11	27	8	0	1	.296
Mickey Rocco	Winnipeg	—	—	—	12	—	.296
Joe Atkins	Carman	53	197	58	7	40	.294
Cowan Hyde	Brandon	62	271	79	0	30	.292
Clarence King	Brandon	70	277	81	4	46	.292
Connie Juelke	Minot	59	245	71	11	49	.290
Chuck Carroll	Minot	66	266	77	3	38	.289
Curly Williams	Carman	57	199	57	12	40	.286
Tom Parker	Brandon	20	49	14	0	9	.286
Don Corcoran	Minot	59	204	58	3	22	.284
Dee Moore	Winnipeg	39	121	34	0	15	.281
Jim Banks	Brandon	33	76	21	1	18	.276
Othello Renfroe	Minot	64	219	60	3	45	.274
Zoonie McLean	Minot	45	173	47	0	20	.272
Sonny Andrews	Carman	62	239	64	5	29	.268
Joe Mitchell	Brandon	60	209	56	2	34	.268
Bob Strader	Winnipeg	73	318	83	8	48	.261
Bob Rittenberg	Winnipeg	69	258	67	1	40	.260
Chuck Wilson	Brandon	66	247	64	9	45	.259
Bill Spaeter	Winnipeg	56	230	59	5	41	.257
Lou Louden	Winnipeg	65	274	69	2	32	.252
Jesse Douglas	Wpg/Bran.	53	206	52	2	25	.252
Joe Massaro	Minot	59	251	63	2	35	.251
Willie Hutchinson	Carman	16	36	9	0	3	.250
Orlando Anduz	Brandon	67	233	57	0	17	.245
Ed Bowman	Minot	60	218	53	0	21	.243
Howard Easterling	Winnipeg	—	42	10	1	10	.238
Jack Berry	Winnipeg	—	21	5	2	6	.238
Willie Wells Sr.	Brandon	21	47	11	0	4	.234
Fred Parker	Winnipeg	14	30	7	1	5	.233
Ed Albosta	Minot	20	30	7	0	2	.233

Batting and Pitching Records

	Team	G	AB	H	HR	RBI	AVE.
Dirk Gibbons	Winnipeg	25	56	13	0	3	.232
Dick Butcher	Winnipeg	74	279	62	7	33	.222
Rafe Cabrera	Bran/Winnipeg	57	189	42	4	27	.222
Mel Triplett	Minot	44	162	35	0	13	.216
Bob Turner	Carman	54	201	41	1	33	.204
Jim Newberry	Carman	31	50	10	0	5	.200
Gread McKinnis	Brandon	26	35	7	0	5	.200
Larry Dempsey	Minot	21	31	6	0	3	.194
Hal Price	Winnipeg	20	45	7	0	3	.156
Pee Wee Jenkins	Brandon	18	22	3	0	3	.136
Neal Lettau	Minot	6	15	2	0	3	.133
Walt McCoy	Carman	23	53	6	0	3	.113
Bus Jackson	Winnipeg	3	9	1	0	0	.111
Bill Washburn	Minot/Winnipeg	23	57	6	0	3	.105
Al Preston	Carman	16	20	2	0	1	.100
Rollie Merrill	Winnipeg	22	45	4	0	0	.089
Felix Pine	Carman	5	6	0	0	0	.000
Mario Amero	Brandon	15	20	0	0	0	.000
Bill Barry	Winnipeg	No Record Available					
Bill Cash	Brandon	No Record Available					
Jack Cooper	Minot	No Record Available					
Jim Hinson	Winnipeg	No Record Available					
Phil Tomkinson	Minot	No Record Available					

PITCHING STATISTICS—1953

	Team	G	GS	CG	W	L	PCT
Mike Kanshin	Winnipeg	11	5	2	4	0	.1000
Chuck Gowett	Winnipeg	6	2	2	2	0	.1000
Ed Albosta	Minot	18	3	3	8	2	.800
Neil Lettau	Minot	6	5	3	4	1	.800
Pee Wee Jenkins	Brandon	16	7	2	5	2	.714
Sugar Cain	Minot	17	17	15	12	5	.706
Barney Brown	Brandon	15	11	7	9	4	.692
Harry Rhodes	Carman	26	3	2	8	4	.667
Hal Price	Winnipeg	14	10	6	4	2	.667
Mal Murray	Minot	5	4	1	2	1	.667
Dirk Gibbons	Brandon/Wpg	19	16	8	10	6	.631
Fred Parker	Winnipeg	12	5	1	5	3	.625
Tom Parker	Brandon	12	11	6	6	4	.600
Bill Washburn	Minot/Wpg	21	29	12	10	7	.588
Gread McKinnis	Brandon	25	11	3	7	5	.583
Bob Griffith	Brandon	21	14	6	8	6	.572
Warren Martin	Minot	10	9	5	4	3	.572
Walt McCoy	Carman	21	14	9	10	8	.556
Andy Porter	Carman	13	12	4	4	4	.500
Al Preston	Wpg/Carman	16	11	2	4	5	.444
Bob Whitchar	Minot	10	6	4	2	3	.400
Larry Dempsey	Minot	14	8	4	3	5	.375
Jim Newberry	Carman	30	15	6	5	9	.357
Carlos Forten	Bran/Winnipeg	19	8	2	3	6	.333

	Team	G	GS	CG	W	L	PCT
Willie Hutchinson	Carman	12	9	5	3	6	.333
Tom Lowe	Minot	3	3	1	1	2	.333
Felix Pine	Carman	5	5	1	1	2	.333
Rollie Merrill	Winnipeg	21	17	7	5	13	.278
Mario Amaro	Brandon	16	7	1	2	6	.250
Roy Chapman	Minot	5	1	0	0	1	.000
Roy Klaudt	Minot	1	1	0	0	1	.000
John Kelly	Minot	2	2	0	0	1	.000
Roy McCoy	Carman	3	3	0	0	1	.000
Othello Renfroe	Minot	1	1	0	0	1	.000
Jim Banks	Brandon	14	3	1	0	1	.000
Lou Lombardo	Minot	6	3	2	0	3	.000
Bill Cleveland	Winnipeg	9	3	2	0	5	.000
Chet Brewer	Carman	3	2	0	0	0	.000
Paul Beck	Winnipeg	1	0	0	0	0	.000
Mike Williams	Wpg/Minot	4	0	0	0	0	.000
Willie Wells	Brandon	4	0	0	0	0	.000
Lillard Cobb	Carman	1	0	0	0	0	.000
Dee Moore	Winnipeg	4	0	0	0	0	.000
Wilmer Fields	Brandon	2	1	0	0	0	.000
Chick Longest	Carman	1	0	0	0	0	.000

League Leaders—1953

Batting:	Dean Scarborough	Minot	.356
Home Runs:	Pete Hughes	Winnipeg	13
RBI:	Pete Hughes	Winnipeg	66
Wins:	Sugar Cain	Minot	12
Best Record—Pitcher	Ed Albosta	Minot	8—2 .800

Batting Statistics—1954

	Team	AB	H	D	T	HR	RBI	AVE
Sugar Cain	Minot	82	37	5	5	2	20	.451
Roy Weatherly	Williston	194	80	11	1	14	58	.412
Ron Bowen	Brandon	112	41	6	0	7	28	.366
Benny Lott	Carman	232	83	17	2	7	53	.358
Othello Renfroe	Minot	229	80	14	2	3	39	.349
Yogi Giammarco	Minot	128	44	—	—	9	30	.344
Duke Bowman	Minot	252	85	18	4	3	57	.337
Don Stewart	Brandon	228	76	13	4	8	41	.333
Bob Miller	Carman	81	27	6	1	1	13	.333
Lloyd Gearhart	Williston	239	79	21	2	17	61	.331
Dean Scarborough	Minot	274	90	14	4	2	60	.328
Joe Massaro	Minot	283	92	10	0	7	66	.325
Walt Thomas	Carman	100	32	7	0	0	12	.320
Frank Mascaro	Brandon	284	90	11	6	6	60	.317
Zoonie McLean	Minot	255	80	14	4	2	20	.314
Leon Day	Brandon	137	43	5	3	1	17	.314
Dick Baxter	Williston	106	33	3	0	0	11	.311
Bill Spaeter	Brandon	216	66	14	4	4	28	.306

Batting and Pitching Records

	Team	AB	H	D	T	HR	RBI	AVE
Sammy Drake	Carman	276	84	11	4	1	30	.305
Don Corcoran	Minot	259	77	11	3	7	42	.297
Joe Lutz	Williston	65	19	3	0	8	20	.292
Gerry MacKay	Brandon	306	89	16	7	8	42	.291
Tony Campos	Williston	249	72	12	4	6	39	.289
Jesse Douglas	Carman	238	68	16	1	1	44	.286
Almer McKerlie	Carman	46	13	2	0	0	6	.283
John Chalfont	Williston	161	45	9	1	4	33	.280
Connie Juelke	Minot	244	68	10	8	7	46	.279
Lou Louden	Brandon	227	63	5	1	0	21	.278
John Washington	Carman	249	69	11	2	1	36	.277
Chick Longest	Carman	246	68	13	1	4	37	.276
Bill Cleveland	Bran/Will	285	77	23	5	3	38	.270
Ronnie Martin	Williston	216	57	6	4	0	17	.264
Buddy Owens	Brandon	108	28	6	3	3	18	.259
Dee Moore	Brandon	112	29	4	0	3	19	.259
Hal Daugherty	Brandon	222	57	5	2	1	45	.257
Lester Lockett	Carman	242	60	16	1	3	31	.248
Ed Bowman	Minot	215	53	4	6	0	32	.247
Dewey Williams	Williston	69	17	4	2	1	10	.246
Norm Robinson	Carman	254	62	7	1	2	23	.244
Weldon Ridley	Carman	144	32	4	0	3	19	.222
Jim Michalec	Williston	121	35	3	1	3	11	.207
Felipe Jiminez	Carman	87	18	1	1	0	6	.207
Buddy Afremow	Williston	234	44	4	1	2	28	.188
Willie Greene	Minot	33	6	0	1	0	3	.182
Walt Bowman	Minot	54	7	0	0	0	2	.130
Ron Smith	Williston	No Record Available						
Charlie Ferguson	Williston	No Record Available						
Jim Shupe	Brandon	No Record Available						
Lou Almendariz	Brandon	No Record Available						
Ray Sisler	Brandon	No Record Available						
Ralph Blinn	Williston	No Record Available						

Pitching Statistics — 1954

	Team	IP	H	BB	SO	W	L	PCT.
Morley McFarlane	Brandon	9	4	5	12	1	0	1.000
Murray Richardson	Brandon	9	7	7	8	1	0	1.000
Dick Myers	Brandon	—	—	—	—	1	0	1.000
Sugar Cain	Minot	106	69	34	98	11	1	.917
Neal Lettau	Minot	131	109	74	52	13	2	.867
Bill Washburn	Minot	80	64	35	60	7	2	.778
Harry Taylor	Williston	115⅔	98	39	59	9	4	.692
Ed Albosta	Carman	71	81	22	30	4	2	.667
Rod MacKay	Brandon	61⅔	82	7	22	4	2	.667
Willie Greene	Minot	16⅔	22	8	4	2	1	.667
Cliff Lemme	Minot	22⅔	22	11	16	2	1	.667
Dirk Gibbons	Brandon	54⅔	177	47	70	11	7	.611
Dan Ahtipis	Brandon	136⅓	143	80	77	10	7	.588
Warren Martin	Minot	127⅔	130	59	58	7	5	.583

	Team	IP	H	BB	SO	W	L	PCT.
Red Rose	Brandon	93⅓	128	37	52	7	5	.583
Dick Schoonover	Williston	91⅔	94	41	52	6	5	.545
Danny Patton	Williston	35	41	15	12	1	1	.500
Ernie Canada	Minot	—	—	—	—	1	1	.500
Walt McCoy	Carman	126	144	57	70	8	9	.471
Vic Michalec	Williston	103⅓	117	37	32	6	8	.421
Mort Wright	Brandon	68⅓	96	38	24	3	4	.429
Ed Williams	Williston	36⅔	45	14	25	2	3	.400
Buddy Woods	Carman	79⅔	118	52	47	5	8	.385
Bob Miller	Carman	90⅓	97	30	31	3	6	.333
Dean Scarborough	Minot	—	—	—	—	1	2	.333
Fred Parker	Min./Will./Bran.	84⅓	105	45	33	3	7	.300
Dick Baxter	Williston	79⅔	93	42	41	2	6	.250
Rollie Merrill	Minot	22⅓	29	13	5	1	3	.250
Walt Thomas	Carman	8	12	5	1	0	1	.000
Ed Mazur	Carman	—	—	—	—	0	1	.000
Leon Day	Brandon	11	20	6	6	0	2	.000
John Murray	Carman	42⅔	35	41	11	0	3	.000
Kent Geisler	Williston	40⅓	47	37	23	0	3	.000
Felipe Jiminez	Carman	57⅓	64	54	36	0	5	.000
Gil Pantel	Carman	—	—	—	—	0	1	.000
Harold Dark	Williston	—	—	—	—	0	1	.000
Don Betzen	Williston	No Records Available						
Bert Shepard	Williston	No Records Available						

League Leaders—1954

Batting	Roy Weatherly	Williston	.412
Home Runs	Lloyd Gearhart	Williston	17
RBI	Joe Massaro	Minot	66
Wins	Neal Lettau	Minot	13
Best Record — Pitcher	Sugar Cain	Minot	11 — 1
Strikeouts	Sugar Cain	Minot	98

Batting Statistics—1955

	Team	AB	H	D	T	HR	RBI	AVE
Don Orwiler	Dickinson	55	21	2	2	4	7	.382
George Wopinek	Minot	21	8	2	1	1	5	.381
Roy Weatherly	Williston	299	111	23	4	21	61	.371
Butch Davis	Minot	255	94	21	3	6	37	.369
Bill Hockenbury	Bismarck	134	49	8	2	10	30	.366
Ray Dandridge	Bismarck	328	118	25	7	8	43	.360
Bob Easterbrook	Bismarck	276	99	23	2	18	68	.359
Bill Cash	Bismarck	255	91	10	5	15	61	.357
Zoonie McLean	Minot	276	97	18	2	13	57	.351
Art Pennington	Bismarck	229	80	11	2	11	46	.349
Bill Pinckard	Minot	46	16	4	1	1	11	.348
Dolph Regelsky	Williston	184	57	18	2	14	53	.348
Bob Betz	Williston	289	99	15	3	8	68	.343
Ray Berns	Williston	160	53	5	4	7	36	.331
Bill Jankowski	Bismarck	311	103	15	9	3	38	.331

Batting and Pitching Records

	Team	AB	H	D	T	HR	RBI	AVE
Bill Raehse	Williston	283	91	26	8	8	59	.323
Duke Bowman	Minot	305	98	20	3	2	53	.321
Lloyd Gearhart	Bismarck	119	38	8	1	8	28	.319
Ron Bowen	Dickinson	280	89	10	1	18	68	.318
Joe Monteiro	Minot	249	78	20	2	14	51	.313
Don Petschow	Dickinson	197	61	9	0	15	40	.310
Terry Hayes	Williston	26	8	0	1	1	1	.308
Don Fischer	Dickinson	333	71	8	2	2	23	.305
Dick Jok	Dickinson	202	61	5	1	6	32	.302
Ron Martin	Williston	255	77	14	0	3	28	.302
Don Corcoran	Minot	289	87	17	5	11	55	.301
Frank Roelandt	Williston	220	66	14	0	3	30	.300
Ev Johnson	Dickinson	282	84	13	7	6	39	.298
Tom Gatts	Minot	64	19	3	2	0	8	.297
Dennis Healy	Bismarck	128	38	4	2	0	9	.297
Bob Geels	Dickinson	155	46	9	4	1	20	.297
Ed Bowman	Minot	277	82	14	5	0	29	.296
Fred Vaughan	Will/Bismarck	174	51	8	0	7	31	.293
Milt Joffee	Dickinson	321	94	11	9	7	31	.293
Dean Scarborough	Minot	301	87	20	1	2	42	.289
Al Cihocki	Bismarck	160	46	5	1	11	36	.288
Willie Patterson	Minot	70	20	4	0	1	13	.286
Dan Chepkauskas	Williston	50	14	3	2	2	10	.280
Dick Morgan	Dickinson	329	92	11	1	6	42	.280
Joe Massaro	Minot	226	63	13	0	2	37	.279
Tom McDevitt	Williston	61	17	3	1	0	6	.279
Bob Bourbeau	Dickinson	213	58	9	2	6	26	.272
Bill Sharp	Williston	321	87	13	2	5	31	.271
Jack Wilson	Williston	104	28	6	1	3	19	.269
Buddy Afremow	Dickinson	314	83	16	2	1	34	.264
Sugar Cain	Minot	59	15	3	0	1	6	.254
Sam Scarpone	Bismarck	112	27	5	0	0	17	.241
Dick Baxter	Dickinson	77	18	1	0	1	8	.231
Preston Gomez	Bismarck	238	55	12	1	5	30	.251
Dewey Williams	Minot	152	35	7	0	5	23	.230
Ray Tabacchi	Dickinson	96	19	1	2	0	7	.198
Pius Wolf	Bismarck	128	19	6	1	1	10	.148
Charley Frey	Minot	No Record Available						

Pitching Statistics — 1955

	Team	IP	H	BB	SO	W	L	ERA
John Fitzgerald	Bismarck	8	7	4	3	1	0	1.13
Bobby Hogue	Williston	5	3	1	1	2	0	1.18
Preston Elkins	Williston	73	59	12	40	7	0	2.34
Sugar Cain	Minot	107	108	48	91	8	4	2.94
Mike Lotz	Bismarck	110	100	25	79	8	2	2.95
Jonas Gaines	Bismarck	113	102	39	70	8	3	3.27
Don Lee	Williston	74	70	26	60	5	2	3.65
Dick Schoonover	Williston	147	176	55	73	8	10	3.67
Roger Higgins	Bismarck	117	121	11	51	8	3	3.69

	Team	IP	H	BB	SO	W	L	ERA
Robbie Cartledge	Minot	44	45	16	33	1	3	3.89
Ed Williams	Williston	113	130	41	78	6	5	4.22
Ken Heintzelman	Bismarck	64	82	14	48	5	2	4.50
Mel Duncan	Minot	26	25	14	20	2	1	4.50
Bill Hockenbury	Bismarck	87	95	58	47	7	6	4.55
Red Rose	Dickinson	149	161	32	70	10	10	4.65
Art Worth	Bismarck	32	29	16	13	2	3	4.78
Dan Ahtipis	Minot	38	32	15	21	2	3	4.98
Stan Milankovich	Minot	43	51	27	29	4	2	5.23
Joe Rancher	Bismarck	12	19	9	4	0	1	5.25
Tom Mulcahy	Williston	101	125	31	53	7	5	5.26
Ed Beneke	Dick/Bismarck	58	65	24	32	4	1	5.27
Jim Michalec	Dickinson	152	164	52	68	5	7	5.33
Tom Horton	Minot	91	91	73	43	3	4	5.34
Dirk Gibbons	Minot	100	133	46	59	5	7	5.44
Norm Rynard	Dickinson	16	18	8	5	1	1	5.63
Fred Parker	Williston	65	82	26	28	2	5	5.68
Bill Washburn	Minot	55	71	26	28	3	2	6.06
Stan Karpinski	Williston	50	70	12	22	3	3	6.12
Walt Mitchell	Williston/Dickinson	74	57	77	36	3	5	6.33
Walt McCoy	Bismarck	56	83	33	25	3	6	6.85
Tom Edmunds	Minot	62	85	27	35	4	3	6.82
Dick Baxter	Dickinson	92	121	53	33	3	6	6.85
Phil Haugstad	Williston	13	16	11	7	0	1	6.92
Fred Brenzell	Dickinson	116	139	60	40	5	10	6.98
Jack Dean	Dickinson	21	24	8	13	1	2	7.71
Gail Burnhart	Dickinson	8	11	4	4	0	1	7.88
Don Orwiler	Dickinson	65	116	19	44	1	6	8.17
Joe Cincotta	Dickinson	12	19	3	8	0	2	8.25
Neal Lettau	Minot	63	99	36	37	3	6	8.29
Barny Brown	Minot	21	34	7	11	0	3	9.00
Bill Furlong	Bismarck	19	37	10	8	0	3	9.00
Warren Martin	Minot	21	20	37	8	2	2	13.28
Murray Richardson	Minot	1	1	4	1	1	0	18.00
Eldon Russell	Dickinson			1	0			
Bob Ebkor	Minot			0	0			

LEAGUE LEADERS—1955

Batting:	Roy Weatherly	Williston	.371
Home Runs:	Roy Weatherly	Williston	21
RBI:	Bob Easterbrook	Bismarck	68
	Ron Bowen	Dickinson	68
	Bob Betz	Williston	68
Best Record—Pitcher:	Preston Elkins	Williston	7—0

BATTING STATISTICS—1956

	Team	AB	H	D	T	HR	RBI	AVE
Dean Scarborough	Minot	44	17	3	0	1	6	.386
Dolph Regelsky	Williston	271	98	17	4	19	68	.362

Batting and Pitching Records

	Team	AB	H	D	T	HR	RBI	AVE
Art Pennington	Bismarck	294	105	10	11	10	51	.357
Carl Paylor	Williston	155	54	11	3	1	22	.348
Tex Dargie	Bismarck	301	104	20	6	3	33	.346
Sam Hill	Bismarck	322	108	19	2	20	73	.335
Bill Raehse	Williston	325	107	20	0	17	60	.329
Sugar Cain	Minot	86	28	—	—	1	10	.325
Ed Barr	Minot	253	82	11	2	12	62	.324
Roy Weatherly	Will./Bism.	176	57	8	1	9	39	.324
Dennis Healy	Williston	106	34	7	0	1	15	.321
Hal Daugherty	Minot	322	103	22	3	12	56	.320
Zoonie McLean	Minot	262	83	20	3	6	50	.317
John Kropf	Bismarck	228	72	13	5	13	43	.316
Bob Van Eman	Minot	208	65	12	1	8	46	.313
Ev Johnson	Dickinson	225	70	13	2	5	32	.311
Pete Spatafore	Williston	119	37	7	6	2	15	.311
Bob Hockenbury	Bismarck	293	90	9	4	18	59	.307
Garland Lawing	Dickinson	270	83	10	3	19	73	.307
Al Cihocki	Bismarck	310	95	30	1	5	51	.306
Nelly Daehn	Williston	345	105	31	5	4	36	.304
Bill Sharp	Williston	250	75	7	0	0	18	.300
Preston Elkins	Williston	50	45	5	0	14	40	.300
Duke Bowman	Minot	284	82	22	2	6	45	.292
Dan Chepkauskas	Will./Dic.	257	75	6	0	6	30	.292
Al Lyons	Williston	45	13	2	1	0	5	.289
Gerald Didier	Dickinson	231	66	7	3	3	33	.286
Al Leap	Bismarck	305	87	14	0	23	61	.285
Mike Perez	Bismarck	204	56	7	2	0	26	.275
Jim Leavitt	Williston	272	74	9	2	5	30	.272
Bill Jankowski	Dickinson	290	78	11	3	3	31	.269
Chick Orner	Minot	113	30	6	3	4	20	.265
Andy Anderson	Minot	141	37	7	0	7	18	.262
Milt Joffe	Dickinson	287	74	10	5	8	31	.258
Carl Bush	Minot	297	76	15	6	11	38	.256
Ray Berns	Williston	312	79	12	6	7	48	.253
Earl Johnson	Dickinson	220	55	6	0	1	32	.250
Fred Brenzel	Dick./Bism	80	20	2	1	0	10	.250
Dee Moore	Williston	28	7	1	0	0	3	.250
Buddy Afremow	Dickinson	235	58	8	1	2	21	.247
Rocky Krisnich	Dickinson	58	14	0	0	2	6	.241
Bob Karbowski	Will./Dick.	90	21	3	0	2	13	.233
Dewey Williams	Minot	154	35	0	1	1	9	.227
D. Boyer	Dickinson	58	13	1	1	1	7	.224
Connie Juelke	Minot	59	13	6	0	4	12	.220
Bill Spaeter	Williston	59	13	2	0	0	4	.220
Don Corcoran	Minot	262	56	9	3	4	25	.214
Don Smith	Minot	48	10	0	0	2	4	.208
Bob Ball	Bismarck	21	4	2	0	0	3	.190
Pius Wolf	Bismarck	25	4	1	0	2	7	.160
Dan Phalen	Williston	17	2	0	1	0	0	.118
Don Miller	Minot	No Record Available						

Pitching Statistics — 1956

	Team	IP	H	BB	SO	W	L	ERA
Sugar Cain	Minot	130	127	44	82	10	5	2.29
Bill Hockenbury	Bismarck	27	25	14	9	2	1	2.33
Al Lyons	Williston	44	37	6	29	4	1	2.46
Preston Elkins	Williston	176	163	37	110	15	4	2.71
Pete Taylor	Minot	110	100	24	37	8	7	2.86
Jack Sanoff	Williston	156	130	47	83	14	3	3.00
Ed Williams	Williston	91	95	20	45	5	6	3.37
Dick Kelly	Minot	95	90	25	35	6	5	3.50
Vic Michalec	Dickinson	138	141	66	78	8	9	3.78
Vic Stryska	Bismarck	140	165	28	67	9	7	3.86
Joe Piercey	Minot	38	39	12	9	1	2	4.02
Gene Nelson	Bismarck	44	53	24	13	3	1	4.10
Gerald Fahr	Dickinson	146	190	25	62	7	10	4.31
Chuck Donley	Williston	61	72	21	37	4	3	4.43
Tom Guderian	Minot	43	47	25	16	3	1	4.50
Norm Johnson	Williston	83	87	41	45	5	5	4.55
Mike Schultz	Minot	37	42	13	6	2	1	4.63
Roger Higgins	Bismarck	121	157	25	62	12	1	4.91
Dirk Gibbons	Minot	109	127	32	58	6	7	4.95
Don Herman	Williston	38	38	14	19	1	3	4.98
Walter Bryja	Dickinson	71	84	19	30	3	3	5.07
Don Smith	Minot	16	21	11	5	0	1	5.07
Mel Heim	Dickinson	139	166	62	80	6	10	5.18
Fred Brenzel	Dick/Bism.	105	132	42	48	5	8	5.23
Chuck Eisemann	Bismarck	15	19	6	11	1	0	5.40
John Fitzgerald	Bismarck	84	97	45	53	4	7	5.46
Malcom Landry	Bismarck	98	115	79	29	9	3	5.51
Charles Griffith	Minot	11	11	6	3	0	0	5.72
Bill Oster	Minot	34	34	16	29	1	2	5.82
Whitney Ulrich	Williston	33	29	23	7	1	4	6.00
Red Rose	Dickinson	31	45	8	19	1	4	6.09
Tony Garcia	Bismarck	120	152	38	44	4	7	6.30
Bob Laskowski	Dickinson	35	61	13	16	0	3	7.46
Mel Duncan	Minot	29	32	29	14	3	1	7.76
Bill Washburn	Minot	11	20	9	7	0	0	8.18
Gread McKinnis	Minot					0	2	
Wymon Carey	Minot					0	0	
Bruce Haroldson	Minot					0	0	
Harry Wise	Bismarck					0	0	

League Leaders

Batting:	Dolph Regelsky	Williston	.362
Home Runs:	Al Leap	Bismarck	23
RBI:	Sam Hill	Williston 73, Butch Lawing Dickinson	73
Wins:	Preston Elkins	Williston	15
Best Record —Pitcher:	Roger Higgins	Bismarck	12—1
Strikeouts:	Preston Elkins	Williston	110

Batting Statistics—1957

Name	Team	AB	H	D	T	HR	RBI	Ave
Bill Lynn	Williston	122	56	7	1	5	33	.459
Len Van De Hey	Bismarck	280	113	20	5	10	66	.404
Zoonie Mclean	Minot	274	100	26	3	9	58	.365
Jessie Rogers	Minot	292	106	20	9	14	66	.363
Jerry Adair	Williston	101	36	5	2	0	8	.356
Bill Sharp	Williston	167	58	4	0	1	18	.341
Carl Bush	Minot	287	97	15	3	11	55	.338
Gideon Jarvis	Minot	156	46	11	2	5	26	.338
Gene Johnson	Bismarck	259	87	13	7	11	36	.336
Joe Massaro	Williston	268	90	21	2	2	55	.336
Al Lyons	Brandon	229	76	9	2	12	46	.332
Bill Raeshe	Williston	261	85	15	2	19	88	.326
Al Leap	Bismarck	260	83	11	0	14	53	.319
Sugar Cain	Minot	88	28	—	—	0	8	.318
Bill Hockenbury	Bismarck	192	60	9	3	11	52	.313
Tom Giuliano	Brandon	272	84	11	4	1	24	.309
Willard Brown	Minot	150	46	9	9	9	29	.307
Jack Ackers	Bismarck	184	56	12	0	9	44	.304
Clyde McNeal	Bismarck	247	75	16	6	16	61	.304
Ed Bowman	Williston	89	27	5	0	0	7	.303
Duke Bowman	Minot	137	41	9	3	3	23	.299
Carl Paylor	Williston	289	86	17	2	10	39	.298
Doug Lewis	Brandon	286	84	12	6	2	37	.294
Steve Molonari	Williston	130	38	1	0	4	17	.292
Preston Elkins	Williston	152	44	8	1	6	25	.289
Garland Lawing	Brandon	229	66	12	3	6	39	.288
Frank Neri	Bismarck	258	73	11	2	11	30	.283
Chuck Orner	Minot	233	64	19	4	2	28	.275
Benny Lott	Brandon	165	45	4	3	2	21	.273
Jack Sanoff	Williston	11	3	1	0	0	2	.273
Buddy Messina	Minot	242	65	9	2	12	33	.269
Dick Thonn	Bismarck	238	64	7	2	3	26	.269
Dee Moore	Brandon	56	15	1	0	0	8	.268
Gerry MacKay	Brandon	265	70	10	1	4	27	.264
Roy Weatherly	Williston	65	17	7	0	2	9	.262
Lou Louden	Brandon	195	50	5	0	3	24	.256
Ralph Wilcox	Brandon	179	45	6	2	9	37	.256
Bob Ball	Wiliston	16	4	4	1	0	0	.250
Andy Anderson	Minot	293	73	11	4	10	37	.249
Frank Tanana	Williston	59	14	2	0	4	8	.246
Pete Konyar	Williston	92	22	1	1	1	8	.239
Dennis Healy	Williston	126	30	7	2	0	18	.238
Bruce Meland	Bismarck	8	2	0	0	0	0	.225
Howard Morgenstern	Minot	9	2	0	0	0	1	.222
Bob Rous	Brandon	188	41	4	5	7	25	.218
Don Smith	Minot	191	22	3	0	1	14	.218
Mike Perez	Bismarck	166	36	4	2	0	14	.217
Rudy Mayling	Minot/Williston	133	28	7	0	10	22	.211
Dewey Williams	Williston	26	5	0	1	0	1	.166
Tom Rowan	Williston	31	4	0	0	0	0	.129

Name	Team	AB	H	D	T	HR	RBI	Ave
Billy Munyer	Williston	2	0	0	0	0	0	.000
Jerry Cabana	Minot	No Record Available						
Jerry Henrick	Minot	No Record Available						
Don Hunter	Brandon	No Record Available						
Duane Hummel	Bismarck	No Record Available						
Jim Slevin	Brandon	No Record Available						

PITCHING STATISTICS — 1957

Name	Team	W	L	WK	SO	ERA
Jerry Adair	Williston	1	0	2	5	0.00
Dee Moore	Brandon	1	0	6	10	1.10
Jack Sanoff	Williston	3	0	6	26	2.07
Al Lyons	Brandon	9	4	19	42	3.08
Jack Bowes	Bismarck	10	5	45	73	3.34
Bob Bennett	Brandon	7	10	76	98	3.62
Sugar Cain	Minot	7	5	34	61	3.94
Bill Upton	Minot	7	6	29	40	3.96
Bill Hockenbury	Bismarck	0	1	15	13	4.23
Dirk Gibbons	Minot	3	9	60	51	4.33
Bill Oster	Minot	9	5	59	58	4.27
Bob Yanen	Williston	7	9	41	62	4.41
Al Leap	Bismarck	0	1			4.50
John Fitzgerald	Bismarck	6	4	59	44	4.75
Gib McGlothin	Brandon	7	4	42	31	4.89
Frank Schwartz	Bismarck	7	6	39	60	5.09
John Andre	Minot	3	3	43	35	5.37
Jack Hale	Minot	6	6	63	46	5.49
Jack Ackers	Bismarck	10	6	84	55	6.21
Jay Smith	Williston	0	1	8	4	6.23
Bill Best	Williston	5	4	25	42	6.38
Ed Williams	Williston	2	6	21	41	6.49
Tom Rowan	Williston	0	1	2	7	6.75
Kaye Bachmann	Bismarck	6	9	64	21	6.79
Preston Elkins	Williston	6	6	35	48	7.03
Garland Lawing	Brandon	1	2	20	22	7.04
Bob Rous	Brandon	2	2	18	10	7.23
Elwin Hahn	Williston	3	1	12	28	7.47
Norm Johnson	Will./Bran.	7	10	68	31	7.52
Al Gettel	Williston	1	4	2	12	7.82
Roy Mathews	Williston	1	1	1	1	9.01
Andy Anderson	Minot	1	0	2	2	12.00
Frank McCollum	Minot	0	1			
Gerry Cashill	Brandon	0	1			
Ed Funai	Brandon	0	1			
Mel Hein	Brandon	0	1			
Norman Budz	Minot	0	0			
Gerry Harder	Bismarck	0	0			
Mort Wright	Brandon	0	0			
Don Orwiler	Brandon	No Record Available				
Mort Wright	Brandon	No Record Available				

LEAGUE LEADERS 1957

Batting Average:	Len Van de Hey	Bismarck	.404
Home Runs:	Bill Raeshe	Wiliston	19
RBI:	Bill Raeshe	Williston	88
Most Wins:	Jack Bowes	Bismarck	10
ERA:	Al Lyons	Brandon	3.08

MANDAK LEAGUE RECORDS

Batting Average:	Butch Davis	Winnipeg Buffaloes	.456	1950
Hits:	Ray Dandridge	Bismarck Barons	118	1955
At Bats:	Nellie Daehn	Williston Oilers	345	1956
Singles:	John Washington	Brandon Greys	81	1953
Doubles:	Al Cihocki	Bismarck Barons	30	1956
Triples:	Art Pennington	Bismarck Barons	11	1956
Home Runs:	Al Leap	Bismarck Barons	23	1956
Runs Batted In:	Bill Raehse	Williston Oilers	88	1957
Total Bases:	Sam Hill	Bismarck Barons	232	1955
Slugging:	Roy Weatherly	Williston Oilers	.686	1955
Put Outs in a Season:	Ron Bowen	Dickinson	750	1955
Assists:	Buddy Afremow	Dickinson	297	1955
Games Won:	Preston Elkins	Williston Oilers	15	1956
Strikeouts:	Hal Price	Winnipeg	130	1952
Strikeouts in a Game:	Taylor Smith	Winnipeg Buffaloes	17	1950
E.R.A.:	Sugar Cain	Minot Mallards	2.29	1956

PLAYOFF CHAMPIONS

1950 — Winnipeg Buffaloes
1951 — Brandon Greys
1952 — Minot Mallards
1953 — Minot Mallards
1954 — Minot Mallards
1955 — Minot Mallards
1956 — Williston Oilers
1957 — Bismarck Barons

Appendix III
Rosters

BISMARCK BARONS

1955 — Ed Beneke[1] (P), Bill Cash (C), Al Cihocki (2B/MGR), Ray Dandridge (3B), Bob Easterbrook (1B), Bill Furlong[2] (P), John Fitzgerald (P), Jonas Gaines (P), Lloyd Gearhart (OF), Preston Gomez (SS), Ken Heintzelman (P), Dennis Healy (UT), Roger Higgins (P), Bill Hockenbury (3B), Bill Jankowski (1B), Al Leap (SS), Mike Lotz (P), Art Pennington (1B), Joe Rancher (P), Sam Scarpone (C), Fred Vaughan (2B), Pius Wolf (UT), Art Worth (P)
[1]*Played part of the season with Dickinson Packers*
[2]*Played part of the season with Williston Oilers*

1956 — Bob Ball (UT), Fred Brenzell[1] (P), Al Cihocki (2B/MGR), Tex Dargie (RF), Chuck Eisemann (P), John Fitzgerald (P), Tony Garcia (P), Sam Hill (OF), Roger Higgins (P), Bill Hockenbury (P/3B), Connie Juelke (OF), John Kropf (OF), Malcom Landry (P), Al Leap (SS), Walt McCoy (P), Gene Nelson (P), Art Pennington (OF), Mike Perez (C), Vic Stryska (P), Roy Weatherly[2] (OF), Harry Wise (P), Pius Wolf (UT)
[1]*Played most of the season with Dickinson*
[2]*Played part of the season with Williston Oilers*

1957 — Jim Ackers (LF), Bob Ball (C), Kaye Bachmann (P), Jack Bowes (P), John Fitzgerald (P), Gerry Harder (P), Bill Hockenbury (MGR/3B), Duane Hummel (C), Gene Johnson (LF), Al Leap (SS), Clyde McNeal (2B), Bruce Meland (1B), Frank Neri (CF), Mike Perez (C), Frank Schwartz (P/LF), Ray Thonn (1B), Len Van De Hey (RF)

BRANDON GREYS

1950 — Rafe Cabrera (P/OF), Mario Chacon (P), Carl Dent (SS), Percy Fenwick (MGR), Dirk Gibbons (P), Manuel Godinez (P), Art Hunt (P), Tom Johnson (P), Ian Lowe (3B), Gerry MacKay (OF), Winslow Means (P), Pedro Naranjo (P), Charles Peete (OF),Leonard Pigg (C), Ramon Rodriquez (C), Victor Savingne (OF), Armando Vasquez (UT), Dick Vinson (P), Frank Watkins (P), Murray Watkins (3B), Chuck Wilson (2B)

1951— Bill Anderson (P), Pepper Bassett (C), Harry Butts (P), Rafe Cabrera (P/OF), Frank Evans (RF), 223 Amancio Ferro (P), Ed Finney (2B), Art Hunt (P), Clarence King (LF), Ian Lowe (3B), Gerry MacKay[1] (OF), Gread McKinnis (P), Joseph Mitchell[2] (2B), Pedro Naranjo (P), Alonzo Perry (1B/P), Ramon Rodriquez (C/OF), Armando Suarez (P), Jim Valentine (2B/P), Armando Vasquez (UT), Murray Watkins (3B), Frank Watkins[3] (P)
[1]*Was released and signed with Minot Mallards*
[2]*Played part of the season with Elmwood Giants.*
[3]*Played part of the season with Minot Mallards*

1952 —(Alexander), Mario Amaro (P), Cesar Argudin (3B), Norman Banks (OF), Barney Brown (P), Bruni[1] (P/INF), Butch Buttgereit (OF), Harry Butts (P), Rafe Cabrera (P/OF), Irvan Castille (3B), Chuck Chohalis, Luther Clifford (C), Jose Colas (OF), Decker (INF), Pee Wee Jenkins (P/OF), Clarence King (LF), Gus Kyle (C), Glen Lewis (C), Linek (1B/P), Enriqe Maroto (P/OF), Maze (P), Joseph Mitchell (2B), Frazier Robinson (C), Norm Robinson (RF), Lou Tost (P), Al Tehero[2] (3B), Jim Valentine (2B), Armando Vasquez (UT), Murray Watkins (3B), Willie Wells (MGR), Junior Williams (P)
[1]*Some players were with teams only briefly, and their last names alone appeared in box scores.*
[2]*Played some games with the Winnipeg Giants*

1953 — Mario Amaro (P), Orlando Andux (SS), Jim Banks (P), Barney Brown (P), Harry Butts (P), Rafe Cabrerra[1] (OF), Bill Cash[2] (C), Jesse Douglas (INF), Howard Easterling (INF), Wilmer Fields (OF), Bob Griffith (P/OF), Cowan Hyde (OF), Pee Wee Jenkins (P/OF), Clarence King (LF), Gread McKinnis (P), Joseph Mitchell (2B), Tom Parker (P), Jim Valentine (P), John Washington (1B), Willie Wells (MGR/UT), Chuck Wilson (2B/OF)
[1]*Was released and signed by Winnipeg*
[2]*Played part of the season with Elmwood Giants.*

1954 — Dan Ahtipis (P), Lou Almendariz (SS), Ron Bowen[1] (1B), Leon Day (P/3B), Hal Daugherty (2B), Dirk Gibbons (P), Jeminez (1B), Clarence King (OF), Lou Louden (C), Morley McFarlane (P), McGill (P), Gerry MacKay (OF), Rod MacKay (P), Dennis Magnuson (C), Dee Moore (MGR/UT), Frank Mascaro (OF), Dick Myers (P), Buddy Owens (SS), Murray Richardson (P), Red Rose (P), Ray Sisler (C), Ron Smith (3B), Bill Spaeter (OF), Donald Stewart (UT), Trann (SS), Mort Wright (P)
[1]*Played most of the season with Williston Oilers.*

1957 — Bob Bennett (P/1B), Bob Betz (OF), Gerry Cashill (P), Charles Dana (C), Ed Funai (P), Tom Giuliano (SS), Mel Heim (P), Don Hunter (OF), Norm Johnson[1] (P), Benny Lott (INF), Lou Louden (C), Al Lyons (P), Butch Lawing (RF), Doug Lewis (1B), Dee Moore (MGR/C), Gerry MacKay (OF), Gib McClothin (P/INF), Harry McIlvaine (P), Don Orwiler (P), Bob Rous (3B/P), Jim Slevin (C), Gerry Smith (P), Ralph Wilcox (3B), Dewey Williams[2] (C), Mort Wright (P)
[1]*Played most of the season with Williston Oilers*
[2]*Played some games with Minot and Brandon, then finished season with Williston.*

CARMAN CARDINALS

1950 — Joe Adams (P), Sonny Andrews (SS), Luke Chojnowski (INF), Lillard Cobb (P), Ed Dorohoy (OF), Gord Elliot (INF), Red House (3B, MGR), Gentry Jessup (P), Bob Johnson (1B), Bill Malone (OF), Bob Manning (P/OF), Mac Massingale (OF), Almer McKerlie (C), Clint McKerlie (P), Ray McWhorter (P), Ed Novak (MGR), Don Reid (P), Jack Schaefer (1B), Ron Teasley (1B/OF), Walt Thomas (C), Dan Webster (P/C), John Wingo (P)

1951— Andy Anderson (OF/P), John Bass (P), Sonny Andrews (SS), Joe Bestudik[1] (OF), Fred Brenzel (P), T. J. Brown[2] (2B), Earl Bumpus (P/OF), Lillard Cobb (P),
[1]*Was released and signed with Minot Mallards*
[2]*Was traded to Elmwood Giants*

Joe Degrazia[3] (INF), Joe Greene[4] (C), Billy Horne (INF), Willy Hutchinson (P/OF), Al Jacowski (P), Gentry Jessup (P), Bob Johnson (1B), Chick Longest (OF), Almer McKerlie (C), Weldon Ridley (U), Jack Schaefer (1B/MGR), Gene Smith (P), Herb Souell (3B/OF), Al Spearman (P), Walt Thomas (C), Joe Wiley (2B/OF)

[3]Was released and joined the Minot Mallards
[4]Was traded to Elmwood Giants

1952 — Sonny Andrews (SS), Dick Ashley (LF), Lyman Bostock (1B), Ernie Boushy (1B), Fred Brenzell, 225 (P), Pee Wee Carlisle (SS), Ed Conley (INF), Mel Gelleges (C), Sam Hill (OF), Willie Hutchinson (P/OF), Gentry Jessup (P), Chick Longest (INF/OF), Almer McKerlie, Andy Porter (P), Harry Rhodes (P), Murray Richardson (P), Willie Richardson (P), Weldon Ridley (2B), Jack Schaefer (MGR), Herb Souell (3B), Ray Tabacchi (2B)

1953 — Sonny Andrews (SS), Joe Aikins (OF), Chet Brewer (MGR/P), Lyman Bostock (1B), Willie Hutchinson (P/OF), Lester Lockett (INF/OF), Chick Longest (INF/OF), Benny Lott (INF/OF), Roy McCoy (P), Walter McCoy[1] (P), Almer McKerlie (C), Jim Newberry (P), Felix Pine (P), Andy Porter (P), Al Preston[2] (P), Harry Rhodes (P), Norm Robinson (OF), Herb Souell (3B), Bob Turner (C), Curly Williams (3B/OF)

[1]Played briefly for Elmwood Giants that season.
[2]Played part of the season with Elmwood Giants.

1954 — Ed Albosta (MGR/P), Jesse Douglas (SS), Sammy Drake (3B), Benny Garrett (P), Felipe Jimenez (P/UT), Lester Lockett (INF/OF), Chick Longest (INF/OF), Benny Lott (INF/OF), Walter McCoy (P), Almer McKerlie (C), Ed Mazur (P), Bob Miller (P), John Murray (P), Gil Pantel (P), Win Phelps (P), Weldon Ridley (C), Norm Robinson (RF), Jim Swanton (2B), Walt Thomas (C) John Washington (1B), Buddy Woods (P)

DICKINSON PACKERS

1955 — Buddy Afremow (SS), Dick Baxter (P/UT), Ed Beneke[1] (P), Bob Bourbeau[2] (3B), Ron Bowen (1B/MGR), Fred Brenzel (P), Gail Burnhart (P), Joe Cincotta (P), Jack Dean (P), Don Fischer (SS), Bob Geels (2B), Tom Guiliano (SS), Mel Heim (P), Dick Jok (OF), Milt Joffe (CF), Earl Johnson (C/OF), Ev Johnson (C), Stan Karboski, Dan Lewandoski (P), Jim Michalec (P), Walt Mitchell[3] (P), Dick Morgan (LF), Don Orwiler (P), Don Petschow[4] (LF), Bill Rose (P), Eldon Russell (P), Norm Rynard (P), Ray Tabacchi (2B)

[1]Played part of the season with Bismarck
[2]Played first part of the season with Williston
[3]Started the season with Williston
[4]Played part of the season in Minot

1956 — Buddy Afremow (SS), D. Boyer (P), Fred Brenzell[1] (P), Walter Bryja (P), Dan Chepkauskas[2] (OF), Jerry Didier (2B), Gerald Fahr (P), Tom Guiliano (SS/2B), Jack Gore[3] (OF), Mel Heim (P), Bill Jankowski (1B), Milt Joffe (CF), Earl

[1]Finished the season with Bismarck
[2]Played part of the season with Williston Oilers
[3]Traded to Bismarck for Bob Karbowski

Johnson (C/OF), Ev Johnson (C), Ed Kalski (P), Bob Karbowski[4] (INF), George "Otts" Kram[5] (NP), Rocky Krsnich (3B), Bob Laskowski (P), Butch Lawing (RF), Jim Michalec (P), Bill Rose (MGR/P)

[4]*Traded from Bismarck for Jack Gore*
[5]*No position listed (NP)*

MINOT MALLARDS

1950 — Andy Anderson (P), Bill Anderson (P), Jack Bruton (P), Willie Cathey (P), Bob Danielson (P), Gervis Fagen (INF), Ev Faunce (OF), Norm Felde (1B), Ted Fowler (1B/3B/OF), Leo Henry (P), Roy Hughes (P), Cliff Kempf (C), Harvey Lapides (OF), Lefty Lefebvre (MGR/P), Zoonie McLean (SS), Joe Mack (OF), Satchel Paige (P), Jimmy Peet (P), Frank Pickens (P), Fred Shepard (OF), Henry Smith (2B), Artis Stewart (P), Marley Strong (C), Ted Strong (P/3B), Brad Tolson (P), Del Triplett (OF), Paul Wasseth (3B), Tim Witherspoon (OF/P), Steve Wylie (P)

1951— Harvey Beaster (CF), Don Berg (OF), Joe Bestudik[1] (OF), Willie Blackshire (INF), Jack Bruton (P), Nip Bruton (P), Sugar Cain (P), Willie Cathey (P), Joe Degrazia[2] (2B), Vallie Eaves (P), Norm Felde (INF), Jonas Gaines (P), Jimmy Grant (3B), Otto Huber (MGR), Walter Jako (OF), Connie Juelke (OF), Leonerd Johnson (P), Jim Kamis (P), Cliff Kempf (C), Henry McHenry (P), Gerry MacKay[3] (OF), Zoonie McLean (SS), Joe Mack (OF), Rollie Miles (3B/OF), Othello Renfroe (UT), Harold Schacker (P), Fred Shepard (P), Ed Sudol (1B), Brad Tolson (P), Bob Turner (C), Frank Watkins[4] (P), Bob Wiles (P), Charles Wiles (C),

[1]*Played briefly with the Carman Cardinals*
[2]*Played briefly with the Carman Cardinals*
[3]*Played part of the season with Brandon Greys*
[4]*Played part of the season with Brandon Greys*

1952 — Eddie Allen (P), Ed Albosta (P), Quincy Barbee (1B), Duke Bowman (3B), Al Bryant[1] (P), Sugar Cain (P), Don Corcoran (CF), Lefty Gaines (P), Yogi Giammarco (RF), Whit Graves (P), Willie Greene (P), Walter Jako (OF), John Kelly (OF), John Kennedy (2B), Bob Landers (P), Zoonie McLean (MGR/SS), Warren Martin (P), Joe Massaro (C), Mel Murray (P), Roland Summers (P), Bob Tiller (C)

[1]*Was released to Elmwood Giants.*

1953 — Ed Albosta (P/MGR), Willy Blackshear (OF), Duke Bowman (3B), Ed Bowman (2B), Sugar Cain (P), Chuck Carroll (RF), Roy Chapman (P), Jack Cooper (OF), Don Corcoran (CF), Larry Dempsey (P), Willy Greene (P), Connie Juelke (LF), John Kelly (P), Roy Klaudt (P), Whitey Landsen (P), Lefty Lettau (P), Lou Lombardo (P), Tom Lowe (P), Zoonie McLean (SS), Warren Martin (P), Joe Massaro (C), Mal Murray (P), Othello Renfroe (UT), Mickey Rocco[1] (1B), Dean Scarborough (1B), Phil Tomkinson (C), Bill Washburn[2] (P), Bob Whitchar (P), Mike Williams[3] (P)

[1]*Played most of the season with the Winnipeg Royals.*
[2]*Played most of the season with Winnipeg Royals*
[3]*Pitched half the season for the Royals*

1954 — Duke Bowman (3B), Ed Bowman (2B), Walt Bowman (INF), Sugar Cain (P), Ernie Canada (P), Don Corcoran (CF), Yogi Giammarco (RF), Willie Greene

(UT), Connie Juelke (LF), Cliff Lemme (P), Neal Lettau (P), Joe Massaro (C), Warren Martin (P), Rollie Merrill (P), Zoonie McLean (MGR/SS) Fred Parker (P), Othello Renfroe (UT), Murray Richardson (P), Dean Scarborough (1B), Bill Washburn (P)

1955 — Dan Ahtipis (P), Jack Bishop (C), Duke Bowman (3B), Barney Brown (P), Bernard Busse (MGR), Sugar Cain (P), Lou Ciola (P), Don Corcoran (OF), Robert Cartledge (P), Butch Davis (OF), Mel Duncan (P), Bob Ebkor (P), Ted Edmunds (P), Charlie Frey (OF), Tom Gatts (UT), Dirk Gibbons (P), Tom Horton (P), Neil Lettau (P), Zoonie McLean (SS), Joe Massaro (C), Warren Martin (P), Stan Milankovich (P), Joe Monteiro (LF), Willie Patterson (UT), Don Petschow[1] (1B), Bill Pinckard (UT), Murray Richardson (P), Dean Scarborough (1B), Bill Washburn (P), Dewey Williams[2] (C), George Wopinek (OF)
[1]*Finished the season with Dickinson*
[2]*Finished the season with Minot*

1956 — Andy Anderson (UT), Ed Barr (RF), Duke Bowman (3B), Carl Bush (1B), Sugar Cain (P), Wyman Carey (P), Don Corcoran (CF), Hal Daugherty (2B), Mel Duncan (P), Dirk Gibbons (P), Charles Griffith (P), Tom Guderian (P), Bruce Haroldson (P), Gabby Hormann (C), Dick Kelly (P), Joe Lutz (MGR), Gread McKinnes (P), Zoonie McLean (SS), Don Miller (C), Chuck Orner (C), Bill Oster (P), Joe Peircey (P), Dean Scarborough (1B), Mike Schultz (P), Don Smith (UT), Pete Taylor (P), Bob Van Eman (LF), Bill Washburn (P), Dewey Williams (C)

1957 — Andy Anderson (UT/P), John Andre (P), Duke Bowman (3B), Willard Brown (OF), Norman Budz (P), Carl Bush (1B), Jerry Cabana (OF), Sugar Cain (P), Dirk Gibbons (P), Gideon Jarvis (OF), Jack Hale (P), Jerry Hendrick (2B), Frank McCollum (P), Zoonie McLean (SS), Buddy Messina (2B), Rudy Mayling[1] (OF), Howard Morgenstern (OF), Chuck Orner (C), Bill Oster (P), Jessie Rogers (OF), Don Smith (UT), Bill Upton (P), Dewey Williams[2] (C)
[1]*Was released early in the season, then signed with Williston*
[2]*Played with Brandon for a few games then finished the season with Williston.*

WILLISTON OILERS

1954 — Buddy Afremow (SS), Ralph Blinn (OF), Ron Bowen[1] (1B), Dick Baxter (P/UT), Don Betzen (P), Tony Campos (2B), John Chalfont (C), Bill Cleveland (OF), Harold Dark (P), Paul Dyke (RF), Charles Ferguson (2B), Flori (SS), Lloyd Gearhart (MGR/OF), Kent Geisler (P), George (3B), King (NP), Joe Lutz (1B), Dennis Magnuson (C), Ronnie Martin (3B), Vic Michalec (P), Danny Patton (P), Dick Schoonover (P), Bert Shepard (P), Jim Shupe (INF), Ron Smith (INF), Harry Taylor (P), Dewey Williams (C), Ed Williams (P), Roy Weatherly (OF)
[1]*Played most of the season with Williston, then signed with Brandon Greys.*

1955 — Ray Berns (OF), Bob Betz (OF), Bob Bourbeau[1] (SS/3B), Dan Chepkauskas (OF), Preston Elkins (P), Tom Gatts (3B), Bruce Haroldson (P), Phil Haugstad (P), Terry Hayes (C), Bobby Hogue (MGR/P), Dick Jok (LF), Stan Karpinski (P), Jim Leavitt (C), Don Lee (P), Al Lyons (P), Ron Martin (3B/OF), Walt Mitchell[2] (P), Dee Moore (C),Tom Mulcahy (P), Tom McDevitt (2B), Fred Parker (P), Bill
[1]*Played the last half of the season with Dickinson Packers*
[2]*Played briefly for Dickinson*

Raehse (1B), Dolph Regelsky (SS), Frank Roelandt (C), Jack Sanoff (P), Dick Schoonover (P), Bill Sharp (2B), Fred Vaughan[3] (INF), Roy Weatherly (OF), Dewey Williams[4] (C), Ed Williams (P), Jack Wilson (OF)

[3]*Played part of the season with Bismarck*
[4]*Finished the season with Minot*

1956 — Ray Berns (OF), Dan Chepkauskas[1] (UT), Nelly Daehn (RF), Chuck Donley, Preston Elkins (MGR/P), Jack Gore[2] (OF), Dennis Healy (UT), Don Herman (P), Norm Johnson (P), Bob Karbowski[3] (UT), Jim Leavitt (C), Dee Moore (MGR/C), Carl Paylor (3B), Dan Phalen (1B), Bill Raehse (1B), Dolph Regelsky (SS), Jack Sanoff (P), Bill Sharp (2B), Bill Spaeter (OF), Pete Spatafore (SS), Whitney Ulrich (P), Roy Weatherly[4] (OF), Ed Williams (P)

[1]*Played part of the season with Dickinson Packers*
[2]*Traded from Dickinson for Bob Karbowski*
[3]*Traded to Dickinson for Jack Gore*
[4]*Played most of the season with Bismarck Barons*

1957 — Jerry Adair (SS), Bill Best (P), Ed Bowman (2B), Denis Brodeur (SS), Al Gettel (P), Preston Elkins (MGR/SS), Elwood Hahn (P), Dennis Healy (UT), Norm Johnson[1] (P), Pete Konyar (3B/OF), Bill Lynn (OF), Rudy Mayling[2] (CF), Joe Massaro (C), Roy Matthews (P), Steve Molinari (OF), Billy Munyer (C), Carl Paylor (3B), Bill Raehse (1B), Tom Rowan (OF), Jack Sanoff (P), Bill Sharp (2B), Jay Smith (P), Frank Tanana (RF), Roy Weatherly (OF), Ed Williams (P), Dewey Williams[3] (C), Bob Yanen (P/RF)

[1]*Played last part of the season with Brandon*
[2]*Started the season with Minot Mallards, when released signed with Williston*
[3]*Played for Minot and Brandon, early in the season*

WINNIPEG BUFFALOES

1950 — Lorne Benson (P), Lyman Bostock (1B), John Britton (3B), Spoon Carter (P), Butch Davis (LF), Leon Day (UT/P), Sam Hill (CF), Stamps Holly (OF), Percy Howard (C/OF), John Kennedy (2B), Jim Newberry (P), Nicholson (P), Andy Porter (P), Frazier Robinson (C), Taylor Smith (P), Joe Taylor (RF), Willie Wells Jr. (SS), Willie Wells Sr. (MGR/INF)

1951— Red Barnes (P), Lyman Bostock (1B), Pee Wee Butts (SS), Butch Davis (LF), Leon Day (UT/P), Wilbert Hammond (OF), Percy Howard (C/OF), Sam Hill (CF), Pee Wee Jenkins (P), Clarence Jones (P), John Kennedy (2B), Zell Miles (3B/OF), Cy Morton[1] (INF), Jim Newberry (P), Buddy Owens (3B), Frazier Robinson (C), O.B Robison (P), Larry Soffer (OF), Taylor Smith (P), Othello Strong[2] (P), Charlie White (3B), Al Wilmore (P), Willie Wells (MGR/INF)

[1]*Played first half of the season with Elmwood Giants*
[2]*Played briefly with Minot Mallards*

(WINNIPEG) ELMWOOD GIANTS

1950 — Bill Antoniak (OF), Marshall Boney (C), John Cowan (INF), Bob Cunningham (P), Solly Drake (CF), Ray Finch (P), Len Gzebb (SS), Curly Haas (MGR), Cowan Hyde (OF), Paul Jones (P), Bob Kaye (OF), Ed Leier (OF), Red

Longley (C/INF/OF), Pat Patterson (3B), Andy Phillips (3B), Al Preston (P), Rheddick (3B), Hickey Redd (SS), Terry Sawchuk (1B), Cy Snead (2B/SS/OF), Jack Warwick (1B), Amos Watson (P), Joe Wiley (2B)

1951— John Alexander (P), Wes Barrow (MGR), Red Berry (P), T.J. Brown (INF), Jim Bolden (P), John Britton (3B), Ducky Davinport (OF), Jesse Douglas (INF), Ray Finch (P), Joe Greene[1] (C), Curly Haas (MGR), Dave Hall (P), Bob Harvey (RF), Cowan Hyde (OF), Willie Jefferson (P), Lou Louden (C), Johnny Lloyd (OF), Albert Lombard (2B), Joe Mitchell[2] (OF), Barney Morris (P), Cy Morton[3] (INF), Tom Parker (P), Ted "Double Duty" Radcliffe (MGR/P), Joe Spencer (2B, SS), Roy Swanson (C/OF), Frank Thompson (P), John Washington (1B), Joe Wiley[4] (2B/OF), Sam Williams (P), Coney Williams (SS)

[1]*Started the season with Carman Cardinals.*
[2]*Was released and joined Brandon Greys.*
[3]*Finished the season with Winnipeg Buffaloes.*
[4]*Traded to the Carman Cardinals for Joe Geene and T.J. Brown*

WINNIPEG GIANTS

1952 — Al Bryant[1] (P), Nick Canulli (3B), Bill Cox (P), Earl Christian (P), Jack Deskin (UT), Jesse Douglas[2] (INF), Al Endriss (1B), Arnie Fernandez (P), Ray Finch (P), Cliff Gonzales (OF), Haifield (P), Bob Harvey (OF), Cowan Hyde (INF/OF), Kevin King (P), Lester Lockett (INF/OF), Don Loewen (OF), Lou Louden (C), Walter McCoy[3] (P), Tom Parker (P), Bill Peterson (MGR/P), Jerry Powell (SS), Hal Price (P), Ted Radcliffe (P/C), Lou Sabo (OF), Al Spearman (P/OF), Othello Strong (P), Al Tehero[4] (OF), John Washington (1B), Ray White (1B), Danny Wilson (INF)

[1]*Played briefly with Minot Mallards*
[2]*Sold to Chicago White Sox and assigned to Colorado Springs (Western League)*
[3]*Early in the season was released and joined the Carman Cardinals*
[4]*Finished the season with Brandon Greys*

WINNIPEG ROYALS

1953 — Jack Barry (1B), Bill Barry (2B), Paul Beck (P), Danny Brown (OF), Dick Butcher (LF), Rafe Cabrerra[1] (P/OF), Bill Cleveland (UT), Jack Deskin (C/UT), Jesse Douglas[2] (INF), Carlos Forten (P), Mel Gallegos (C), Dirk Gibbons (P), Chuck Gowett (P), Jim Hinson (UT), Pete Hughes (OF), Bus Jackson (LF), Mike Kanshin (P), Lou Louden (C), Rollie Merrill (P), Dee Moore (UT/MGR), Ken Myers (MGR), Fred Parker (P), Al Preston[3] (P), Hal Price (P), Bob Rittenberg (3B), Mickey Rocco[4] (1B), Bill Spaeter (CF), Bob Strader (SS), Bill Washburn[5] (P), Mike Williams (P)

[1]*Played ½ season with Brandon*
[2]*Was released and signed by Brandon Greys*
[3]*Also played for Carman Cardinals that season.*
[4]*Played briefly with Minot Mallards that season*
[5]*Played briefly with Minot Mallards that season*

Bibliography

Bohn, Terry. *The Story of the Minot Mallards*. Published by the author, no date.
Clark, Dick, and Larry Lester. *The Negro League Book*. Cleveland, Ohio: SABR, 1994.
Craw, Don. *ManDak Statistics 1950 to 1953*. Unpublished compilation based on reports in the *Winnipeg Tribune* and *Winnipeg Free Press,* March 24, 1982.
Finch, Robert A. *50 Golden Years and Who's Who in the American Association, 1951.* Minneapolis, Minnesota: Syndicated Publishing Co., 1951.
Johnson, Lloyd, and Miles Wolff. *The Encyclopedia of Minor League Baseball*. 2nd ed. Durham, North Carolina: Baseball America, 1997.
Riley, James A. *The Biographical Encyclopedia of Negro League Baseball*. New York: Carroll and Graf, 1994.
Thorn, John, and Peter Palmer. *Total Baseball, 2nd ed*. New York: Time Warner Books, 1991.

Newspapers

Bismarck Tribune, 1955–1957
Brandon Sun, 1950–1954, 1957
Minot Daily News, 1950–1957
Williston Herald, 1954–1957
Winnipeg Free Press, 1950–1954, 1957
Winnipeg Tribune, 1950–1953, 1957

Personal Interviews

Adelson, Jim. June 12, 2005
Albosta, Ed. November 28, 2002
Bostock, Lyman, Sr. June 19, 2002
Fields, Wilmer. September 26, 2002
Higgins, Roger. June 29, 1999
Leier, Ed. March 7, 2002
Loeppky, Abe. August 4, 2001
MacKay, Gerry. March 17, 2001
McKerlie, Almer. March 16, 2001
Molinari, Steve. March 17, 2001
Teasley, Ron. February 14, 2001
Williams, Dewey. April 6, 2001
Williams, Ed. February 27, 2000

Index

Aberdeen Pheasants 124
Ackers, Jim 61–62, 65
Ada Herefords 141
Adair, Jerry 59, 62, 65
Adams, Joe "Smokey" 17, 21, 66
Adelson, Jim 36, 37, 64
Afremow, Buddy 43–44, 65–66
Ahtipas, Dan 43–44, 46
Alabama-Florida League 92, 144
Albosta, Ed 11, 32–33, 35–38, 42–43, 45, 66
Albuquerque Dukes 170
Alexander, John 67
Allen, Ed 67
Almendariz, Lou 67
American Association 73, 86, 115, 124, 127, 131, 136, 142, 152, 159, 163, 165–166, 168, 177
Amero, Mario 32, 67
Anderson, Andy 57, 67
Anderson, Bill 68
Anderson, Orenthal "Andy" 68
Andre, John 59–60, 68
Andrews, Sonny 13, 19, 22, 33, 69
Andux, Orlando 39, 69
Antoniak, Bill 181
Appalachian League 76, 122
Argudin, Cesar 69
Arizona-Mexico League 91, 97, 100, 105, 148, 175
Arkansas-Missouri League 72
Ashley, Dick 69
Atkins, Joe 35, 38, 69, 96
Atlanta Black Crackers 108, 160
Atlanta Brown Bombers 87

Bakersfield Boosters 134
Ball, Bob 70
Baltimore Colts 101
Baltimore Elite Giants 70, 103, 151, 156, 178

Baltimore Orioles 65, 139, 141, 167, 176
Banks, Jim 70
Barbee, Quincy "Bud" 29–30, 32, 34, 70
Barr, Ed 56–57, 70
Barrow, Wes 11
Barry, Bill 71
Barry, Jack 71
Basin League 63, 77, 94, 99, 150, 179
Bassett, Lloyd "Pepper" 24, 26–27, 71
Baxter, Dick 52, 71
Bearden, Gene 106
Beaster, Harvey 25, 72
Beck, Dick 72
Benecke, Ed 52, 72
Bennett, Bob 61, 72
Benson, Lorne "Boom Boom" 72
Berg, Don 73
Berns, Ray 56–57, 73
Berry, Mike "Red" 73
Best, Bill 73
Bestudik, Joe 73
Betz, Bob 51–52, 74
Big State League 88, 99, 110, 122, 138, 144, 170
Birmingham Black Barons 71, 74–75, 79, 82, 86, 118, 123, 133, 144, 147, 152, 154, 156, 160, 177
Bishop, Jack 74
Bismarck Barons 78, 204
The Bismarck Tribune 63, 113
Blackshire, Willy 74
Blinn, Ralph 74
Bolden, Jim 74
Boney, Marshall 75
Border League 160
Bostock, Lyman 2, 8, 10, 13, 18–21, 25, 28–29, 33, 37, 75
Boston Braves 12, 22, 49, 54, 114–115, 122, 132, 136, 159, 166, 169, 175

Boston Bruins 125
Boston Red Sox 25, 65, 109, 113, 127, 162–163
Bourbeau, Bob 75
Boushy, Ernie 76
Bowen, Ron 12, 42, 46, 51–52, 76
Bowes, Jack 60–61, 76
Bowles, Ted 63
Bowman, Duke 32–33, 35, 37, 39, 42, 44–46, 48, 53, 57, 77
Bowman, Ed 34, 39, 77
Bowman, Walt 44, 47
Brandon Cloverleafs 59, 134, 180–181
Brandon Greys 204–205
Brantford Red Sox 102
Brenzel, Fred 26, 52, 55, 78
Brewer, Chet 11, 37, 78
Britton, John 9, 13, 79
Brodeur, Dennis 79
Brooklyn Cuban Giants 6, 18, 90
Brooklyn Dodgers 2, 14, 73, 89, 96, 100, 111, 119, 122, 126, 136, 141, 154, 163–167
Brooklyn Royal Giants 75
Brown, Barney 32, 38–39, 41, 49–50, 79, 109
Brown, Danny 80
Brown, T.J. 80
Brown, Willard 59, 62, 80
Bruni, Louis 80
Bruton, Jack 10, 80
Bruton, Nip 81
Bryant, Al "Lefty" 81
Bryja, Walter 56, 81
Budz, Norm 81
Bumpus, Earl 82
Bush, Carl 56, 82
Busse, Bernard 12, 82
Butcher, Dick 82
Butts, Harry 83
Butts, Thomas "Pee Wee" 22, 24, 27, 29, 83
Byrd, Bill 95

Cabana, Jerry 83
Cabrera, Rafe 10, 13, 16–18, 21–22, 27, 63, 83
Cain, Ben 143, 165
Cain, Sugar 2, 4, 22, 26–27, 29–30, 32–34, 37–39, 42–43, 45–46, 48–53, 55–57, 59–60, 84, 143, 165
California Angels 65, 127
California League 105, 113, 126, 134, 145, 161, 163

California Mohawks 25
Campos, Tom 85
Canada, Ernie 85
Canadian-American League 112, 126, 128
Canadian National Baseball Team 132
Can-Am League 122
Caps, Regina 37
Carey, Wyman 85
Carlisle, Pee Wee 85
Carman Cardinals 205–206
Carolina League 72, 85, 103
Carrigan, Jack "No No" 12
Carroll, Chuck 35, 37, 39, 86
Carson, Johnny 100
Carter, Ernest "Spoon" 8, 86
Cartledge, Robbie 51–52, 86
Cash, Bill "Ready" 86
Cashill, Jerry 87
Castille, Irvan "Chuck" 87
Cathey, Willie 10, 16, 19, 22, 25, 27, 87
Cedar Rapids Indians 144
Central Association 77
Central League 76, 86, 106, 121, 137
Chacon, Mario 87
Chalfont, John 87
Champions, Playoff 203
Chapman, Roy 88
Chattanooga Choo Choos 74
Chepkauskas, Dan 56, 88
Chicago American Giants 30, 68, 75, 82, 113–114, 118, 120, 129, 136, 140–141, 145, 151–152, 154, 160, 163–164
Chicago Black Hawks 127, 138
Chicago Colored Giants 22
Chicago Cubs 9, 42, 59, 68, 71, 86, 97–99, 103–104, 107, 120, 127, 132, 144, 152, 176–177, 179
Chicago White Sox 25, 55, 65, 72–73, 84, 86, 95, 99, 106, 121, 124, 134, 149–150, 157
Chojnowski, Luke 88
Christopher, Thad 88
Cihocki, Al 12, 88, 171
Cincinnati Buckeyes 114
Cincinnati Clowns 162
Cincinnati Crescents 87, 162
Cincinnati Red Sox 87
Cincinnati Reds 54, 111, 115, 117, 120, 126, 139–141, 152, 159, 167, 169
Ciola, Lou 89
Claussen, Ed 12

Index

Cleveland, Bill 39, 89
Cleveland Buckeyes 69, 74, 91, 100, 102, 114, 163, 179
Cleveland Indians 24, 55, 71, 73, 76–77, 87, 89, 101, 105, 108, 111–112, 120, 146, 156, 163, 166, 173, 181
Clifford, Luther 30, 90
Coastal Plains League 96
Cobb, Jerry 32
Cobb, Lillard 10, 13–14, 16–17, 19–20, 90
Cohen, Mickey 8
Colas, Jose 30, 90
Collins, Rip 24
Colonial League 107, 151
Colorado Springs Sky Sox 73
Columbia Reds 159
Columbus Blues 171
Columbus Elite Giants 109
Columbus Redbirds 142
Conley, Howard "Butch" 90
Cooper, Jack 90
Cope, Bob 91
Corcoran, Don 29–30, 44, 47–48, 51, 91
Corpus Christi Aces 149
Cottingham, Sherman 146
Cotton States League 92, 95, 124, 141, 149, 153, 165
Cowan, John 14, 91
Cox, Bill 91
Crue, Marty 92
CUAC Blues 181
Cunningham, Bob 13–14, 92

Daehn, Nellie 92
Dana, Dave 92
Dandridge, Ray 2–3, 49–50, 52, 64, 92–93
Danielson, Bob 16, 93
Daugherty, Hal 12, 42–44, 46, 55, 57, 93
Dauphin Red Birds 76, 173
Davenport, Lloyd "Ducky" 22, 94
Davidson, W.S., Jr. 54
Davis, Butch 4, 8, 17–19, 21, 24–27, 49, 94, 137, 180
Day, Leon 2, 4, 8, 16–17, 19–21, 23–25, 27–28, 42, 64, 93–95
Dean, Jack 52, 95
Dean, Roy 36
Degrazia, Joe 95
Dempsey, Larry 39 41, 96
Dent, Carl 96

Denver Bears 81
Deskin, Jack 96
Detroit Black Sox 115
Detroit Red Wings 38
Detroit Stars 98, 115, 150, 170
Detroit Tigers 50, 93–94, 113, 117, 130–131, 134, 168
Detroit Wolves 109, 115, 119, 136
Dickinson Packers 206–207
Didier, Gerald 96
DiMaggio, Joe 13
Donley, Chuck 96
Doster, Leroy 146
Douglas, Jesse 11, 22, 25, 30, 39, 43–44, 97, 166
Drake, Sammy 42–44, 97
Drake, Solly 9, 14, 18, 21, 97
Duluth Dukes 140
Duncan, Mel 51, 53, 98
Dunn, James "Jimmy" 7, 22
Durham Bulls 66

East Texas League 99
Easterbrook, Bob 51–52, 98
Easterling, Howard 35, 98
Eastern League 71, 76, 90, 93–94, 100, 106, 112, 117, 121, 133, 157–159, 166–168, 176, 180
Eastern Shore League 100
Eaves, Valle 99
Ebkor, Bob 99
Edmonton Eskimos 140
Edmunds, Ted 52–53, 99
Eisemann, Chuck 99
Elkins, Preston 12, 49, 51–52, 55–57, 62, 100
Elliot, Gord 16, 100
Endriss, Al 100
Estevan Maple Leafs 25–26
Ethiopian Clowns 162
Evangeline League 96, 132
Evans, Frank 6, 100

Face, Elroy 147
Fagen, Gervis 101
Fahr, Gerald "Jerry" 55–56, 101
Far West League 122, 142
Fargo-Moorhead Twins 93, 165
Faunce, Ev 14, 101
Felde, Norm 14, 101
Fenwick, Percy 8
Ferguson, Charles 102

Ferro, Amancio 27–28, 102
Fields, Wilmer 35, 102
Finch, Ray 17, 25–26, 29, 102
Finney, Ed 27, 103
Fitzgerald, John 53, 103
Florida International League 69, 74, 85, 104, 140
Florida State League 89, 95, 122
Flynn Mark 174
Fonda, Henry 106
Fowler, Ted 103
Fox, Nellie 147, 152
Frey, Charlie 51, 53, 103
Funai, Ed 103
Furlong, Bill 104

Gaines, Jonas "Lefty" 22, 29–30, 32, 34, 50
Garcia, Tony 55, 104
Gatts, Tom 104
Gearhart, Lloyd 12, 42–43, 45–46, 50, 105
Geels, Bob 105
Geisler, Kent 46, 105
Georgia-Florida League 11, 70
Georgia State League 105, 134
Gettel, Al 105
Giammarco, Yogi 29–30, 32, 34, 43, 106
Gianes, Jonas 104
Gibbons, Dirk 16–17, 19–21, 35, 39, 42–44, 46, 50, 52–53, 55, 57, 59, 61, 106
Gillium, Junior 83
Giuliano, Tom 107
Godinez, Manuel 10, 14, 20, 22, 107
Gomez, Preston 50, 52, 107
Gonzales, Wilfredo 18
Gore, Jack 107
Gowett, Chuck 35, 107
Grand Forks Chiefs 159
Grant, Jimmy 107
Graves, Whit 108
Green, Pumpsie 25
Green Bay Packers 140
Greene, Joe 108
Greene, Willy 30, 44, 108
Griffith, Bob 39, 109
Groat, Dick 147
Groves, Morrell 109
Guderian, Tom 109
Gulf Coast League 99
Gzebb, Len 110

Haas, Curly 8, 11, 14, 30, 33, 36, 42, 110, 162
Hahn, Elwin 62, 110
Hale, Jack 61, 110
Hankyu Braves 144
Harlem Globetrotters 6, 8, 14, 18, 140, 165
Haroldson, Bruce 110
Harvey, Bob 26, 111
Haugstad, Phil 111
Havana Cuban Giants 148
Havana Cubanos 119
Hayes, Terry 111
Healy, Dennis 62, 111
Heim, Mel 112
Heintzelman, Ken 50–52, 112
Hendrick, Jerry 112
Henry, Leo 112
Herman, Don 113
Hermman, Ed 15
Higgins, Roger 50, 52, 54–56, 103, 113, 130
Hill, Sam 13, 29, 54, 56, 113
Hinson, Jim 113
Hockenbury, Bill 12, 52, 55, 61, 114
Hogue, Bobby 12, 49, 52, 114
Hollywood Stars 158, 169
Homestead Grays 71, 86, 90, 98, 102, 115, 179
Horne, Billy 114
Horton, Tom 53, 115
House, Red 8, 11, 109, 115, 136–137, 174
House of David 6
Houston Astros 107, 127
Houston Eagles 111
Howard, Percy 14, 115
Howe, Gordie 38
Huber, Otto 12, 23–25, 63, 73
Hughes, Pete 35, 38–39, 115
Hunt, Art 17–21, 116
Hunter, Don 59, 181
Hutchinson, Willie "Ace" 27, 30, 33, 39, 116
Hyde, Cowan 4, 9, 18, 22, 29, 35, 39, 116

Illinois League 115
Illinois State League 12
Indian Head Rockets 32, 30, 38
Indianapolis Clowns 10, 83–84, 87, 96, 106–109, 113, 120, 143, 148, 150, 154, 165, 177–179

Index

Inter County League 83, 102
International League 28, 70, 89, 94–95, 98, 102, 106, 121, 131, 134, 149, 166, 168
Inter-State League 128, 152

Jacowski, Al 27, 117
Jako, Wally 12, 27, 32, 117
Jankowski, Bill 56, 117
Jarvis, Gideon 60, 117
Jefferson, Paul 24
Jefferson, Willie 117
Jenkins, Pee Wee 6, 32, 39, 109, 118
Jersey City Giants 131
Jessup, Gentry 4–5, 10, 16–17, 19–22, 25, 29–30, 33–34, 63, 118
Jimenez, Felipe 119
Joffe, Milt 119
Johnson, Bob 17, 21, 27, 119
Johnson, Earl 119
Johnson, Ev 53, 56, 119–120
Johnson, Glen 61
Johnson, Leonard 120
Johnson, Norm 60, 120
Johnson, Tom 18, 120
Johnson, Woody 54
Johnstown Johnnies 154
Jok, Dick 120
Jones, Clarence "Lefty" 121
Jones, Johnny 25
Jones, Paul 14, 18, 121
Jones, Rex 146
Juelke, Connie 24, 30, 35, 37–39, 73, 121

Kalski, Ed 121
Kamis, Joe 121
Kansas City A's 110, 138
Kansas City Monarchs 14, 70, 78, 80–82, 90, 98, 108–109, 116, 125, 138, 146, 153, 162, 165, 169, 180
Kansas City Royals 65
Kansas-Oklahoma-Missouri League 164
Kanshin, Mike 122
Karpinsku, Stan 122
Kelly, Dick 57, 122
Kelly, John 32–33, 122
Kempf, Cliff 13, 123
Kennedy, John 3, 9, 16, 20–21, 25–26, 29, 32–33, 70, 77, 123
Keokuk Kernels 148

King, Clarence 26, 28, 123
King, Kevin 123
Kirby, Clay 107
Kitty League 66, 73, 78, 81–82, 87, 164
Klamath Falls Gems 154
Klaudt, Roy 123
Kline, Ronnie 147
Konyar, Pete 51, 59–60, 124
Kropf, John 124
Krsnich, Rocky 56, 124
Kyle, Gus 125

The Lacombe Globe 6
Landers, Bob 31, 125
Landry, Mal 125
Landsen, Whitey 125
Lapides, Harvey 125
Las Vegas Wranglers 139
Laskowski, Bob 125
Laurentian League 90
Lawing, Garland "Butch" 55, 59, 126
Leap, Al 55–56, 59, 62, 126
Leavitt, Jim 57, 126
Lee, Don 49, 51–52, 126
Lefebvre, Lefty 8, 11, 21, 63, 68, 125, 127
Leier, Ed 13, 127
Lemme, Cliff 127
Lettau, Neal 38–39, 42–45, 127
Lewandowski, Don 50, 128
Lewis, Doug 128
Lloyd, John 128
Lloydminster Meridians 79
Lockett, Lester 29, 35, 128
Lollar, Sherman 106
Lombardo, Lou 129
Longest, Chick 10, 32, 39, 43–45, 129
Longhorn League 65, 82, 101, 139
Longley, Red 129
Los Angeles Dodgers 98
Lott, Benny 35, 37, 42–43, 45–46, 130
Lotz, Mike 50–51, 130
Louden, Lou 24, 29, 39, 41, 43–46, 130
Louisiana Travelers 14, 18, 149, 160, 163
Louisville Black Caps 86
Louisville Black Colonels 133, 154
Louisville Buckeyes 121
Louisville Colonels 170
Lowe, Ian 2, 8, 10–11, 14, 17–22, 27–28, 130
Lowe, Tom 131
Lucas, Stan 24

Lutz, Joe 12, 43, 46, 131
Lynn, Bill 62, 132
Lyons, Al 54, 56–57, 59, 61–63, 132
Mack, Joe 136
Mack, Ray 106
MacKay, Darcy 13
MacKay, Gerry 10, 13, 16, 20, 22, 27, 46, 59, 132
MacKay, Rod 46, 133
Malone, Bill 136
Mancao, Chris 15
Manitoba Baseball Hall of Fame 76, 110, 127, 131–132, 138, 154, 172, 180
Manitoba Junior League 110, 127
Manitoba-Saskatchewan League 143, 150
Manitoba Senior League 1, 59, 69, 84, 88, 90, 97, 106, 110, 119, 127, 131, 138–139, 143, 151–152, 157, 162, 166–167, 172–173, 180
Manitoba Sports Hall of Fame 131
Manning, Bob 137
Maroto, Ricky 137
Martin, Ron 46, 137
Martin, Warren 32–33, 43, 45, 137
Mascaro, Frank 4, 43, 137
Massaro, Joe 2, 29–30, 32, 35, 38–39, 43, 45–46, 48, 50–51, 60, 62, 70, 137, 143
Massingale, Mack 138
Matthews, Roy 138
Mayling, Rudy 138
Mays Willie 130
Mazur, Ed 138
McClothin, Gib 134
McCollum, Frank 133
McCoy, Roy 133
McCoy, Walt 32, 37, 39, 42–43, 46, 133
McDevitt, Tom 133
McFarlane, Morley 46, 134
McGowan, Curtis 134
McHenry, Henry 134
McIlvain, Harry 134
McKerlie, Almer 14, 16, 22, 29, 45, 78, 134–135
McKerlie, Clint 135
McKinnis, Gread "Lefty" 23, 26–28, 38–39, 109, 135
McLean, Zoonie 3, 10, 12, 19, 25, 27, 29–30, 32–36, 38, 44, 47–48, 50, 52, 57, 59, 61–63, 82, 115, 135
McNeal, Clyde 61–62, 136
McWorter, Roy 14, 136
Means, Winslow 139
Memphis Red Sox 6, 30, 80, 90–91, 116, 129, 134, 154, 170, 175–176, 180
Messina, Buddy 112, 139
Mexican League 67, 78, 85–86, 96, 98, 133, 139, 150, 153, 157, 171
Michalec, Jim 56, 139
Michalec, Vic 46, 139
Mid-Atlantic League 74, 88, 120, 154
Milankovich, Stan 140
Miles, Roland "Rollie" 140
Miles, Zell 15, 26, 140
Miller, Bob 44, 46, 140
Miller, Don 140
Millon, Herald 141
Milwaukee Braves 22, 115, 119, 144, 169, 175
Milwaukee Brewers 136, 165
Minneapolis Millers 108, 124, 127, 168
Minneapolis Clowns 6
Minnesota Twins 127
The Minot Daily News 13–14, 50, 168
Minot Mallards 207–208
Minot Merchants 2, 81, 108, 135, 164–165, 168–169, 180
Minot Oscars 123
Mississippi-Ohio League 82, 102
Mississippi–Ohio Valley League 116, 144, 152, 164
Mitchell, Joe 28, 32, 39
Modesto Reds 145
Molinari, Steve 59–60, 124, 141
Montana State League 91
Montiero, Joe 50–51, 141
Montreal Canadians 138
Montreal Expos 153
Montreal Royals 136
Moore, Dee 11–12, 42–44, 57, 59, 63, 141
Moorhead Red Sox 101
Morgan, Dick 52, 142
Morganstern, Howard 142
Morrus, Barney 142
Morton, Cy 142
Moultrie Athletics 11
Mt. Vernon Braves 12, 115
Mulcahy, Dick 52
Mulcahy, Tom 143
Munyer, Billy 143

Murray, John 143
Murray, Mal 14
Muskogee Cardinals 18
Muskogee Giants 125
Myers, Ken 11, 35–36

Naranjo, Pedro 10, 16–19, 22, 26–28, 143
Nashville Elite Giants 109
National Hockey League 158
Nelson, Adrian 58
Nelson, Gene 144
Neri, Frank 61, 144
New England League 67, 117
New Orleans Creoles 6, 74, 129
New Orleans Eagles 129
New York Black Yankees 88, 106, 109, 147, 151, 162
New York Cubans 75, 83, 118, 142, 167, 171
New York Giants 55, 88, 98, 105–106, 119–120, 122, 124–126, 129, 133, 146, 157, 170, 173
New York Mets 97
New York Rangers 125
New York Yankees 70, 76, 85, 103, 105–106, 113–114, 127, 132, 145, 157–158, 164, 173, 179
Newark Eagles 95, 104, 111, 174, 176
Newberry, Jim 17, 19–20, 23–25, 35, 38, 144
North Atlantic League 169
North Carolina League 109
North Carolina State League 138
North Central League 101
Northern League 54, 63, 70, 72–73, 87, 93, 95, 105, 108, 111, 113, 120, 124, 133, 140–141, 144, 146, 149, 157–160, 164–165
Northern Longhorn League 146
Northwest League 97–98, 166
Novak, Ed 11

Oakland A's 65
Oakland Oaks 169
Ogden Dodgers 11
Ogden Reds 147
Ohio State League 103
Omaha Rockets 6
Ontario League 175
Orner, Chuck 145
Orwiler, Don 53, 145

Oster, Bill 54, 57, 61, 145
Owens, Buddy 145

Pacific Coast League 63, 71, 96, 99, 106, 133, 149, 156, 158, 167, 169, 175, 179
Paige, Satchel 2, 14, 64, 68, 78–79, 84, 86, 97, 145–146, 148, 153, 155–156, 180
Palmer, Betsy 106
Pampa Oilers 128
Parker, Fred 39, 44, 46, 146
Parker, Tom 35, 109, 147
Patterson, Pat 147
Patterson, Willie 51, 53, 147
Paylor, Carl 51, 56, 58, 147
Peet, Jimmy 147
Peete, Charley 20–21, 148
Penn State League 100
Pennington, Art "Superman" 49, 52, 54, 56, 148
Peoria Chiefs 166
Perez, Mike 148
Perkins, Anthony 106
Perry, Alonzo 22–24, 149
Peterson, Bill 11
Petschow, Don 50, 149
Phalen, Dan 149
Philadelphia A's 54, 74, 76, 89, 99, 114, 135, 145, 159, 167, 170, 178
Philadelphia Meteors 143, 165
Philadelphia Phillies 51, 82, 85, 98, 106, 112, 117, 123, 134, 138, 141, 144, 154, 173, 176
Philadelphia Stars 86, 95, 106, 109, 142, 175, 178
Pickens, Frank 149, 163
Piedmont League 76, 82, 104, 107–108, 115, 124, 138–139, 141, 148, 162
Piercey, Joe 12, 150
Pigg, Lenny 32, 150
Pinckard, Bill 150
Pine, Felix 39, 150
Pine Bluff Judges 124
Pioneer League 11, 71, 109, 111, 133, 142, 145, 147, 154, 157, 165, 170
Pittsburgh Crawfords 71, 84, 86
Pittsburgh Pirates 67, 78, 83–84, 86, 100, 112, 124, 126, 132, 169, 175, 180
Plainview Ponies 128
Pocatello Cardinals 142
Pollack, Syd 10
Pony League 82, 87, 89, 104, 177
Port Arthur Sea Hawks 144

Porter, Andy 6, 20, 32, 34, 150
Porterville Comets 11
Powell, Jerry 151
Preston, Al 151
Price, Hal 4, 30, 151

Quebec Braves 126
Quebec Provincial League 69–70, 76, 83, 86, 129
Quinn, Bus 171

Radcliffe, Ted "Double Duty" 11, 22, 24, 30, 151
Raehse, Bill 51, 55–58, 61–62, 152
Rancher, Joe 152
Records, League 203
Redd, Hickey 152
Regelsky, Dolph 49, 52, 55–56, 58, 152
Regina Braves 55
Regina Caps 18, 125, 140, 169
Reid, Don 153
Reimer, Roy, 8 29, 35, 42, 192
Renfroe, Othello 22, 35, 39, 42, 44–45, 153
Rhodes, Harry 29, 153
Richardson, Ab 12
Richardson, Murray 33, 45, 154
Richardson, T.W. 32, 154
Richmond Colts 141
Ridley, Weldon 154
Riley, James 2, 146
Rio Grande Valley League 149
Rittenberg, Bob 41, 154
Riverside Canucks 173
Robinson, Frazier 8, 19–21, 24, 27–29, 155
Robinson, Jackie 1, 8, 75, 173
Robinson, Norm 156
Robinson, Sugar Ray 51
Robinson, Winnie 155
Robison, O.B. 25, 27, 156
Rocco, Mickey 2, 5, 35, 64, 156, 172
Rodriguez, Ramon 17, 21, 27, 156
Roelandt, Frank 157
Rogers, Jesse 61, 157
Rose, Bill "Red" 12, 46, 51–52, 157
Rous, Bob 62, 157
Runyan, Damon 151
Russell, Eldon 50, 158
Rynard, Norm 158

Sabo, Lou 181
Saginaw Bears 86
Saginaw Jacks 137
St. Boniface Native Sons 138, 172
St. Cloud Rox 124
St. Louis Browns 25, 59, 80, 114, 131, 146, 149, 162
St. Louis Cardinals 50, 67, 69, 91, 103, 106, 111, 119–120, 128, 133–134, 139, 142, 148, 167, 169
St. Louis Stars 114
St. Paul Saints 131
St. Petersburg Saints 140
Salina Blue Jays 172
Salisbury Pirates 138
Sally League 129, 153
Salt Lake City Bees 154, 170
San Bernardino Pioneers 137
San Diego Padres 107
San Francisco Giants 93
Sanoff, Jack 56–57, 60, 124
Santa Barbara Dodgers 66
Saperstein, Abe 8
Saskatoon Gems 144
Savannah Indians 74, 114
Sawchuk, Terry 158
Scarborough, Dean 35, 37–38, 44, 48, 50, 57, 158
Scarpone, Sam 159
Sceptre Panthers 78, 151
Schacker, Hal 22, 159
Schaefer, Jack 11, 14, 21, 159
Schoonover, Dick 43–44, 46, 159
Schultz, Mike 54, 159
Schwartz, Bill 61
Schwartz, Frank 160
Seattle Rainiers 169
Sharp, Bill 51, 58, 62, 160
Shepard, Bert 160
Shepard, Fred 160
Shreveport Sports 68
Shupe, Jim 160
Shurey, Dave 146
Sioux Falls Canaries 132, 144
Sisler, Ray 161
Slevin, Jim 59, 181
Smith, Don 161
Smith, Gene 22, 27, 161
Smith, Henry 161
Smith, Jay 161
Smith, Jerry 59, 181
Smith, Maurice 13, 63

Index

Smith, Taylor 13–14, 17, 21, 23–24, 162
Snead, Cy 11, 13, 162
Society for American Baseball Research 146
Soffer, Larry 162
Sooner State League 141
Souell, Herb 22, 27, 29, 162
South Atlantic League 74, 97, 104, 114, 119, 122–123, 131, 142, 159, 169
South-Eastern League 163
South West League 151
Southern Association 99, 129, 153, 159, 170
Southern League 85, 105, 124
Southern Minny (Minnesota) League 89, 93, 109, 111, 129, 149, 158, 176
Southwest International League 11, 89, 96, 130, 139, 169
Southwestern League 130
Spaeter, Bill 162
Spatafore, Pete 163
Spearman, Al 10, 22, 35, 33, 163
Spencer, Joe 163
Statistics: batting (1950) 183–184; (1951) 186–187; (1952) 189–190; (1953) 192–193; (1954) 194–195; (1955) 196–197; (1956) 198–199; (1957) 201–202; pitching (1950) 185; (1951) 188–189; (1952) 191; (1953) 193–194; (1954) 195–196; (1955) 197–198; (1956) 200; (1957) 202
Stewart, Artis 163
Stewart, Don 43, 46, 164
Stone, Toni 6
Strader, Bob 35, 164
Strong, Marley 164
Strong, Othello 27, 29
Strong, Ted 10, 18, 164
Stryska, Vic 165
Suarez, Armando 25–28, 165
Sudol, Ed 165
Summers, Roland 165
Sunset League 11, 35, 71, 82, 107, 113, 116, 137
Superior Blues 72, 157
Swanton, Jim 166

Tabacchi, Ray 53, 166
Tallahassee Rebels 140
Tanana, Frank 166
Tanner, Chuck 147
Taylor, Harry 42–44, 46, 166

Taylor, Joe 9, 19–21, 23
Taylor, Pete 57, 167
Teasley, Ron 1, 6, 10, 13–14, 17–20, 167
Texas City Texans 170
Texas League 68, 71, 76, 92, 117, 119, 122, 130, 139, 150, 167
Thomas, Walt 25, 168
Thonn, Ray 168
Three-I League 91, 97, 115, 117, 122, 136, 144, 148–149, 159, 166, 175, 181
Tiller, Bob 168
Tolson, Brad 168
Tomkinson, Phil 168
Toronto Maple Leafs 24–26, 28, 49, 95, 103, 175
Tost, Lou 169
Traub, Coleman 29
Trenton Giants 98
Triplett, Del 169
Tri-State League 76, 93, 170
Turk, Alex 8, 22
Turner, Bob 35, 169

Ulrich, Whitney 169
Upton, Bill 170
Utica Blue Sox 106

Van Buren, Mark 13, 16, 21, 24
Van de Hey, Len 61–62, 170
Van Eman, Bob 170
Vantin, Glenn 59
Vasquez, Armando 10, 14, 16–17, 30, 32, 171
Vaughan, Fred 53, 171
Veeck, Bill 25
Vinson, Dick 171

Warwick, Jack 13, 172
Washburn, Bill 35, 39, 43, 47, 172
Washington, John 35, 39–40, 42, 172
Washington Senators 50, 81, 93, 104, 107, 119, 127, 160, 171–172, 180
Wasseth, Paul 172
Watkins, Frank 13, 16, 18–19, 27, 172
Watkins, Muray 17, 173
Watkins, Skeeter 16–18, 25, 28
Watson, Amos 173
Weatherly, Roy 4, 12, 42–44, 45–46, 49–51, 54, 57, 173
Webster, Dan 14, 174
Wells, Jack 16
Wells, Willie, Jr. 14, 175

Wells, Willie, Sr. 2, 8, 11, 13, 16, 18, 20–21, 25, 27, 29, 35, 38, 45, 64, 83, 93, 118, 174
Welsh, Bill 24
West Texas–New Mexico League 76, 104, 122, 128, 180
Western Association 88, 95, 97, 125, 179
Western Baseball League 131
Western Canada Baseball League 36, 54, 72, 74, 79, 108, 121–122, 125–127, 130, 132, 136, 140, 143–144, 154, 161, 164, 169–170, 176–177
Western Carolina League 85
Western International League 83, 92, 95, 99, 122–123, 133, 137, 180
Western League 68, 73, 108–109, 112, 117, 125, 150, 153, 169–170, 177, 179
Western Minnesota League 91
Western Wisconsin League 161
Whitcher, Bob 175
White, Charlie 22–25, 27, 175
Whiteside, Mrs. 10
Wichita Transit 124
Wilcox, Ralph 62, 175
Wiles, Bob 176
Wiles, Chuck 24, 176
Wiley, Joe 14, 27, 176
Williams, Curly 39, 176
Williams, Dewey 42–44, 176–177
Williams, Ed 42–43, 46, 52, 55, 57, 93, 170, 177
Williams, Jimmy 18
Williams, Len 177
Williams, Sam 30, 177
The Williston Herald 51, 62–63, 73, 145, 152

Williston Oilers 208–209
Willows Cardinals 142
Wilmore, Al 24, 26–27, 63, 176
Wilson, Chuck 14, 20–21, 37, 39, 178
Wilson, Danny 178
Wilson, Don 107
Wilson, Jack 178
Wingo, John 14, 18–19, 179
Winnipeg Blue Bombers 73
Winnipeg Buffaloes 209
Winnipeg Elmwood Giants 209–210
Winnipeg Evening Tribune 78
The Winnipeg Free Press 12–13, 16, 24–25, 36, 63
Winnipeg Giants 209–210
Winnipeg Goldeyes 160
Winnipeg Reos 181
Winnipeg Rosedales 138, 153
Winnipeg Royals 210
Winnipeg Senior League 158
The Winnipeg Tribune 12–13, 21
Wisconsin League 157
Wisconsin State League 112, 125
Wise, Harry 57, 179
Witherspoon, Lester 179
Wolf, Pius 179
Woods, Buddy 45–46, 179
Woods, Parnell 14
Wopinek, George 53, 180
Worth, Art 180
Wright, Mort 59, 180
Wylie, Steve 14, 87, 180

Yanen Bob 181

Zedd, Stanley 7, 11, 22, 25

www.ingramcontent.com/pod-product-compliance
Lightning Source LLC
Chambersburg PA
CBHW020813230426
43666CB00007B/1000